SOCIAL INSURANCE IN EUROPE

Other titles available from The Policy Press include:

Beyond the threshold: the measurement and analysis of social exclusion edited by Graham Room ISBN 1 86134 003 6 £13.95

The Gypsy and the state: the ethnic cleansing of British society (2nd edn) by Derek Hawes ISBN 1 86134 011 7 £14.95

The rise of international social policy by Peter Townsend ISBN 1 86134 002 8 £4.95

Global restructuring and social policy: the need to establish an international welfare state by Peter Townsend and Kwabena Donkor ISBN 1 86134 007 9 £4.95

[All the above titles are available from The Policy Press, University of Bristol, Rodney Lodge, Grange Road, Bristol BS8 4EA, Telephone 0117 973 8797 Fax 0117 973 7308]

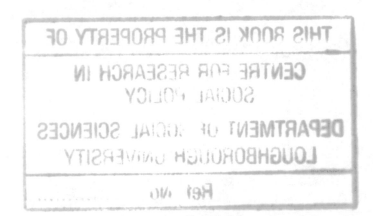

SOCIAL INSURANCE IN EUROPE

Edited by Jochen Clasen

First published in Great Britain in 1997 by

The Policy Press
University of Bristol
Rodney Lodge
Grange Road
Bristol BS8 4EA

Telephone (0117) 973 8797
Fax (0117) 973 7308
e-mail: tpp@bris.ac.uk

© Jochen Clasen, 1997

British Library Cataloguing in Publication Data
A catalogue record for this book is available from the British Library

ISBN 1 86134 0

Jochen Clasen is Senior Lecturer in Social Policy at the University of Stirling.

Cover design: Qube, Bristol.

The Policy Press works to counter discrimination on grounds of gender, race, disability, age and sexuality.

Printed in Great Britain by H. Charlesworth & Co Ltd, Huddersfield.

Preface

This book originates from the seminar on 'Social insurance in Europe', held in July 1996, which was sponsored by the British Social Policy Association. I am grateful to the Association for their support and also to participants for their contributions to the seminar. I gratefully acknowledge the help I received from Fiona Milburn and Angus Erskine, who both provided invaluable support and advice throughout the process of producing this book.

Jochen Clasen
Stirling
April 1997

Contents

Notes on contributors   ix

one   Social insurance – an outmoded concept of social
protection?
Jochen Clasen   1

two   Retrenchment or restructuring? The emergence
of a multitiered welfare state in Denmark
Jon Kvist   14

three   Sweden: on the way from standard to basic security?
Ann-Charlotte Ståhlberg   40

four   Social insurance in Germany – dismantling or
reconstruction?
Jochen Clasen   60

five   A 'liberal' dynamic in the transformation of the
French social welfare system
Bruno Palier   84

six   Switzerland: institutions, reforms and the politics
of consensual retrenchment
Giuliano Bonoli   107

seven   The withering of social insurance in Britain
Angus Erskine   130

eight   Social protection and social insurance in Portugal
Jack Hampson   151

nine   Social insurance and the crisis of statism in Greece
Theodoros N. Papadopoulos   177

ten   Social insurance in Hungary: the individualisation
of the social?
Tony Maltby   205

eleven   Social security and social insurance in the Czech
Republic
Mita Castle-Kanerova   223

twelve   Social insurance in Europe – adapting to change?
Angus Erskine and Jochen Clasen

Bibliography   251

Index   279

Notes on contributors

Giuliano Bonoli is a researcher and teaching assistant at the Institut des Sciences Sociales et Pedagogiques at the University of Lausanne, and a PhD candidate at the Department of Social Policy, University of Kent. His research interests are comparative social policy and the politics of welfare. Among his recent publications are 'Entre Bismarck et Beveridge: crises de la sécurité sociale et politique(s)', *Revue Française de Sciences Politiques*, vol 45, no 4, 1995 (with Bruno Palier); and 'Classifying welfare states: a two-dimension approach', *Journal of Social Policy*, vol 26, no 3, 1997.

Mita Castle-Kanerova is a senior lecturer in social policy at the University of North London and an honorary professor at the Charles University in Prague. Her research interests are the socio-political history and social policy of East and Central European countries, comparative social policy and women and social policy. Recent publications include 'Social security in the Czech Republic: the market, paternalism or social democracy?' in M. May, E. Brundson and G. Craig (eds) *Social Policy Review*, no 8, 1996, and 'Social policy in Czechoslovakia', in B. Deacon (ed) *The new Eastern Europe*, London: Sage, 1992.

Jochen Clasen is a senior lecturer in social policy in the Department of Applied Social Science, University of Stirling. His research interest is in the area of comparative research in social policy, with a particular emphasis on unemployment and social security. Recent publications include *Social policy in Germany* (ed, with Richard Freeman), Hemel Hempstead: Harvester, 1994; and 'Stability and change in welfare states: Germany and Sweden in the 1990s' (with Arthur Gould), *Policy and Politics*, vol 23, no 3, 1995.

Angus Erskine is a senior lecturer in social policy in the Department of Applied Social Science, University of Stirling. His research and teaching interests are in the fields of poverty, social security and unemployment. He has edited *Changing Europe: some aspects of identity, conflict and justice,* Aldershot: Avebury,

1996, and has jointly edited *The students companion to social policy* (with Pete Alcock and Margaret May), Oxford: Blackwell, 1997.

Jack Hampson is a senior lecturer in the Department of Social Studies at the University of Central Lancashire. His research interests are comparative social policy, with specialisation in healthcare systems. He has been a visiting lecturer at the Instituto Superior de Serviço Social in Oporto since 1990. Recent publications include *Modelos do estaba de bem-estar*, Oporto: Instituto Superior de Serviço Social, 1992 and 'Social policy in the Latin rim: the case of Portugal', in M. May, E. Brundson and G. Craig (eds) *Social Policy Review*, no 9, 1997.

Jon Kvist is a researcher at the Centre for Welfare State Research which is a joint venture between the Danish National Institute of Social Research and the University of Odense. His main research interests include welfare states, social security, taxation and inequality in an international perspective. Recent publications include 'Comparing tax welfare states' (with Adrian Sinfield) in M. May, E. Brundson and G. Craig (eds) *Social Policy Review*, no 9, 1997, and *Social security in Europe: development or dismantlement?* (with Niels Ploug), The Hague: Kluwer Law International, 1996.

Tony Maltby is a lecturer in social policy in the Department of Social Policy and Social Work at the University of Birmingham. His main research interest is the comparative study of pensions and income in later life. He has recently published (with Alan Walker) *Ageing Europe*, Buckingham: Open University Press, 1996, which presents findings from the European Union's Observatory on Ageing and Older People.

Bruno Palier is a temporary lecturer in political science at the University Paris I La Sorbonne. He also works for Mission Inter-ministerielle Recherche et Experimentation (MIRE), which forms part of the French Ministry of Social Affairs and for which he has organised international conferences comparing social welfare systems in Europe. His main research interest is the social protection system in France. Recent publications include 'Entre Bismarck and Beveridge: crises de la sécurité sociale et politique(s)', in *Revue Française de Sciences Politiques*, 1995, and 'Reclaiming welfare' in

South European Society and Politics, vol 1, no 3, 1996 (both with Guiliano Bonoli).

Theodoros N. Papadopoulos is a lecturer in social policy at the University of Bath. His DPhil thesis was a comparative study of social policy responses to unemployment in the EU. His research interests include comparative research methodology, the decommodification potential of welfare programmes and social policy in southern Europe, and his publications include '"Family", state and social policy for children in Greece', in J. Brannen and M. O'Brien (eds) *Children in families: research and policy*, Lewes: Falmer Press, 1996.

Ann-Charlotte Ståhlberg is an associate professor of economics at the Swedish Institute for Social Research, Stockholm University, and a senior lecturer at the School of Social Work, Stockholm University. She was an expert in the Swedish official pension investigation 1984-90, in the following Swedish official pension investigation of 1991-93, and in the committee on sickness and occupational injuries 1993-96. Her major research interests are the economics of social insurance, lifetime distribution of income and questions of moral hazard. Recent publications include 'Pension reform in Sweden' and 'Women's pensions in Sweden', both in *Scandinavian Journal of Social Welfare*, vol 4, 1995.

one

Social insurance – an outmoded concept of social protection?

Jochen Clasen

Introduction

Although initially providing very moderate old age pensions, invalidity pensions or sickness benefits for only small parts of society, conservative and liberal elites as well as moderate social reformers in many European countries regarded social insurance programmes as the answer to the 'social question' of how to integrate a growing industrial working class into the existing social and political order. By contrast, many socialists and trade union activists opposed mandatory social insurance as undermining existing workers' mutual support schemes and thus working class solidarity, as attempting to establish social control over workers and as unnecessarily delaying the inevitable collapse of capitalism.

Once introduced, social insurance schemes soon allowed some sort of class compromise, which in turn enabled existing programmes to expand to other groups than the core industrial sector and to include more types of risk, such as unemployment. Achieving real improvement in material living standards for many workers, while at the same time contributing to the preservation of existing social structures and power relations, the 'conservative–revolutionary dual nature' (Heimann, 1929) of social policy in general, and of social insurance programmes in particular, became evident to both capital owners and working class leaders. In Germany, for example, social democratic forces changed from early opposition to firm support of a further extension of social insurance when it became obvious that particular features, such as self-administration by employers and employees, graduated contributions and benefits and separate funds outside the state budget, actually strengthened rather than weakened the link between workers and their organisations (Hennock, 1987; Ritter, 1983).

Of course, there were national differences in the extent and form of social insurance programmes, but a shift from 'social policy from above', that is, the setting up of social insurance schemes by conservative and liberal elites between the 1880s and the First World War, to a period of 'social policy from below', when social democratic forces became involved in the expansion of social insurance during the interwar years, was characteristic in many European countries (Alber, 1987). However, the real triumph of social insurance came after the Second World War, when, based on high economic growth rates, generally low unemployment levels and broad political compromises, new types of risk were covered and benefits were improved, and in many countries were more closely linked to earnings with more social groups included. It was hoped that social insurance would promote solidarity and social cohesion by bringing together workers, the middle classes and employers, who would all contribute to and benefit from the system. In short, social insurance programmes, providing benefits on the basis of employment, became the cornerstones of the growth of modern welfare states, relegating, it was hoped, the role of means testing to a residual and exceptional type of public support in many European countries.

This optimism has all but vanished in the late 1990s. In many European countries means testing has become more rather than less important, while the role of social insurance is being seriously questioned because of the impact of a number of changes in economy and society, rendering outmoded the assumptions on which traditional social insurance programmes rested (see Baldwin and Falkingham, 1994). Most crucially, changes in the labour market over the past three decades or so call into question a type of social protection that requires full-time, continuous participation in paid employment as the eligibility criterion for maximum benefit entitlement. Moreover, implicitly, and at times explicitly, social insurance has relied on the notion of nuclear families headed by a male breadwinner, with men in paid employment and wives and children merely entitled to 'derived' benefits via the husband's membership in social insurance. Gaps in social insurance have opened up and widened not only as a consequence of persistent mass and high levels of long-term and youth unemployment but also as a result of changes in employment patterns, including a growth of part-time and other types of 'atypical' work (which, owing to low earnings or too few hours worked per week, is increasingly not covered by social insurance schemes), rising levels of female participation in the labour market, the growth in single-person and lone-parent households and the decline of one-earner and the growth of no-earner households (European Commission, 1994; Webb, 1995). Moreover, demographic changes in Europe are bringing about an increasingly adverse relationship between the share of economically active population and those in retirement, putting financial pressure on social insurance based pay-as-you-go pensions and on care insurance systems in particular. Rising healthcare costs too are putting increasing pressure on health insurance schemes.

In short, a number of changes are putting pressure on social insurance programmes because of their inherent normative orientation towards a social and economic context which seems to be rapidly disappearing. On a broader level, questions about the future shape of welfare states in general, and the role of social insurance schemes in particular, have been asked in the light of further political integration within Europe (Leibfried, 1993; Leibfried and Pierson, 1995) as well as changes within national and international economic contexts which, some argue, imply a transition from Fordist Keynesian welfare states to post-Fordist Schumpeterian workfare states (Jessop, 1993; 1994).

Within social science, these changes and pressures have been noted for some time and have been central to a body of research on the origins, development and future of modern welfare states (for a recent example, see Esping-Andersen, 1996a). Early studies on these topics centred on social expenditure, or 'welfare effort', as the main indicator for welfare state development (Wilensky, 1975). Later, the timing of social insurance legislation, the scope of risks included and the degree of coverage became parameters in research that was interested in testing theories based on structural changes as an explanation of welfare state development versus theories based on political conflict (Flora et al, 1977; Flora and Heidenheimer, 1981; Flora, 1986). Indeed, perhaps the most influential contribution to comparative studies of welfare states in recent times continued to focus on characteristics of three major social insurance schemes (pension, unemployment and sickness insurance) as an indicator of the degree of 'de-commodification' inherent in different welfare states (Esping-Andersen, 1990), even though a shift in focus towards particular properties of national social insurance programmes and their respective impact on social stratification and social conflict indicated a recognition of cross-national differences which had been somewhat neglected in previous studies. However, the debate on welfare state typologies since then (for a summary and overview, see Kvist and Torfing, 1996) has been remarkable in terms of the many contributions pointing out the need to focus on welfare indicators other than social insurance, thus reinforcing the impression that social insurance programmes might have had their day as a major type of social protection and might become marginal in future European welfare states.

Questions about long-term viability or desirability of statutory social insurance programmes based on pay-as-you-go principles are also becoming increasingly important in political debates. This is particularly the case in Britain, the European country that has perhaps moved furthest away from an erstwhile comprehensive social insurance legacy. However, the adherence to traditional principles is currently also being questioned in countries that still have a very strong social insurance orientation, such as France and Germany.

In political debates two main alternatives to social insurance can be distinguished. Advocating a continuing role of the state, those on the left of the political spectrum point to the need to fill increasing gaps within social insurance by providing a form of social protection that is not (or at least is less) based on employment and is based more on citizenship (or residence) as an entitlement criterion. If social insurance schemes are not to be replaced by some type of basic or citizens' income, existing programmes should at least be reformed in order to allow the inclusion of groups currently not participating in insured employment, such as carers. By contrast, favouring a reduced role for the public sector and more scope for private provision, those on the right tend to put more emphasis on means tested forms of social security. This would allow one to distinguish better between those who really need support and those who do not, and would also reduce the level of overall public expenditure and encourage more individualised, private forms of social protection purchased on markets or provided by companies for their employees.

Against this background of both changing socioeconomic contexts within which social insurance programmes operate and doubts expressed in political and academic debates as to the viability or desirability of social insurance, the overall objective of this book might be summarised as an attempt to provide some answers to the question of to what extent social insurance has already become, or is likely to become, an outmoded concept of social protection in Europe.

Social insurance and other forms of social protection

Of course, there are differences in the particular design and role of national social insurance programmes. For example, Britain has a strong history of social (national) insurance as a comprehensive system of income protection. However, providing flat-rate benefits and originally an alternative to the Poor Law, its orientation differs considerably from social insurance schemes in Germany or France, which aimed at status maintenance via a close association between earnings related benefits and contributions and a strong involvement of social partners in the management of social insurance funds. In other countries, such as Sweden and Denmark, earnings related social insurance cover was to supplement universal schemes, such as basic national pensions, and the fiscal balance between contribution financing and progressive taxation is tilted much more towards the latter than elsewhere. Other differences between and within countries regarding social insurance programmes include the scope of coverage, the level of contributions, qualification criteria, benefit ceilings, etc, raising the question as to what the term 'social insurance' actually implies.

On the surface, a definition of social insurance seems straightforward when contrasted with the two other main principles upon which statutory social protection schemes rest (social assistance and universal benefits) on the one hand, and the differences between social and private insurance on the other. The term 'social assistance' has come to be generally applied to means tested benefits aimed at preventing, or alleviating, poverty (Eardley et al, 1996), while universal benefits are paid irrespective of need to all or a group of citizens, or residents, of a country, such as pensioners. By contrast, entitlement to social insurance benefit is neither based on need nor conferred as a social right per se, but is conditional on compulsory contributions to one (or several) social insurance funds while in employment. Thus, participation in paid work is generally the key criterion for social insurance. The two crucial differences to private insurance are the compulsory membership and the payment of contributions that are not determined by risk categories.

However, a brief glance at existing welfare state programmes reveals that the picture is more diverse and complex than this and that there are many grey areas, not simply because of a lack of a uniform terminology (eg, the term 'national insurance' rather than 'social insurance' in Britain). A complication is certainly the existence of what might be called 'hybrids', that is, social protection programmes which comprise principles of, for example, both social insurance and social assistance. Entitlement to earnings related unemployment assistance in Germany, for example, is dependent on a contributory record but is also subject to a means test. In principle, benefits might be universally available to all citizens, but there might be an earnings ceiling excluding those with incomes above it, which is increasingly the case in Denmark (see Chapter two in this volume). The compulsory character is not always absolute either. Unemployment insurance in both Sweden and Denmark is voluntary, while higher income earners in some countries are allowed to leave some types of statutory social insurance and to opt for private insurance cover instead. Benefit ceilings in some countries mean that insurance benefits, although in principle earnings related, reflect previous earnings only to a very limited degree. In the UK insurance benefits, except for the state earnings related pension scheme, are not related to previous earnings and levels are very close, or even below, the level of assistance benefits.

Social insurance programmes deliver predominantly cash transfers (unemployment, pensions, sickness), but some benefits in kind (eg, healthcare, long-term residential care) are common in many countries. What is more, in most countries the bulk of insurance benefits is funded by contributions, but some degree of tax subsidies is common especially in those countries where a tripartite contribution basis is (or was) conventional, with the state as the third contributor alongside employers and employees.

However, the most crucial 'common denominator' of social insurance programmes across countries is the link between benefit entitlement and paid employment. The fact that this link can sometimes be indirect (eligibility to healthcare for dependants of somebody in employment, contribution crediting for non-waged activities such as caring) does not obscure the fact that, on the whole, social insurance programmes rely on contributions rather than taxation as the main funding source, or that benefits are primarily, but not exclusively, geared towards those in paid employment. Indeed, the link between paid employment and entitlement is the crucial criterion for social insurance, and this connection is at the centre of much criticism from those who advocate the abolition, or at least a substantial reform, of social insurance programmes.

The aims of the book

By illustrating commonalities and differences within and across countries, this book reflects on the current role of social insurance, recent policy changes and pressures for reform in ten European countries. Most of the countries have previously been categorised as belonging to one or another type of welfare 'regime' or 'type' (Esping-Andersen, 1990; Lewis, 1992; Castles and Mitchell, 1992; Leibfried, 1993). To some extent, these typologies have influenced the choice of countries covered in this book since it has deliberately attempted to capture diversity by including the current situation of, and pressures on, social insurance arrangements in 'liberal', 'conservative', 'social democratic', 'Latin Rim' and 'transitional' European countries. However, it also tries to question these typologies by bringing together (with the exception of Britain as the only 'liberal' welfare state) at least two countries in each of these categories in order to reflect on differences and commonalities between them.

Of course, social insurance arrangements form only one section of national welfare states and all countries have their own particular mix of insurance, assistance and universal social protection schemes, and allow for more or less private provision. An examination of social insurance programmes has necessarily to remain, therefore, a partial analysis of welfare states. Nevertheless, social insurance principles and arrangements have played a significant role in many European welfare states. A detailed investigation of the current situation seemed therefore justified and should allow some contributions to the current debate on welfare states and their futures.

Thus, a major aim of the book is to provide information about cross-national differences and commonalities between social insurance schemes in Europe, and to reflect upon their future roles at a time when the balance between social insurance and other types of public and private forms of social protection seems to be shifting. Underlying questions to be addressed are whether and to what extent an erosion of social insurance principles can be observed; how far 'classic' social insurance countries such as Germany or France have responded to socioeconomic pressures and how strong doubts are as to the viability of traditional forms of social protection. Is the role of social insurance arrangements in largely tax-funded Scandinavian welfare states growing or decreasing? Which types of social insurance or other forms of social protection have been introduced in so-called transitional Central and Eastern European countries, and how firmly have these been established? What are the characteristics and the future of social insurance programmes in southern European countries?

The structure of the book

Providing information and context for subsequent sections, all chapters begin with a discussion of aspects such as administration, expenditure and risks covered in order to illustrate the particular role, scope and design of social insurance programmes in particular countries. Second, recent policy changes in major social insurance programmes are discussed which, depending on the countries in question, require more or less extended historical accounts in order to put recent policies in context. Third, there is a reflection upon the significance of different kinds of pressure on social insurance programmes, followed by some, necessarily tentative and speculative, assessment as to the direction of, and future role for, social insurance programmes. While these common themes are addressed in all chapters, country-specific differences made too rigid a structure in the organisation of chapters or emphasis given to particular sections within them neither feasible nor desirable.

The first countries to be discussed are Denmark and Sweden. In Scandinavia, earnings related social insurance schemes are often assumed to be secondary or complementary to tax-funded universal benefits, such as national old age pensions for example. However, as Jon Kvist and Ann-Charlotte Ståhlberg demonstrate, the roles of universal and insurance benefits have changed in the course of the historical development of the Swedish and Danish welfare states. What is more, there are currently a number of substantial reforms under way which will alter the mix of benefit principles and the relative importance of public, occupational and private provision, particularly in Denmark.

Jon Kvist begins his chapter by questioning the conventional perception of social insurance as distinctively different from social assistance or universal benefits and also criticises the failure to analyse social protection programmes without taking account of the role of fiscal and occupational welfare provisions. In order to illustrate these points, he discusses Danish social security arrangements in general and policy changes in the area of pensions in particular. An interpretation of these reforms as merely cost-cutting exercises and as a retreat of the state from the responsibility for social protection would be misguided, Kvist argues. Instead, restructuring rather than retrenchment is taking place which will lead to the emergence of a multitiered welfare state with a new mix between universal public insurance, negotiated occupational schemes and private pension provision.

Ann-Charlotte Ståhlberg maintains that changes in the Swedish welfare state should be seen as responses both to structural problems within social insurance and to economic and demographic pressures. One major change will affect the compulsory earnings related pension scheme which will have adverse distributional consequences for the previously privileged middle classes. Early retirement options have already been made less attractive and, as a way of reducing the rate of absenteeism and to save public expenditure, the total level of sickness compensation has been lowered and stricter qualifying rules for unemployment benefits have been introduced. Overall, Ståhlberg argues, these changes should safeguard and strengthen rather than jeopardise the continuation of public social insurance programmes.

France and Germany are countries where contributory financing of social protection is more prominent than in Scandinavia. In both of those countries, social insurance schemes

are administratively compartmentalised and provide predominantly earnings related benefits for earnings related contributions,
administered by funds which, although subject to some form of
state control, are largely (some exclusively) controlled by
employers and employees. Despite these and other similarities,
there are also many differences. For example, the German system
is comparatively less fragmented but perhaps even more aimed at
maintaining (or reproducing) differences in standards of living
from the market into social security. Nevertheless, as Jochen
Clasen   demonstrates,   some   elements   of   'solidarity',   or
intrapersonal   redistribution,   are   built   into   social   insurance
programmes.   Indeed,   it   is   the   mixture   of   different   principles
which   has   contributed   to   their   historical   resilience   to   change.
However, financial pressure, demographic concern and a rise in
the number of social assistance recipients have brought traditional
mechanisms of social protection into question. What is more,
recent policy changes might undermine the 'moral infrastructure'
of social insurance (Hinrichs, 1996) and thus threaten its role as
predominant type of social protection in Germany. On the other
hand, the introduction of a statutory long-term care insurance
scheme seems to suggest that the Bismarck legacy is by no means
over yet.

By comparison, Bruno Palier argues that social insurance in
France is currently undergoing structural change since the most
pressing problems of the French welfare state have been identified
as characteristics of social insurance (funding modes, coverage of
schemes and a lack of state control). As a consequence, recent
reforms have lowered the share of contributions paid by employers
and simultaneously raised the burden on employees, increased the
role of tax funding in the area of social protection and transferred
a greater degree of control over social insurance funds from
employees to the state. Overall, Palier argues, these changes can
be regarded as having introduced a 'liberal' dynamic into the
transformation of the French welfare system which implies a
greater role to means testing at the expense of social insurance
structures and principles.

Although Switzerland is a latecomer in terms of implementing
social insurance schemes, a low level of unemployment and a
prosperous economy allowed programmes to expand steadily
throughout the 1980s. Since the early 1990s, however, rising
unemployment has led to policy changes which were strongly

influenced by political institutions. Referendums in particular can be a formidable obstacle to policy making as Giuliano Bonoli demonstrates in relation to recent reforms within three main social insurance branches: healthcare, pensions and unemployment. Expansionary trends in all three areas came to a halt in the 1990s and gave way to policies which combined elements of retrenchment and improvement. However, while there is pressure on the traditional consensual pattern of policy making, Bonoli argues that policy changes in the area of social insurance are likely to be incremental rather than radical and that the structure of social insurance arrangements will remain fairly stable in the medium term.

Such a verdict would be questionable for Britain which, as Angus Erskine points out, stands out in a European context since it is not only a remarkably centralised and state controlled system of social insurance but also provides almost exclusively modest flat-rate rather than earnings related benefits. The role of social insurance, however, is not marginal as about half of all social security spending is devoted to contributory benefits; however, Erskine describes the incremental blurring of social insurance and social assistance principles over the past two decades or so, and the increasing extent of means testing on the one hand and the active encouragement of private provision on the other. Recent debates on how to address the problems of costs for long-term care and the future of state pensions indicate that the gradual residualisation of social insurance in Britain is likely to continue.

Compared with other EU countries, one commonality between Portugal and Britain is the relatively high share of tax funding of welfare programmes. Other features are more distinctive to southern European countries generally, such as the effect of long periods of state authoritarianism and the repression of demands for more comprehensive social reforms, as Theo Papadopoulos illustrates for Greece and Jack Hampson for Portugal. Even today, comprehensive social insurance schemes characteristic of more established welfare states have not been implemented in either country. As Hampson demonstrates, a major reform in 1984 aimed at the introduction of a compre-hensive system of social insurance in Portugal with funds expected to be self-financing. However, legislation has been diluted so that the fragmentary nature of schemes, based on occupational differences and political privileges and the lack of a clear financial division between social insurance and social assistance, has continued. This gap between legislation and implementation is an important obstacle which constrains social reforms in Portugal. As Hampson points out, social insurance funds face financial difficulties owing to the debts that many firms have accumulated for the payment of social insurance contributions. In addition, high levels of public sector debt, sluggish economic growth and a significant rise in unemployment since the early 1990s has put considerable strain on the political scope for expansionary social insurance strategies in Portugal.

Greece too has no comprehensive social insurance system. However, operating under complex and diverse contribution and benefit conditions, contributory schemes and social insurance principles are more relevant and extensive than in Portugal. The state has a strong regulatory role, as Papadopoulos emphasises; yet the lack of uniformity is illustrated in different levels of tax subsidies that particular insurance funds receive, which in turn reflects differences in the political clout that individual schemes possess. Overall, the maintenance of patronage, with privileges especially for public sector employees, client networks and indebted insurance funds are major characteristics of Greek social insurance arrangements. High levels of unemployment, demographic changes and the perceived need to meet the criteria for participating in the European Monetary Union provide the policy context in which economic policies take precedence over any attempts to expand or make uniform social insurance schemes.

One similarity between social insurance in southern Europe and the so-called transitional societies in central and eastern Europe is the historically late extension to agricultural labourers. This affected women in particular, as Tony Maltby illustrates in relation to pension insurance in Hungary, since the majority of agricultural workers there are female. Recent reforms in Hungary have included the introduction of separate social insurance funds covering different types of risk. However, moves to firmly establish these funds are met with obstacles. There is a propensity for evading the payment of taxes and social insurance contributions, as this was as an act of political protest under the former communist regime. An extensive informal economy also deprives social insurance funds from revenue. In addition, there was a rapid rise in unemployment between the early and the mid-1990s. Most important, however (Maltby argues), is the role of international financial agencies (such as the International Monetary Fund [IMF] and the World Bank) which often apply such conditions for credit as a reduction in overall social expenditure, and which favour the expansion of means testing rather than social insurance.

Similar external pressure is less pronounced in the Czech Republic owing to the country's buoyant economy and, at least officially, very low levels of unemployment. The recently reformed social protection system has therefore not yet been properly tested. Policy changes during the first half of the 1990s aimed at 'de-monopolising' social insurance, that is, taking it out of state budgets and direct political control. This, on paper, has been completed. However, as Mita Castle-Kanerova argues, rather than creating autonomous social insurance funds, the state remains firmly in control of all three 'pillars' of social protection in the Czech Republic. What is more, as institutional arrangements put heavy emphasis on vertical at the expense of horizontal income redistribution, better-off income groups and the aspiring middle classes are being asked to subsidise pension and sickness insurance heavily. Both aspects have triggered criticism of the social insurance programmes for not adapting to changing social structures, and accusations of neo-paternalism and of state embezzlement of pension funds.

In the concluding chapter, Angus Erskine and Jochen Clasen return to some of the main issues raised in this introduction and reflect on both the diversities and the similarities between social insurance arrangements across the countries covered. In an attempt to identify some of the broad patterns in policy responses in the light of major pressures on current social insurance arrangements, they examine how and to what extent social insurance has adapted to change.

two

Retrenchment or restructuring? The emergence of a multitiered welfare state in Denmark*

Jon Kvist

Introduction

The 'dismantlement of welfare states' is an appellation that has often been used to describe recent changes in the welfare states of industrialised capitalist societies, irrespective of whether countries rely heavily on social assistance like the USA and the UK, or more on social insurance, such as Germany (Pierson, 1994; Esping-Andersen, 1996a; Ploug and Kvist, 1996). The diagnosis of welfare retrenchment has also been applied to Scandinavian welfare states, including Denmark with its emphasis on universal tax-financed benefits. This chapter will question the universality and validity of the retrenchment thesis by looking at developments in Denmark. Moreover, it will question common perceptions of social insurance in the light of recent social security reforms in Denmark.

The chapter addresses three main points. The first relates to the supposed distinctiveness of different types of social protection scheme. When looking in more detail at social security schemes, it is argued, differences between social assistance, social insurance

---

* I would like to thank Jørn Henrik Petersen, Sue Morris and the editor of this volume for useful comments on an earlier draft, and Hans Hansen for tax/benefit calculations.

and universal tax-financed benefits become less clear. Eligibility criteria, benefit formulae and financing have common traits across these three types of social security arrangement in existing national schemes, thus blurring the lines between them. The logic underlying the various types of social security arrangement is, of course, not without significance for issues such as redistribution or stigmatisation, but this is related more to the actual institutional design than to a particular term applied to a scheme.

The second point relates to the changing role of social protection schemes. A renewed trend towards linking entitlement to social security benefits with some sort of activity such as work or education is becoming evident cross-nationally, which adds to the blurring between the three types of social security. More importantly, this trend signals a new policy concern of combating social exclusion in some countries. Thus, a new reintegrative role is envisaged for social security to complement the more established roles of insurance and prevention. This role is being emphasised within social assistance, social insurance and universal tax-financed benefits. Thus, social protection schemes no longer aim merely to secure a minimum level of subsistence, a guarantee of status maintenance or income distribution, but put a renewed emphasis on promoting life chances. This is particularly evident in Denmark.

The final point concerns the inadequacy of traditional social policy analysis in capturing all relevant cash transfers to households. Concentrating merely on public social security programmes fails to take account of the actual benefit package available to people. Different components of benefit packages stem from direct social security programmes as well as from the tax system and occupational sources, which are sometimes interrelated. For example, direct social security benefits are sometimes supported by tax exemption, while occupational schemes often enjoy fiscal privileges. For such reasons, it is important to adopt a broad view of social security.

This chapter is concerned with these three points by investigating the institutional design of social security in Denmark and its recent development. It is organised in four sections. The first deals with theoretical issues within social security in general, by setting out institutional designs, objectives and the multitiered nature of social protection. The second section describes the history and institutional design of the multitiered social security system in Denmark today, while the third discusses recent changes introduced by centre–right and subsequently centre–left governments. The final section discusses both empirical and theoretical findings and provides a tentative prediction of the future of social security in Denmark.

Social security in theory

'Social security' is a label which is often used to encompass social insurance and social assistance. Precise definitions however are largely lacking in comparative social policy literature and are mostly operationalised by reference to existing national laws (Berghman, 1991; Pieters, 1994). Without allowing for national variations, the following definitions of social insurance, social assistance and universal social security will be used in this chapter as reference points for the succeeding discussion:

- **Social insurance** is compulsory or voluntary insurance which provides wage earners in particular with a certain income compensation in the event of a predefined risk. Eligibility is determined through contribution testing. Benefits are earnings related and not income tested and are financed through earmarked contributions.

- **Social assistance** provides benefits for people facing economic hardship who have no rights to other benefits or family support. Eligibility is determined by assessment of needs or means. Benefits are usually means tested against other income in the family. Social assistance is financed through taxation.

- **Universal tax-financed social security** provides a certain income based on a test of citizenship or residence and on membership of a specified risk group, eg, the unemployed or sick. Benefits are flat-rate or earnings related and are not income tested.

In the following, these three archetypical definitions will be used as benchmarks and their usefulness will be discussed in the light of actual schemes. The discussion is based on Danish social security research which has been particularly concerned with the distinction between social insurance and other models of social security (see, eg, Dich, 1964; Andersen, 1971; Petersen, 1972; 1974; Socialkommissionen, 1992; Ploug and Kvist, 1996).

The institutional design of social security

Many questions about the boundaries and distinctiveness of the three types of social security become relevant when actual national social security schemes are categorised and compared. Here only three aspects of such schemes will be considered: coverage; calculation of benefits and financing.

Coverage concerns benefit entitlement, and a distinction is traditionally made between universal and selective benefits. Selectivity is normally associated with targeting benefits to the needy within social assistance and wage earners within social insurance schemes. In contrast, universalism is associated with benefits to the entire population in general, and to certain groups of people such as the aged, the sick and families in particular. Implicitly, it is thus assumed that eligibility criteria within social assistance have the purpose of singling out the needy, originally through an assessment of needs but in later years increasingly through a test of means or income. A test of contributions is the main eligibility criterion in social insurance, which serves to ensure that only true wage earners qualify, whereas eligibility criteria within universal or categorical schemes are thought to be less strict, normally through a test on residence and/or citizenship.

However, a more detailed investigation of actual social security schemes shows that such a trichotomy is misleading (Kvist and Ploug, 1996). Instead, another framework might be suggested in which the 'rationing' of transfers may be described as individuals' passage through three filters (Petersen, 1974). As personal scope of application, a first filter sets out the potential extent of coverage, that is, whether benefits are targeted at everybody within a category (old, unemployed, sick, etc) or are limited to a group within a category (wage earners, the insured, etc). The second filter, the eligibility criteria, sets out the entitlement conditions for a given benefit in relation to claimants' personal, behavioural, family and labour market situation. For example, there might be personal requirements such as age or income, behavioural requirements such as actively seeking work, family requirements such as being a breadwinner, or labour market requirements such as a previous work or contribution record or participation in work or education (see Kvist and Ploug, 1996).

The benefit formulae is a third filter which determines the level and duration of benefits.

The three filters can be found within social insurance, social assistance and universal benefit systems. Indeed, commonalities in the filters blur the lines between the three models of social security. This perspective breaks with the conventional understanding of coverage as mainly a function between benefit and income. Instead, it can be argued that the relationship between benefit and income is only part of one rationing filter which has an impact on coverage, rather than the crucial one which is in fact the personal scope of application and eligibility criteria. In other words, a careful examination of the rationing filters and their implementation are important for an understanding of redistributional effects of social security schemes in the real world.

Focusing on how benefits are calculated in relation to income and contributions, it becomes evident that no clear distinction is possible between the three types of social security. In theory, the level of benefit can be related to current and previous earnings and income, such as transfers positively related to previous earnings (earnings related benefits) and negatively related to current income (income tested benefits), and benefits related to neither earnings nor income (flat-rate benefits). More rarely, benefits may be positively related to former earnings but tested against current income, for example the German unemployment support scheme (*Arbeitslosenhilfe*). The other three benefit–income relationships are often associated with social insurance, social assistance and national insurance (as in Britain), respectively. However, in actual schemes often hybrid forms of social protection rather than archetypes are predominant. For example, a so-called insurance scheme might apply flat-rate benefits (as in the UK) or some degree of income testing (as in the Finnish and German unemployment support schemes).

Another issue is the relationship between contributions and benefits as an indicator as to whether a transfer of income should be categorised as a social insurance benefit or, for example, a universal benefit. Should the relation be in a strict actuarial sense where contributions match the size of benefits, the probability of the risk occurring and an administration fee? More common are links in a less restricted manner. For example, benefits might be conditional on the payment of a certain number of contributions (as for unemployment benefit in the UK), or on the size of contributions (as in the Norwegian unemployment insurance scheme), or on being insured for a certain period or time (as in Denmark). Again, reality turns out to be more complicated than the archetypical definitions allow.

Finally, financing methods also blur the lines between the three types of social security. Traditionally, it is argued that social assistance and universal benefits are tax-financed whereas social insurance is financed via contributions. However, in this strict sense most of the European social insurance schemes would not qualify as such since they typically receive some form of tax-funded state subsidy. If it is merely the existence of contributions in contrast to taxes that defines a scheme as social insurance, then the Danish system of unemployment insurance would qualify as social insurance because of the existence of member fees, despite the fact that the state contributes approximately 80% of the cost of unemployment benefits. However, as Dich (1964) has stressed, it is more important to examine who carries the marginal risk: the state, employers or the insured. In this case, the Danish unemployment insurance would not qualify as social insurance, since there is no variation in 'premiums' paid by the insured, and the state thus covers the whole of the marginal risk entirely.

Objectives of social security

Social security has a wide range of objectives, but the main one is to protect against loss of income resulting from a specified social risk and to provide an income to people who face a particular social contingency. This takes the form of an income to guarantee a minimum level of subsistence and/or income maintenance. Generally speaking, social assistance is supposed to ensure a minimum level of subsistence whereas social insurance should ensure against a dramatic fall in acquired living standards. Generous universal schemes were supposed to do both. In reality, of course, it is questionable whether actual social security schemes live up to their supposed objectives.

However, social security has also been regarded as preventing people from an economic, mental and social *deroute* (Sinfield, 1996) and as fulfilling reintegrative roles, for example by building a bridge into the labour force or by retaining people in vulnerable low paid jobs (Berghman, 1996). This is achieved primarily by making benefit entitlement conditional upon some sort of activity, such as training, education or participation in work schemes. In reality, it can be difficult to distinguish between reintegrative efforts and measures of social control. For example, social assistance has always been subject to conditioning in order to separate the so-called non-deserving poor from the deserving poor. In recent years, however, the practice of attaching conditions to benefit receipt has been used increasingly within unemployment insurance and, although perhaps to a lesser extent, within disability schemes, as in The Netherlands.

Reintegration and control are aims that are difficult to separate. We may start 'blaming the benefit' rather than acknowledging the real cause of the problem, such as unemployment or disability, and there is the danger that the victims will be seen as villains (Sinfield, 1996).

When social insurance benefits are made conditional upon recipients' active participation, the insurance character of the scheme is open to question. This argument can be generalised: the more a benefit is conditional on some sort of test (whether personal, family, behavioural, income or other), the more indistinct the insurance element becomes and more blurred the demarcation line between social insurance and social assistance.

Multitiered social security

Traditional social security analysis comparing national welfare schemes of, for example, public old age pension schemes, faces dangers of ethnocentrism and assumptions regarding functional equivalence. Ethnocentrism is a possible danger because there is rarely cross-national consensus in welfare terminology – social insurance, for example, is defined differently across countries. Problems of functional equivalence can occur because social security schemes of the same name or status might serve different purposes. In order to overcome such problems, it is advisable to adopt a broad view and a working definition of social security as, say, public and private subsidies to persons facing a social contingency. Academic impetus to such a view comes from scholars like Dich (1964), who emphasised public subsidies as the core of social policy, and Titmuss (1958), who pointed to the fiscal and occupational forms of cash benefits. Accordingly, social policy and tax policy serve the same role of providing subsidies to households in the sense that social security benefits function as negative taxation and taxation as negative social security benefits.

This view is crystallised in the concept of 'multitiered social security'. The multitiered social security system is made up of the several public and private cash benefit schemes for persons facing certain social contingencies. Public schemes include direct social security benefits as well as indirect benefits through the tax system in the form of tax exemptions, reliefs, rebates or deductions (Kvist and Sinfield, 1996; OECD, 1996). Private schemes include schemes related to the workplace, whether of an individual or a collective nature. For the individual, it might not matter so much whether the particular benefit stems from a direct social security benefit, from tax benefits or from occupational benefits.

In reality, the difference between public and private is immensely blurred in social security. The institutional design of regulation, administration and financing phase out the distinctiveness of private schemes such as private pensions. For example, regulations stipulate the form and extent of tax-deductible contributions and govern the pension vehicle, which in turn influences the behaviour of both individuals and firms and thus distributional aspects. Administration is related to issues of ownership. Often a scheme is deemed private if it is governed by a private insurance company or a tripartite body. However, both of these pension vehicles are typically heavily regulated, and sometimes the company or tripartite body is not free to decide contribution rates or where to place investments.

Legislation may stipulate that individuals cannot be excluded, as is the case of compulsory social insurance schemes. This is illustrated by the gradual expansion of French social insurance to cover students and artists, and more recently by the extension of the Danish Labour Market Supplementary Pension (ATP) to cover the unemployed and other claimants of social security benefits (see below). Similarly, in its conditions for subsidies the state often dictates benefit and contribution levels, as in the German social insurance schemes.

Finally, financing is rarely completely private. Through tax deductions for contributions and premia to pension vehicles, the public purse subsidises the amounts involved by tax revenue forgone. This is also the case when income to a pension fund is tax-exempt. The state may also provide a direct subsidy in some situations when, for example, a social insurance fund cannot meet its obligations owing to increases in unemployment, disability or demographic changes. In all cases, it is difficult to say whether private funds are completely private because of public regulation or subsidies, either direct or indirect (through the tax system).

Social security in Denmark

Danish public social security schemes, dating back to the 1890s, were deliberately established as counterparts to schemes introduced in Germany at about the same time. Even before Germany decided on a model where cash benefit systems relied on compulsory insurance for wage earners, the Danish debate rejected this approach (Petersen, 1985). Instead, a cash benefit system was established and developed according to principles that would later come to be perceived as characteristic of the Nordic welfare state: a universal scope of application and benefits financed largely through general taxation rather than earmarked contributions. After the Second World War, it also became a characteristic of the Danish system that the assessment of long-term benefits, such as pensions, depended on existing income – which meant that those who already had high incomes were not entitled to benefits. In 1956 the National Pension Act initiated a gradual process of abandoning this principle through the introduction of a minimum pension irrespective of income; this culminated in 1964 in a benefit increase, which effectively made the national pension a flat-rate benefit for all, irrespective of current income.

The 'private' part of the multitiered social security system in Denmark also dates back to the middle of the last century and started, as in many other countries, in the public employment sector. As a predecessor to the first Civil Servants' Pensions Act in 1919, the Constitution of 1849 formalised the privileged position of civil servants, codifying a system of defined benefits according to former wages and length of service. Building on some of the principles of those for civil servants in the 1870s, the financial sector was part of the avant garde in setting up pension schemes for employees. A few other schemes emerged around the turn of the century, including a series of occupational pensions (based on individual firms). This basis of the small unit of the firm created problems of pension security because of a lack of an actuarial link between contributions and benefits. In 1917 some 200 companies signed policies in the newly established Pension Insurance Institution (*Pensionsforsikringsanstalten*, PFA), a life insurance company providing pension schemes, mainly for white collar workers in the private sector. However, such schemes in the private sector remained rare until after the Second World War.

The institutional design of Danish social security

This section sets out the institutional design of unemployment insurance and a number of retirement provision schemes, ie national old age pension, ATP, labour market pensions and individual pensions. It describes the principles of provision, financing and administration.

The main principle of welfare financing in Denmark is taxation. Revenue from social security contributions amounted to a modest 8% of total expenditure on public social security in 1993, that is, excluding civil servants' pensions, the Labour Market Supplementary Pension Scheme (*Arbejdsmarkedets Tillægspension*, ATP), labour market pensions, and private individual pensions (see below). There is only one area within public social security where contribution financing is of any importance, and that is unemployment insurance. The funding of the bulk of public social security benefits is the responsibility of either the state alone or the state in conjunction with the municipalities. However, the ATP and all labour market pensions are financed via contributions.

The state and the municipalities are responsible for the implementation of social policies and the administration of most cash benefits within the limits set by the Danish parliament (*Folketinget*), which has overall responsibility. In addition, the social funds, including the ATP fund and unemployment funds, are involved in social security provision. The ministries involved in the administration of each of the traditional social policy areas provide guidance for, and supervision of, municipalities and social funds. However, labour market pensions are regulated through collective agreements between employers and employees and are administered by private insurance companies under the supervision of public authorities, subject to various types of legislation.

Since 1991, the value of most cash benefits has been linked to wage developments of workers organised in the Danish Confederation of Trade Unions (LO). The levels of unemployment benefit and the national old age pension are adjusted in July each year by the same percentage rate as the increase in LO workers' wages of two years previously. However, this regulation does not extend to ATP, where individual benefit levels are determined by individual contribution records. In addition, the ATP benefit depends on the investment return of contributions. Similarly, there is no indexation of labour market pensions and individual private pensions because they are defined contribution schemes.

Unemployment insurance

Danish unemployment insurance (*arbejdsløshedsforsikring*) differs from that in most other countries because of its voluntary membership, relatively easy access to benefits, a high replacement rate for low income groups, a de facto management by trade unions and its mainly tax-financed character (Ploug and Kvist, 1994). Despite voluntary membership, coverage is high, which is due inter alia to its popular voluntary early retirement pay (*efterløn*) from age 60, which requires 20 years of membership of an unemployment insurance scheme. The main uninsured group consists of those on low incomes who, when unemployed, are often better off financially on social assistance.

Unemployment benefits are equal to 90% of previous gross earnings with a minimum of 429DKK per day and a ceiling of 523DKK per day in 1996 figures. The benefit ceiling is equivalent to around 68% of the wage of an average production worker (APW) who earned 244,000DKK per year in 1996 (about £27,000 – at an exchange rate of 9.05DKK to £1). Because of the ceiling and the effect of taxation, actual net replacement rates in 1996 varied between 98.5% for a person previously earning half as much as an APW, over 65% for an APW and 39.5% for someone previously earning twice as much as an APW (Hansen, 1997). In comparison with other European countries, Denmark has relatively high replacement rates for low income groups and relatively low replacement rates for high income groups.

Total public expenditure for unemployment insurance, that is, unemployment benefits and voluntary early retirement pay, amounted to 47.6 billion DKK in 1993 (employers' payment for the first two days of unemployment not included). Member fees are fixed amounts: they totalled nearly 7.7 billion DKK, equivalent to 16% of expenses with the remaining proportion being funded by general taxation.

Unemployment insurance as a whole is regulated by parliament, which also determines benefit rates. However, it is managed by 39 separate unemployment funds, 37 for wage earners and 2 for the self-employed. Individual unemployment funds cover different employment areas and these generally parallel the major areas of union responsibility. Members of individual unemployment funds are not also obliged to belong to the parallel trade union, but most employees do. Each unemployment fund has its own independent management, including members' representatives and often representatives from the parallel trade union. Thus, there is a strong link between the unemployment fund and the trade union in the area of responsibility for the administration and management of unemployment benefits.

Pensions in Denmark

As an overview, Table 1 displays the features of what can be regarded as the multitiered old age pension system in Denmark. What follows is a brief discussion of its elements.

The national old age pension: the universal national old age pension (*folkepensionen*) is paid at a basic annual rate of 45,576DKK (1996) from age 67. This amount is reduced for those with earnings above a certain level. In addition, an income tested pension supplement of 27,216DKK for single people and 20,016DKK for each partner of a couple is payable, as well as a non-income tested special pension supplement for single people of 17,964DKK. Guaranteed total monthly pensions amount to 7,563DKK and 5,466DKK respectively for single people and for each partner of a cohabiting/married couple. National old age pensions are financed by general taxation and administered by the individual person's municipality of residence. In addition to the national old age pension, people over the age of 67 may receive one or more of three types of supplementary pension – the ATP, a labour market pension and an individual private pension.

Table 1: The multitiered old age pension system in Denmark

	National old age pension	ATP	Labour market pensions	Personal individual pensions
Function	To guarantee a level of income	To guarantee a level of income and a modest supplement	To replace earnings or supplement basic income	To compensate for no supplement or to provide for extra supplement
Participation	Statutory	Statutory	Mandatory via collective agreements	Voluntary
Coverage	Universal (residents)	Collective (wage earners and most social security recipients)	Collective (employees in collective agreements)	Individual
Coverage ratio	100%	70% of all current pensioners 95%-98% of future pensioners	Men: 66% Women: 71%	na
Benefit formulae	Flat-rate, partly income tested	Actuarial (cohort)	Actuarial (individual)	Actuarial or saving
Financing method	Pay-as-you-go	Funded	Funded	Funded or saving
Source of finance	Taxation	Flat-rate contributions	Wage related contributions	Premia or savings
Contributions	–	Usually 2,683DKK per year (1996)	3%-15% of wage	Varies

Sources: Petersen (1995); Finansministeriet (1995); and unpublished material from the European Community Household Panel and information from ATP

The ATP scheme: the Labour Market Supplementary Pension Scheme (ATP) covers all wage earners in Denmark, and since 1996 also most claimants of social security benefits. It is a fully funded, defined-contribution scheme. Benefits are paid out from age 67. Only those who have been full-time members since its inception in 1964 are entitled to the maximum ATP benefit, which was 15,038DKK in 1996. The net replacement rate in 1996 for a single old age pensioner receiving both the national old age pension and the maximum ATP varied between 98% for a person previously earning half as much as an APW, over 54% for an APW and 33% for earnings twice as much as an APW (Hansen, 1997); the replacement rate for a couple with previous earning of one-and-a-half times an APW was 54%. Thus, the national old age pension and ATP together provide low income groups with comparatively high replacement rates, whereas high income groups do not have the same income compensation as in many other European countries.

ATP is financed by a fixed rate of compulsory contributions for all wage earners who work for 10 hours per week or more. The level is related to working hours rather than earnings. For wage earners in full-time employment, for example, it was 2,683 DKK in 1996, equivalent to approximately 1.2% of average private sector wages. One third of the contribution is paid by employees and the remainder by employers. Individual ATP benefits are calculated as a function of total contributions paid by individual members and the interest on those contributions, thus reflecting individual labour market careers and investment profiles of contributions.

A council consisting of representatives of employers, employees and the state is responsible for the administration of ATP. Requiring a majority of both employers and employees, the council decides on the annual level of contributions. There is a limit on how much revenue from contribution can be invested in one single firm, and investments have to find the right balance between scope and security on the one hand and the largest possible yield on the other. The Danish Financial Supervisory Authority oversees the ATP in respect of legal provisions.

For some time, individual labour market pension schemes have become more widespread and important (see below). Taking account of the changing landscape of pension provision in Denmark, policy makers have responded to this with a number of changes to the ATP scheme aimed at compensating those who are less firmly attached to the labour market. In turn, these reforms further underline the multitiered character of the Danish pension system. For example, in 1993 claimants of unemployment benefit, sickness benefit and maternity benefit became eligible for ATP coverage. Benefit recipients pay one third of the contribution and the remainder is paid jointly by all private employers and unemployment funds collectively. For recipients of sickness and maternity benefits, the 'employer contribution' is paid jointly by the state and private employers according to the latter's share of employees receiving benefits.

Moreover, in 1997 and 1998 a reform of the ATP scheme is being phased in which introduces three important changes. First, ATP contributions for people receiving unemployment benefit, sickness benefit or maternity benefit are doubled, while the financing mode remains unchanged. Second, compulsory coverage is extended to recipients of social assistance and a number of other social security benefits, with one third of the contribution paid by the insured and two thirds by the state. Third, voluntary membership becomes possible for some people leaving the labour market before the age of 67, that is, recipients of disability pensions, partial pension and voluntary early retirement pay.

Labour market pensions: making up the bulk of non-mandatory social security schemes in Denmark, labour market pensions (*arbejdsmarkedspensioner*) are regulated within collective agreements for each branch of industry. Despite their non-mandatory nature, they cover about two thirds of the Danish labour force of 2.8 million people.

An estimated number of 150,000 primarily non-skilled workers in the public sector is the main group not covered by labour market pensions because of a relatively long qualifying period of four years' employment, compared with about one year in the private sector. Unlike most social insurance schemes, labour market pensions are entirely funded, defined contribution schemes; that is, contributions are set as a percentage of wages according to collective agreements and benefits vary according to contributions paid and interest.

Contribution rates and waiting rules differ between the areas covered by collective agreements. However, all of these contributions, and the income they yield, enjoy tax privileges, and a considerable amount of public tax revenue is forgone at the expense of subsidising private pensions. (For a detailed discussion, see Kvist and Sinfield, 1996.)

Labour market pensions are either company based pension schemes (*virksomhedsbaserede ordninger*), where agreement has been reached between a single company and a pension fund or life insurance company, or part of collective agreements between the employers and employees (*tværgående ordninger*). The latter model applies to by far the majority of the labour force, covering all public sector employees and all hourly paid workers under the main organisations LO and the Danish Federation of Employers (DA).

Individual pension schemes: finally, there are numerous types of personal or individual pension schemes, and life insurance and savings are also very important in Denmark. Individuals can deduct contributions of up to 31,200DKK per year (in 1996) to private forms of pension (including labour market pensions) from their taxable income. Pensions take the form of either a lump sum, taxed at 40% on receipt, or annuities, which are typically taxed at a higher rate since they are regarded as personal income. Life insurance companies and banks are the main providers of these schemes.

The multitiered old age pension system in Denmark as a whole: the various types of old age pensions, other social security benefits payable to older people and tax benefits are but one example of what often are complex benefit packages which people receive and governments sponsor in the event of certain contingencies such as sickness, unemployment and early retirement. Here I have concentrated on the multitiered old age pension system, since it is the backbone of the Danish welfare state and clearly demonstrates the complexity of, and interaction between, various benefits. What is more, recent policy changes in the area may provide important insights as to the future of social security in Denmark.

Labour market pensions in particular became the focus of fierce discussions during the second half of the 1980s, leading to the introduction of new non-mandatory pension systems based on collective agreements in 1990, which covered about a fifth of the labour force (von Nordheim Nielsen, 1996; Finansministeriet, 1995). There are no regular official statistics, but a recent survey shows that labour market pensions now cover 66% of men and 71% of women in the Danish labour force (unpublished material from the European Community Household Panel). This must be seen in the light of labour market participation rates in Denmark of around 80% for both men and women. Moreover, the Ministry of Finance estimates that 85%-90% of the population at some time during their lives will be covered by labour market pension schemes (Finansministeriet, 1995). Thus, an almost universal tier of pension provision has been introduced via collective agreements rather than government regulation. However, the various labour market pension schemes differ in their design as far as risks are concerned and, perhaps more importantly, in contribution rates, thus laying the foundations for future inequalities in old age.

Of course, it is difficult to make predictions, especially (as noted by the Danish humorist P. Storm) about the future. However, private pensions, whether labour market pension or individual personal pensions, are becoming increasingly important. Pensioners' annual average private pension income rose from 14,000DKK in 1983 to 26,000DKK in 1993 (in constant prices), compared with a corresponding increase of public pension income from 45,000 to 53,000DKK – equal to an annual growth rate of 6.2% for private and 1.6% for public pensions (Finansministeriet, 1996a). As labour market pensions mature, the share of private pension income will continue to increase further, and it is certain that the pension system of 2030 will be very different from today's.

What is more, the significant increase in private pensions has contributed to increased income levels for pensioners in relation to the population of active working age. Between 1983 and 1993 the individual average net income in old age rose by 1.9% annually, from 75% to 81% of the average income of individuals of working age, which increased by only 1% per year during the same period (Finansministeriet, 1996a). This trend is likely to continue as the labour market pension schemes mature.

Danish old age pensioners have gained more during the last 10 years, in both absolute and relative terms. More crucially, the composition of benefit packages has changed. In other words, a restructuring of social security is taking place, rather than a retrenchment. This indicates that it is not sufficient to concentrate on one income component only, say public pensions, in discussions of welfare state development.

Changing benefit packages have, of course, distributional effects. When labour market pensions based on affiliation to the labour market and earnings become dominant, seasonal and unskilled workers as well as women are likely to suffer. However, as discussed below, paradoxically, labour market pensions may still contribute to a reduction in inequality compared with a time where there was no coverage at all for some groups and upside-down effects of individual personal pensions prevailed. This can be illustrated by discussing relevant policy changes of the recent past.

Recent policy changes

The Danish social security system has been heavily criticised from all political angles during the last 15 years. The following discussion regarding political rhetoric and actual changes is divided into a section covering the period between 1982 and 1993 of a right-wing coalition government, followed by a discussion of changes implemented by the left-wing coalition government since then.

Policy changes under right-wing coalition governments

Danish politics is characterised by either two or more parties in a coalition government – which might still be in a minority in parliament – or one political party forming a minority government. In August 1982, the Social Democratic Party (*Social-demokratiet*) were in such a minority in government that passing of legislation was made difficult. As a response to a state deficit, compounded by an economic recession, the government suggested taxing the considerable income of pension funds. Fierce opposition to this plan in parliament eventually led to the resignation of the Social Democratic administration, and to the formation of a coalition government between the Conservatives (*Det konservative folkeparti*), the Liberals (*Venstre*), the Centre Democrats (*Centrumdemokraterne*) and the Christian People's Party (*Kristeligt folkeparti*). The expectation on the part of the Social Democrats of regaining power before too long was misguided. As it turned out, 1982 signalled the beginning of an unprecedented period of right–centre dominance in Danish politics. What is more, one of the new government's first laws introduced the taxation of pension fund income (*realrenteafgiften*).

Despite their declared willingness to 'transform the uncontrolled Leviathan Welfare State', the Conservative-led government did not reduce overall costs. While in 1982 expenditure on cash benefits (in constant prices for 1990) accounted for 18% of GDP, in 1993 the rate stood at 21%, which was equal to an increase of 39% compared with a growth in GDP of only 24%. However, while expenditure on some benefits increased, other types of social spending were cut back.

As in other countries, these outcomes were influenced both by external economic and demographic factors, reflected in the numbers of social security recipients, and by internal factors, such as changes made to benefit levels. Unemployment benefits were more affected by both the economic cycle and political decisions than were national old age pensions. In the period 1982-87 unemployment decreased from 11% to 8%, but then surged to a level of 10.7% in 1993. The period of declining unemployment needs to be considered in the light of favourable economic conditions of rising economic growth and private consumption and declining rates of inflation and interest. From 1987 onwards the increase in unemployment was caused, among other things, by a series of political interventions aimed at improving the balance of payments, which had reached an unprecedented level of 5% of GDP in 1985 and 1986. Two forms of political intervention in particular were aimed at curbing domestic consumption. A tax reform limited the possibilities for deducting the interest paid on private-debts from taxable income, and the so-called 'Potato Cure' further restricted the tax deductibility of interest on credit for private consumption.

Moreover, a series of policy changes brought about a slight decrease in benefit expenditure per claimant between 1982 and 1988. Measures were aimed at reducing expenditure on unemployment benefit in particular and also at increasing the gap between benefit levels and minimum wages. The maximum rate of unemployment benefit was frozen between October 1982 and April 1986, leading to a 17% decrease of its real value (Knudsen, 1987). However, in December 1987 the government reached an agreement with the Social Democrats and other opposition parties which resulted in a 10% increase in both benefit levels and the rate of voluntary early retirement pay. This U turn has to be seen in the light of political bargaining and negotiations between the government and the Social Democrats surrounding the budget. Furthermore, in spring 1990 the Danish parliament decided that in future cash benefits were to be linked to wages, as described earlier.

Contribution rates to unemployment insurance were raised in the 1980s, but in 1988 employers became exempt from contributions. However, since then employers have been obliged to pay benefits to insured persons for the first day of unemployment. This was later extended to the first two days, with the aim of discouraging employers from short-term layoffs. However, because of the failure of some employers to implement this change, one in four unemployed people do not receive benefits for the first two days out of work, despite their entitlement (Andersen and Høgelund, 1995).

In contrast to unemployment benefits and other social security schemes, interventions left the perhaps politically more sensitive area of national old age pensions remained remarkably untouched. In fact, old age pensioners experienced an improvement in the value of their benefits during the reign of right-wing coalition governments. For example, a freeze of indexation on most social security benefits and, noticeably, wages did not affect national old age pensions. Pensions were indexed to the cost of living (*dyrtidsreguleringen*), which meant that pension values increased by an annual average of 1.6% compared with 0.6% for wage earners between 1983 and 1993 (Finansministeriet, 1996a). The Social Democrats argued for further increases in benefit levels during the negotiations with the government over the 1987 budget. As a result, basic pension levels were increased, including a rise of supplementary elements by 5% for single people and by 7% for married pensioners, on top of the indexation for 1988. However, for those aged between 67 and 69, an income test for part of the national old age pension was implemented in 1984. Overall, expenditure on national old age pensions increased by 20.9% in real terms between 1982 and 1993, but the share of GDP remained stable (at 5.9% and 5.8% respectively).

Policy changes under a Social Democrat-led coalition government

In January 1993, the Conservative-led government resigned as a result of a refugee scandal (the Tamil case) and a new government took over under the leadership of the Social Democratic Party in coalition with the three centre parties – the Christians, the Centre Democrats and the Social Liberals. During their first year in office a number of reforms were passed, including a tax reform, phased in between 1994 and 1998, and a labour market reform which took effect from January 1994. Both reforms had an impact on social security. The new government made a commitment not to reduce the level of cash benefits for individual claimants but to create a more coherent and transparent system and, in the case of the labour market reform, to strengthen the bond between rights and obligations.

One of the most important elements of the 1994 labour market reform was to set the maximum period during which claimants are entitled to unemployment benefits to seven years, although this may be extended by another two years in respect of educational leave, by up to one year (per child) in the case of parental leave and by six months in the case of maternity leave; furthermore, recipients may continue receiving unemployment benefits after the age of 50 without being excluded from the system. New, and improved, leave-of-absence from work schemes (educational, parental and sabbatical) and more flexible training and vocational training programmes were other important elements of the labour market reform. Unemployment rates increased from 10.7% in 1993 to over 12% in 1994. Since then unemployment has decreased, mainly as a result of an economic upturn, but also because of an increase in the number of people participating in the improved leave-of-absence schemes and activation measures (L. Pedersen, 1996; Ingerslev and Pedersen, 1996).

The main objectives of the 1994 tax/benefit reform were to reduce marginal tax rates, to widen the tax base and increase the sources of taxation, and to make the costs of social protection more visible to the public (Skatteministeriet, 1994). These objectives were generally in line with the preceding tax reform of 1987 and also in line with the tax reforms of most capitalist countries during the 1980s and early 1990s (Pechmann, 1988). Of particular importance to the issue of social insurance was the introduction of a so-called 'labour market contribution' based on wages, which is earmarked to finance unemployment benefit, sickness benefit and various forms of active labour market measures. However, the contribution is not linked to actual expenses, nor are benefits linked to the contributions. Thus, one could argue that it has little to do with social security contributions in terms of social insurance, but simply represents a gross tax. Responding to recommendations made by various commissions, especially the Social Commission (Socialkommissionen, 1993) and by a working group under the Ministry of Social Affairs (Socialministeriet, 1991), the tax reform also achieved greater transparency of the social security system and benefit comparability with income from work through the abolition of certain tax allowances for old age pensioners and recipients of social assistance. Benefit increases compensated for the higher level of taxation.

Also in 1994, the basic amount of the national old age pension became income tested in relation to earnings from work. Those with earnings exceeding a certain amount now receive a reduced basic amount of the old age pension – or no pension at all. Moreover, the supplement element of the old age pension has also become income tested, taking into account income from other pensions. In practice, this means that people in old age with considerable income from earnings will not receive a national old age pension, and people with significant income from other pensions will receive only the basic amount. From a Danish perspective, this does not mean that the national old age pension is no longer a universal benefit, since the income test relates merely to the calculation of the pensionable amount and not to eligibility.

The future of social security in Denmark

There is now a multitiered social security system in Denmark in which the first tier of public social security is fairly uniform and gives the state a major role in financing and providing benefits, and where the whole population is covered in the event of social contingencies. Only a few schemes adhere to the principles of social insurance and the Danish unemployment insurance, is the only programme that qualifies as a social insurance system in purely rhetorical terms. In contrast to the first tier, the second tier of private schemes is fairly fragmented and covers the labour force by offering variable income protection arrangements depending on economic sector and branch of industry. Again, there is no conformity to social insurance principles. Instead, benefits and funding characteristics are more closely related to aspects of private insurance. Since the first tier aims to guarantee all citizens a basic income in the event of certain social contingencies, it provides comparatively generous benefits for low income groups. In contrast, the second tier provides some income replacement for middle and high income groups.

The historical development of Danish social security is not one of sweeping reforms but rather is characterised by incremental steps. Roughly two periods can be identified (Kvist and Petersen, 1997). During the first fifty years, reforms gradually included more and more social groups into the system of first-tier protection and made benefits independent of income testing. This process culminated in 1964 with the universal national old age pension, a flat-rate benefit which was not subject to an income test and was financed by taxation on a pay-as-you-go basis. The first period thus can be characterised as progress towards universalism and the ending of income tests in public schemes.

The year 1964 also marked the start of the second period with the establishment of the ATP scheme, that is, a supplementary benefit scheme. Its logic was in sharp contrast to the inherent logic of the national old age pension. Benefits were based on attachment to the labour market, financed through social security contributions on a funded basis, and to individual benefit levels, determined by contributions paid and their derived interest. In other words, a direct link between contributions and benefits was established. This distinguished ATP from civil servants' pensions, where benefits were expressed as part of previous earnings and financed in the same way as other cash benefits.

Second-tier or supplementary schemes for economically active people have continued to develop since 1964. In particular, they provide labour market pensions for people with a disability, surviving dependants and the old, but they also include sickness and maternity benefits. Labour market pensions and similar supplementary benefits have become major issues in negotiations and collective agreements between social partners. In other words, the second period of social security in Denmark is characterised by the development of a second tier of cash benefits for the working population.

Most of these second-tier schemes are financed through employers' and employees' contributions on a strictly funded basis, and benefits are of a more significant order than ATP, especially for middle and high income groups. Greater inequalities both within and between generations will occur as these schemes mature. It can even be argued that the second tier is more likely to become an alternative, rather than merely supplementary, to first-tier schemes of social security. In particular, middle and high income groups are likely to receive generous benefits while they might be excluded from the income tested national old age pension.

Paradoxically, however, labour market pension schemes may be instrumental in actually reducing income inequalities since they provide protection for low and middle income groups (Petersen, 1995). In the absence of these collective schemes, individuals would have to make their own savings for old age, which was the case in the early 1980s. At that time there was a clear tendency towards a dualisation of the Danish welfare state, with low income groups relying on the national old age pension while those on a higher income made their own arrangements which were generously subsidised by the tax system (Vesterø-Jensen, 1985). The supplement element of the national old age pension is income tested, which includes income from other pensions. Thus, as labour market pension schemes mature and pay out higher pensions, many more employees will be affected by some reduction of their national old age pension. This means that tax resources will be saved and income inequality reduced. This can be seen as an example of policy makers implementing a mechanism that does not at present affect many current pensioners and voters, but will gradually come to be of increasing importance.

Compared with ten years ago, the debate about the welfare state today focuses much more on claimants' obligations than on claimants' rights and 'passive' cash benefits, indicating a shift in welfare discourse away from entitlements based on citizenship and towards activation measures, and attaching conditions to benefit eligibility. Social Democrats and other socialist groups today advocate selectivism, just as Liberals promoted universalism a hundred years ago (Nyrup Rasmussen, 1996; Nielsen, 1994). In fact, with the aim of shifting the financial burden of poor relief from the municipalities and land taxes on to the state and income taxes, Liberals in Denmark were among the strongest proponents of universalism and state provision at the time when the Danish welfare state was founded (Dich, 1973). In other words, the same tools of social policy can be used over time for different reasons by opposing political parties.

Social Democrats in Denmark today are among the advocates of claimants' obligations as well as rights and, sometimes, of rationing benefits through income testing. Their stated motives are not to dismantle the welfare state, but to enhance the link between rights and obligations, to target benefits on the needy and to promote the conjunction of work and family life rather than a complete independence of the labour market (Lykketoft, 1994; Socialdemokratiet, 1995; Finansministeriet, 1996b; Nyrup Rasmussen, 1996). In other words, the social democratic 'project' in Denmark is no longer just about wages and benefit increases, but also about the more qualitative aspects of life, that is, the reconciliation of work and family life and giving everybody a chance to work, with the tools of targeting and activation becoming increasingly prominent.

However, there are discrepancies between political rhetoric and policy in practice. For example, lack of funding and other resources has rendered many activation initiatives hollow. Also, political rhetoric does not always match actual policies, sometimes as a result of competing policy objectives. For example, the possibility for unemployed workers to take educational, parental or sabbatical leave from their unemployment, which was introduced in 1994, does not fit well with the idea of making benefits conditional on activation, but contributes towards another stated objective – that of lowering unemployment. Also, changes in public social security spending and increases in the number of recipients are due largely to changes in economic and demographic contexts rather than to policy decisions, with the exception of the new leave-of-absence schemes and activation measures.

Conclusion

The dichotomous framework of residual and institutional welfare states has an inherent bias in supporting retrenchment theses as soon as changes are made to public social security schemes since it does not allow for a sufficient understanding of change over time within one country. Recent developments in Denmark point to the necessity of including not just state welfare in social policy analysis, whether national or cross-national, but also tax and occupational welfare. More attention should be paid to the institutional design of welfare states, that is, the complex world of social security, taxation and other welfare schemes. A narrow focus on state provided or state regulated welfare does not enable the researcher to depict the perhaps equally important channels of welfare based on collective solutions in the labour market, not least occupational pensions in some countries.

The gradual transformation of the Danish welfare state, the emergence of a truly multitiered social security system, is a 'silent revolution' without much monitoring and discussion (Petersen, 1995). Nevertheless, this revolution will most likely result in a restructuring of the Danish welfare state. This future multitiered social security system will include a basic income guarantee, underpinned by universalism and tax financing, but with an increased emphasis on activation as implemented through the attaching of conditions to benefit eligibility. Other schemes will be based on funding and actuarial principles and will provide partial income compensation for working people. Both types of scheme deviate from the social insurance models in other countries.

three

Sweden: on the way from standard to basic security?[*]
Ann-Charlotte Ståhlberg

Introduction

In the 1990s, social insurance has become a central issue in Sweden. For sickness insurance, the level of compensation has been reduced and a qualifying no-benefit day has been introduced. A proposal on guiding principles for a radically different system of old age pensions has been passed by parliament. The widow's pension has been eliminated. In future, no one will be able to receive an early retirement pension for reasons related to problems in the labour market. A government commission has proposed a higher level of income protection in the event of occupational injury than in cases of work-related sickness. Compensation levels in unemployment insurance have been lowered, and further changes are under discussion.

Compared with the expansion in the 1970s and 1980s, the 1990s appear to mark a dramatic turning point in the development of social insurance. Where is Sweden heading? Is the standard security provided by the Swedish social insurance system gradually dwindling into basic security? These questions are examined in this chapter: first, by discussing historical developments, and second, by analysing and assessing the structure and purpose of

---

[*]I would like to thank the Stockholm Centre for Organizational Research for financial support

recent reforms within the principal components of the social insurance system: pensions, sickness insurance, occupational injury insurance and unemployment insurance.

Social security in outline

There are various ways and means by which individuals and households can protect themselves from loss of income as a result of unemployment, sickness, occupational injury and old age, and these are often combined. In international debates, it has become customary to speak of the different tiers or pillars of income security. In the first tier there is social insurance, which in many cases comprises a part that is independent of income and a part that is tied to income. A second tier is made up of negotiated occupational insurance schemes, but also of insurance agreements and unilateral commitments entered into by individual companies. The third tier encompasses group insurance schemes, private insurance policies and also private savings.

The public element is very strong in the Swedish social security. With the exception of unemployment insurance, which is voluntary, social insurance schemes are mandatory and universal. They consist of uniform, publicly administered programmes, based mainly on the principle of compensation for loss of income. In all essentials, they are financed by (earmarked) earnings related contributions, that is, fixed percentages of wages paid by employers but ultimately borne by employees in the form of lower direct remuneration.[1] Social insurance schemes are set up as pay-as-you-go systems.

Complementary schemes, principally in the form of negotiated occupational insurance schemes, have many features in common with social insurance. The terms of the former schemes are defined in agreements reached by the parties in the labour market. In practice, they are compulsory and universal in scope, and insurance entitlements are transferable between jobs. The benefits are income related and are financed mainly by charges levied on employers, but borne by employees.[2] The negotiated insurance schemes in the public sector, national and local, are constructed as pay-as-you-go systems, while those in the private sector are wholly or partially set up as funded systems. Negotiated insurance schemes cover the same areas as social insurance and complement the latter by raising the level of compensation and by compensating for the loss of income over and above the level of earnings covered by social insurance schemes.

For most people, both the social and the occupational insurance schemes entail a redistribution of income over a lifetime (intertemporal equalisation). In certain periods they pay in, and in others they receive benefits. In addition, insurance schemes redistribute income, first, between individuals at varying risk of being affected by sickness, occupational injury, unemployment, etc, and second, between different income categories.

There are two aspects of income redistribution within the public social risk insurance schemes. The first is an outcome of universal schemes without risk differentiation. People who constitute a higher risk in terms of sickness or early retirement pay the same percentage of wages as people who constitute a lesser risk. The second type of redistribution results from the fact that social insurance schemes compensate for loss of income only below a certain ceiling, while contributions are paid on the entire income, that is, also on the part of the income that is over and above that ceiling. The latter is equivalent to 7.5 so-called 'base amounts'. Tied to the consumer price index, one 'base amount' was equivalent to about 20% of an average industrial worker's pay before taxes in 1996.

The negotiated insurance schemes do not aim to redistribute income in the same way as social insurance schemes. However, there are also elements of redistribution in the negotiated schemes. First, they are universal insurance schemes without risk differentia- tion. For example, the risk of early retirement varies between employees, while the premiums and terms of compensation are the same. A second element of redistribution results from the fact that in the majority of cases negotiated insurance schemes also compensate for loss of income above the ceiling of 7.5 'base amounts', and that the degree of compensation is considerably higher for these portions of income. In these cases, redistribution takes place within the insurance scheme – premiums are paid as a fixed percentage of the payroll. For certain groups, the two redistributional effects mentioned can compensate for one another. People who spend more years in education, for example, have generally lower rates of absence from work because of illness and early retirement than people who have had fewer years of education. On the other hand, it is much more common for people with more education to have incomes above 7.5 'base amounts'. Which type of redistribution predominates cannot be determined without detailed empirical studies.

The element of the social insurance system that is independent of earnings (made up almost exclusively of the national basic pension) is financed jointly by the entire working population who pay a fixed percentage of their wages. This means that people with a high income pay more for this type of uniform income security than those with low incomes. On the other hand, as far as the public national supplementary pension (ATP) is concerned (see below), there is no systematic redistribution from higher to lower wage earners. Instead, as discussed elsewhere (Ståhlberg, 1989; 1990), its design is disadvantageous to those who work for most of their adult life and have a weak wage growth profile (often people on low incomes), while it favours those who work less and whose incomes are unevenly distributed over their lifetime.

Lessons of history

Based on research into British, Danish and German unemployment compensation schemes, Toft (1995) has argued that basic frameworks established in the early construction of social insurance have a tendency to be long-lived and self-reinforcing. What would this mean for Swedish social insurance? In order to address this question, a brief account of what characterises the essential framework of the systems seems appropriate.

The beginning of Swedish social insurance is generally associated with S.A. Hedin's parliamentary bill of 1884, proposing old age and accident insurance for workers. The bill was inspired by the reforms in imperial Germany at the beginning of the 1880s, and the process of official inquiry got under way soon after the presentation of Hedin's bill, albeit with scant results. As late as 1910, there was only one piece of legislation, dating back to 1901, which imposed a limited liability on employers to compensate workers in the event of occupational injury, and an embryonic voluntary sickness insurance movement which received some state subsidies (Edebalk, 1994).

While the beginnings were slow, therefore, a few years later a change occurred in the sociopolitical climate, and in the years around 1910, parties of all political complexions became more or less decided advocates of social policy reform, indicating that a new view of the state's role and its capacity for solving social issues had been established. In 1913, parliament decided by a very large majority to establish a public pension insurance system which was to cover the entire population. It consisted of two parts. The first was a pension financed by individual contributions, inspired by the compulsory insurance system in Germany. The second part was a tax-financed, means tested supplementary pension. This part was introduced in order to give insurance coverage immediate effect (Edebalk, 1994).

Three years later, it was decided to substitute employers' liability for compensation with the introduction of an occupational injury insurance scheme. This covered the entire labour force and benefits were paid according to the principle of compensation for lost wages at a rate of two-thirds of previous income. This was the first time the principle of compensation for loss of income was applied in the Swedish social insurance system (Edebalk, 1996).

A proposal for mandatory public sickness insurance, which enjoyed strong political support, was presented in 1919. At the same time, sickness benefits were to be payable according to the principle of compensation for loss of income, with the same wage replacement rate as the occupational injury insurance. Two thirds of this scheme was to be financed by contributions and one third by taxation. However, the proposal was not implemented. The deflationary crisis intervened and state sickness insurance had to be postponed (Edebalk, 1996).

Overall, the second decade of this century marked the definitive breakthrough of the idea of social insurance in Sweden. In principle, social insurance was to cover the entire population and was to be administered by the state. Where benefits were concerned, the principle of compensation for loss of income was accepted. However, unemployment insurance was then, as now, assigned a place outside the system of public social insurance. The trade union movement found it hard to attain a compromise on a Ghent system (with unemployment insurance organised by unions but subsidised by the state) and an agreement was not reached until 1934 (Edebalk, 1996).

After the Second World War, in a changed economic and political situation, Gustav Möller, the Social Democratic Minister of Social Affairs, intended to introduce an entirely new system of social insurance, involving tax-financed basic security. The principle of minimum standards is a manifestation of Möller's sociopolitical ideology. Strongly influenced by Beveridge, Möller advocated that insurance coverage over and above minimum subsistence requirements ought to be left to the individual, 'on the basis of his or her own sense of responsibility'. Mandatory insurance schemes were to provide basic insurance, which people were then supposed to complement with voluntary insurance. However, unlike Beveridge, Möller envisaged a system financed by taxation, thereby contributing to an equalisation of incomes. When Möller resigned in 1951, Gunnar Sträng succeeded him as Minister of Social Affairs in the Social Democratic government, leading to a continuation of the reforms that had begun before 1920. State subsidies to and the terms of the Ghent system were improved, enabling a significant expansion in unemployment insurance. Mandatory state sickness insurance, based on the principle of compensation for loss of income, came into force in 1955, and the triumph of the principle of compensation for loss of income paved the way for the general supplementary pension, ATP, which took effect in 1960.

In the 1990s, Möller's idea of basic security with voluntary additional coverage has been advanced anew as a way of changing the Swedish system of social insurance. However, if Toft's thesis is correct, the principle of compensation for loss of income is probably too deeply rooted in the Swedish welfare state to be overthrown.

The problems

Swedish social insurance schemes are set up as pay-as-you-go systems and are therefore sensitive to changes in the factors that determine expenditure and the total wage sum. Early exit from the labour force, high absenteeism for reasons of sickness, high unemployment and long-term unemployment reduce the number of contributors to the system and increase the number of those receiving benefits, resulting in a greater financial burden on those in employment.

In the 1970s and 1980s Sweden experienced a trend towards increased absenteeism from illness, increasing numbers of people taking early retirement and people receiving benefits for occupational injuries. This is illustrated by changes in the sickness rate, which is measured as the average number of days of illness for which each person with sickness insurance receives benefits from the public sickness insurance system in the course of one year. At the beginning of the 1980s, the rate was about 20 days per year; this rose to just over 26 days in 1988. What is more, the proportion of the population taking early retirement more than doubled over 30 years, from about 3% in 1963 to 7.3% in 1993. During the 1980s, about 50,000 new early retirement pensions were granted each year. The number of cases of work related sickness covered by occupational injury insurance rose from about 7,000 in 1980 to over 56,000 in 1991. In addition, the proportion of older people in the population is rising and is expected to peak around 2010, when the large groups born in the 1940s reach retirement age.

Finally, unemployment has become a problem. Until the late 1980s Sweden had very low unemployment with rates below 2%, compared with many countries in Europe which were experiencing rates of over 10%. However, in September 1996 open unemployment stood at 8.6% of the labour force; an additional 4.2% were engaged in labour market policy programmes (retraining schemes, etc).

Pay-as-you-go systems are based on the assumption that, in the course of their lives, the vast majority of people are both contributors (paying into the system in certain periods) and recipients (receiving benefits in other periods). If an increasing number of people are excluded from the working population and become permanent benefit recipients, it becomes less certain whether the 'social contract' that a pay-as-you-go system implies will hold. In the long run, standard security could be at risk and could be reduced to a mere essential basic security in accordance with the principle of minimum standards. In addition, there are those who believe that it is the design of the social insurance system itself that provides disincentives to work and therefore contributes, at least to some extent, to the increase in the proportion of benefit recipients. Consequently, in order to break that causal connection, structural reforms are necessary.

How far do these scenarios reflect developments in the 1990s? Are reforms gradually replacing standard security with basic security, or have the changes that have occurred so far been implemented mainly for the purpose of correcting the underlying structure of social insurance, so that standard security can remain tenable in the long term? These are the questions that will be addressed in the following sections which focus on particular aspects of social insurance in Sweden.

A new system of old age pensions

The current public old age pension system consists of a portion independent of income (national basic pension) and a portion tied to income (ATP). The rights to a national basic pension are based either on residence or on income giving rise to an ATP pension. Up to 1993 citizenship was required, but this was changed when rules were introduced in line with EU regulations. On average, the smallest annual amount old age pensioners receive is about 2 'base amounts' (ie, about 40% of an average industrial worker's wage before tax; see above). Normally, the national basic pension and ATP combined make up about 65% of a person's previous gross income up to the so-called ATP ceiling (7.5 'base amounts'). Negotiated occupational pensions provide a further 10% of income up to that ceiling. In addition, most negotiated schemes provide a pension based on earnings over and above the ATP ceiling with a replacement rate of 65% for that part of previous earnings. Both the public pension and the negotiated occupational pension are defined benefits, which means that the level of benefits is fixed, requiring contributions to be adjusted accordingly.

Some problems and technical details of the new supplementary pension (the reformed ATP) are still to be resolved before it can be introduced, with 1999 as the preliminary year of implementation. As presented in the 1994 parliamentary bill, the new scheme will be compulsory and earnings related. What is new is that it will be based on defined contributions rather than defined benefits; also, it is index linked to wages. The current ATP is protected against inflation but there is no wage indexing. What is more, while the new ATP will be organised mainly as a pay-as-you-go system (with a certain buffer fund element), according to the parliamentary decision a small part is to be invested in pension funds. It is proposed that the pension contribution should be 18.5% of employees' wages (and of the incomes of self-employed people). Of these, 16.5 percentage points are to be paid into the pay-as-you-go system and 2.0 percentage points into funds. In the pay-as-you-go system no actual deposits in accounts are made:

instead individual accounts are simulated. Also, contributions to the pay-as-you-go system will be indexed to changes in real wages, while revenue for the funded system will be dependent on the rate of return on capital. Subject to further consideration, it has been proposed that half of the total pension contribution is to be paid by the employer and half by the employee. In the short run, this would be disadvantageous for wage earners. It is only in the long run that employees' real wages will increase (all things being equal) by an amount equal to their pension contribution.[3] Consequently, some Swedish wage earners have objected to the proposal, preferring employers to continue making the payments formally.

The new ATP envisages a flexible retirement age from 61 onwards. When a person retires, the pension rights he or she has earned will be divided by the number of years which, statistically, the particular cohort has left to live. The quotient arrived at equals the annual pension amount. Roughly calculated, a person who works for 40 years will receive a pension equivalent to nearly 60% of his or her previous average lifetime income. Parents of small children will be subsidised by being awarded 'free' pension rights during their children's infancy. It is possible that pension rights earned will be divided between spouses.

A person who has earned no ATP pension or only a low ATP pension will receive a 'guaranteed pension', that is a basic pension financed jointly by all taxpayers. The level of this pension will be about the same as the present national basic pension. It will be automatically adjusted for inflation. Naturally, transitional rules will be applicable for a long time.

All these intended changes are aimed explicitly at enhancing the stability of the pension system. If it had been merely a question of improving public finances, the formula could have been simpler: reduced pension benefits and/or higher contributions. A pension system has to be robust, so that rules and regulations do not change with political majorities. This is because the need to adapt to new regulations is not unproblematic, and repeated changes which create uncertainty about what will apply in the future, serve to undermine the legitimacy of the system in the long run. If a pension system is to be stable, it has to be designed in a way that is acceptable to a majority of people as reasonable and generally fair, thus avoiding conflicts between different groups and continuous demands for changes by those who feel disadvantaged.

In the present, defined benefit ATP system, all adaptations to changes in demographic and economic contexts are effected by means of changes in the rate of contributions charged, that is, the adaptation is laid in its entirety on the section of the population that is gainfully employed. In a pay-as-you-go system, where pension payments are financed by wage-related contributions, an increase in the number of pensioners will result in a heavier financial burden on those in employment. Moreover, if the proportion of people in employment diminishes for other reasons, such as a rise in unemployment, an increase in the minimum school leaving age or longer parental leave, the burden of payment per employed person grows still further. This causes tensions between pensioners and the working population which might threaten the existence of a pension system.

Such a tendency is greatly intensified by the fact that there is no link at present between the level of individual pensions received and the wages of those who are gainfully employed – a design that is not very common in other countries. Instead, the amount of the present individual ATP pension is determined solely by the person's previous income. It is adjusted to changes in the consumer price index, but is not affected by changes in the wages of the working population. In other words, the scope pensioners have for consumption is fixed, no matter what happens to the economy. This means that in 'lean' years pensioners' living standards rise relative to that of the working population, whereas in 'fat' years the reverse is the case. If growth rates were to remain very low over a long period, the average public pension could become as large as the income of members of the working population (Ståhlberg, 1991; 1995). In other words, the adaptation to swings in the economy is laid entirely on the working population.

The new ATP system is intended to change this. The working population is to be relieved of some of the pressure through the introduction of a wage-indexing of pensions, which implies that pensions and wages keep in step with one another. In good years the 'fruits are shared', so that pensioners too enjoy a share in increased productivity; in bad years, both groups alike are hit.

In the present ATP system, the working population also takes on all of the increased costs resulting from increased life expectancy. Because of its pay-as-you-go design, a rise in expenditure on pensions has to be matched by increased contribution rates. In this respect, too, the design of the new ATP system aims to relieve wage earners of part of the burden. Under the new scheme, it is the pensioners themselves who bear the cost resulting from demographic change, since individual pension rights are divided by the number of years a particular age group is expected to have left to live. What is more, variations in the birth rate are known long before they have any impact on pension payments, and for this reason their effect on pension fees can be cushioned with the help of buffer funds, which will be provided for in the new ATP.

In the present ATP pension scheme there is no systematic redistribution between higher and lower wage earners, but there is some redistribution between people with a long working life but weak real wage growth over time and people with a relatively short working life with unevenly distributed lifetime incomes. This is one consequence of ATP's so-called '15- and 30-year' rules, which means that pension levels are determined by the pensionable income during the 15 best paid years, while 30 years of pensionable income are required in order to qualify for a full pension. Those who have their (pensionable) income distributed unevenly over their life (often intermediate level white collar workers and also senior white collar workers whose income does not exceed the ATP ceiling) receive a much higher ATP pension if it is calculated on the basis of their 15 'best years' than they would if it were calculated on the basis of their entire life cycle income. By contrast, pensions for those with a flat (pensionable) life cycle income (often lower level white collar workers and blue collar workers) do not increase more with the '15-year' rule than they would do without it. Thus, since the pension contribution is proportional to the life cycle wage, blue collar workers and lower level white collar workers pay more for their pensions than intermediate level and senior white collar workers (see Ståhlberg, 1989; 1990; 1995a).

The new ATP system is designed to address this. In principle, it will not redistribute income other than over individual life cycles. Each Swedish krona paid into the system will be of equal value. However, there are exceptions. Those with children, for example, will be entitled to 'free' pension rights during the years when the children are young and in need of care. This contrasts with the present rules, which subsidise all non-market types of work, whether the time is spent caring for infants or in some other way. Thus, the accuracy in meeting the targets of redistribution policy will be higher in the reformed system (see Ståhlberg, 1995b).

In sum, the ATP reform has enhanced the chances for the pension system to become economically stable. Compared with the present system, it is better able to adapt to changes in the economy and demography, and it is fairer both within and between generations. Of course, its political acceptance and stability is another question. The present ATP design chiefly favours large middle classes (or, more accurately, intermediate level white collar workers). It remains to be seen whether this group will show social solidarity by supporting a system in which it no longer enjoys a comparative advantage.

Reforms in the sickness insurance system

In 1974, the level of sickness benefit within the social insurance system was raised to 90% of gross income, and made taxable at the same time. In 1987, the last remaining waiting (no benefit) day was eliminated. In practice, replacement rates succeeded 90% because of complementary negotiated occupational benefits. Indeed, between 1987 and 1991 sickness benefits replaced 100% of income lost for virtually everyone, with 90% covered by the public sickness insurance system and the remaining 10% paid out by negotiated insurance plans. However, this trend was reversed in the 1990s when benefits became less generous, a change justified with regard to cost saving and addressing the behavioural implications of sickness benefit.

When insured parties are, in principle, able deliberately to influence insurance payouts (moral hazard), some form of excess is necessary in order to prevent insurance schemes from being exploited. By covering losses in part, insurance policies provide individuals with an incentive to prevent losses. The excess can take the form of compensation lower than 100%, qualifying periods or other types of condition attached to insurance payouts. Another way of reducing moral hazard is to require a certain kind of behaviour on the part of the insured, and then to check that these requirements are being met. The cheaper it is to ascertain whether individuals conform to the demands made, the lower the excess can be. For example, if instead of the sickness insurance scheme there is a period during which employers are responsible for providing sick pay, employers in companies with relatively high rates of absenteeism due to sickness incur higher costs for compensation than employers in companies with a relatively low sickness rate. As a consequence, the control of absenteeism can be firmer than it would be if compensation were provided by a more impersonal and distant insurance system. However, a period of sick pay instead of sickness insurance benefit can lead employers to keep costs for sickness absenteeism down by being selective when appointing new staff, for example, by adopting health screening and not taking on older applicants or those with health problems. The risk of this is greater the longer is the stipulated period of sick pay.

Some types of sickness are easy to diagnose and moral hazard is therefore impossible. In principle, it would thus be possible to provide 100% coverage in these cases; for example, it is self-evident that a serious accident or disability implies absenteeism for reasons of sickness and incapacity to work. Although the official reason was financial savings, in accordance with this line of reasoning, in its 1996 report the Swedish Committee on Sickness and Occupational Injuries proposed that cases of occupational injuries should in future receive a higher compensation than cases of work-related sickness.

However, many types of sickness, such as various kinds of aches and pains, are difficult or prohibitively expensive to subject to medical supervision. In addition, there are mild illnesses which, on a sliding scale, can be classified as falling somewhere between the two extremes 'sick and unable to work' and 'healthy and able to work' (Klevmarken, 1995). In such cases it is not merely a matter of medical assessment of whether a person is sick, but also of the individual being able to judge whether he or she can manage to work in spite of, for example, a cold. The compensation payable in such cases can have a significant impact on the individual's decision. If the excess is low, and the compensation for loss of income therefore high, it is more attractive to stay at home with, say, a mild cold or a slight headache, compared with situations where excess is high and the compensation low.

In Sweden cutbacks in sickness insurance began to be implemented in the 1990s. The first reform, initiated at the end of the 1980s when the economy was still strong, aimed at increasing labour supply by making sickness insurance less generous, but also at keeping down costs (see Lantto, 1994). Thus, in March 1991 the level of compensation in the sickness insurance system was reduced. What is more, sick pay has since been introduced, which means that for the first two weeks of sickness (four weeks from 1997 onwards) the employer rather than the sickness insurance scheme pays compensation. This change was expected to provide both a more effective control mechanism and an incentive for preventive investments in the working environment and for rehabilitative measures. Employers also have an increased responsibility for rehabilitation.

These reforms would not have affected certain groups which are covered by negotiated occupational insurance schemes, since the latter complement social insurance benefits so that periods of sickness do not lead to a loss of income. This anomaly attracted particular attention in political debates for two reasons. First, it was seen as inequitable that certain groups (mainly white collar workers) are able to retain their level of income received when absent from work because of sickness, while others (mainly blue collar workers) have their level of compensation lowered. Second, it was feared that the intended effect in terms of increasing work incentives would not be achieved. Therefore, legislation was enacted with the effect that the lowering of compensation received from the public sickness insurance scheme would also lead to a lowering of the total level of sickness compensation. More specifically, whenever negotiated complementary schemes raise total compensation rates above 90%, sickness insurance benefits are reduced correspondingly. Further, negotiated complementary insurance cover is no longer permitted after 90 days of a period of sickness.

The official reason for the 1991 reform was principally the need to save public expenditure. A reintroduction of waiting days was justified partly by the desire to create a higher excess in the sickness insurance system and partly by the need to cut public expenditure. However, if the government had intended to use the sickness benefit system merely as an instrument to raise revenue, this could have been achieved either by raising employers' contributions or by lowering sickness benefits. To do the latter beyond what would be required as an excess to prevent exploitation implies taxing the sick; by contrast, raising employers' contributions implies imposing a tax on the healthy, assuming that the increase can be shifted on to wages. Yet it seems unlikely that members of parliament have had any intention of imposing a special tax on the sick. Thus, the qualifying no benefit day in the 1993 reform, as well as the reforms lowering the level of sickness benefit, were probably intended to introduce an excess, while the objective of cost saving was used as a pretext. The excess, in turn, was probably implemented in order to curb the exploitation of sickness insurance (see Lantto, 1994).

In March 1991, the total rate of sickness compensation was reduced from 100% to 75% for the first three days of sickness and 90% thereafter until day 90. Only periods of sickness lasting longer were compensated with 100%. The rate of absenteeism due to sickness decreased by about two days between December 1990 and December 1991. In January 1992, employers were made responsible for sick pay for the first 14 days of sickness, and in April 1993 a waiting day was introduced while the total compensation level was lowered to 80% from day 91 onwards. These changes implied that official data now cover only cases of sickness lasting longer than 14 days (approximately 10% of all cases), thus measuring the 'sickness benefit rate' rather than absenteeism due to sickness. In 1990 this rate was 16.4 days, but it dropped to 11.2 days in 1994 (Riksförsäkringsverket, 1995). This decline may indicate that a certain amount of exploitation did occur prior to the reforms, although there might have been other reasons.

The early retirement pension

For some time now, many western European countries have offered improved options of receiving early retirement pensions and partial pensions without signs of an overall decrease in health standards or an increasing degree of invalidity. While obvious impairments in physical or mental functions can make it difficult to carry on working in an increasingly demanding labour market, it has become more common to release employees whose competitiveness in the labour market has declined to a greater or lesser extent and to compensate them for the loss of earnings with an early retirement pension, rather than unemployment benefit.

The incentive to leave working life before the normal retirement age can be influenced by rules governing compensation. When rationalising their operations, employers' first priority may be to release older and (what are regarded as) less effective labour. In general, productivity declines with age and wages for older workers may be higher than what is commensurate with their productivity. Not infrequently, older people are offered either a company based early retirement scheme until the public old age pension system sets in, or a compensation which complements a public early retirement pension. Often these are relatively inexpensive for companies, since the state pays the lion's share of the coverage. In Sweden, the total compensation received by the employee can be as high as his or her previous pay (Wadensjö, 1991).

In the 1960s, structural changes in the Swedish economy led to many older employees becoming unemployed. As a result, the existing early retirement pension law was changed to enable older employees to receive an early retirement pension more readily by combining medical reasons and reasons related to the labour market as entitlement criteria. A few years later, rules were liberalised further to enable older employees to receive an early retirement pension purely for reasons related to the labour market, without any medical examination. In addition, there were the so-called '58.3 year old' pensions, linking unemployment insurance with the early retirement pension for older people whose unemployment insurance had expired. According to the 1975 Occupational Health and Safety Act, the rule 'last in first out' must be observed by companies shedding labour, thereby protecting senior staff from dismissal; however, on the basis of agreements between local unions and employers, it became possible to release employees who were aged 58 years and 3 months on a voluntary basis. The latter would receive a 90% compensation from the unemployment insurance fund for a maximum period of 450 days (hence 58 years and 3 months), followed by an early retirement pension for labour market reasons once the age of 60 was reached. As a result of these rules, the number of early retirees rose sharply in the 1970s.

In order to make early retirement more difficult again, it was later stipulated that, for people aged 57 years or older, departure from the seniority rules laid down in the Occupational Health and Safety Act had to be approved at central level, and not just by local unions. However, redundancies remained heavily concentrated among people aged 58 years or older.

A policy shift occurred in October 1991 when the possibility of receiving an early retirement pension purely for labour market reasons was abolished, putting an end to the '58.3 year old' pension rule. The so-called 'older people's laws' still applied, but only for those between 60 and 65 years of age, which allowed labour market reasons to complement medical assessment. By almost completely depriving the excess in the public social insurance schemes, negotiated occupational supplements and similar arrangements specific to individual companies provide an incentive for some people to leave the labour force early, thus leading to a diminution of labour supply. In periods when the demand for labour is high, this can lead to a rise in wages, with declining competitiveness as a result (see P. Pedersen, 1995). To counteract this to some extent, an increased commitment to rehabilitation, as proposed by the Government Committee on Sickness and Occupational Injuries in its 1996 report, is intended to promote entry into the labour market for people whose capacity for work is impaired or those who have been sick for an extended period.

Occupational injury insurance

In the latter half of the 1970s, the definition of occupational injury was broadened, leading the occupational injury insurance scheme to grant benefits much more extensively than before. Both as a consequence of favourable developments in the way cases were treated and because of the increased number of occupational injuries reported, the cases of work related illness for which benefits were granted rose from about 7,000 in 1980 to over 56,000 in 1991.

In order to reverse this trend, occupational injury became more stringently defined in 1993. At present, positive proof is required that it is the working environment that has caused the injury or illness. A causal connection is accepted only if indicated by a bulk of the evidence, whereas previously occupational injury benefits were granted unless there was considerably strong evidence against it.

Until 1993, occupational injury and sickness benefit guaranteed an income replacement rate of 100%. Owing to new rules introduced since then, no compensation level over and above the level of normal sickness benefit has been awarded. As a consequence of new regulations for assessing and providing benefits for occupational injuries, the number of payments made declined in 1994 and 1995, and is now even somewhat lower than at the beginning of the 1980s (SOU, 1996).

In June 1996, a government commission proposed that the protection of income should be 100% in the case of occupational injuries resulting from accidents, but not in cases of work-related illness. In the case of accidents, moral hazard is excluded, and no excess is therefore required. This may have been the actual reason for proposing different degrees of compensation, even if the official motive was cost saving.

Unemployment insurance

Passive labour market policy consists of compensation from unemployment insurance and cash assistance (KAS). Swedish unemployment insurance is voluntary and applies the so-called Ghent system, which means that the state subsidises union unemployment insurance funds. For union members, membership in the unemployment insurance fund is compulsory, but it is possible to be a member of a union's unemployment insurance fund without being a member of a union. In the past 20 years, over 90% of expenditure on unemployment benefits has been covered by state subsidies, which means that membership fees have been little more than symbolic.

KAS is intended in the first instance for unemployed persons who are not entitled to unemployment insurance because they are not, or have not been long enough, members of a fund (the membership condition), or do not meet benefit qualifying conditions attached to the period of insured employment (the working condition). New entrants into the labour market in particular might find it difficult to fulfil these conditions. Based on agreements between the parties in the labour market, there are also complementary unemployment protection plans which raise the replacement rate of income lost because of unemployment.

Since the end of the 1980s, the unemployment insurance system in Sweden has included a guarantee against exhaustion of insurance cover, which entails that an unemployed person at risk of losing his or her insurance benefit is entitled to participation in a labour market programme. In practice, this guarantee has come to mean that people receiving unemployment compensation have a high probability of being placed in such programmes when the point at which their insurance expires approaches.

In the summer of 1996, parliament passed a resolution for changes in unemployment insurance which included, among other things, a time limit on unemployment compensation and considerably tougher qualifying conditions. What is more, in October 1996 a government commission proposed dividing unemployment benefits into two parts, a basic amount to which all who fulfil the qualifying conditions are entitled, and a voluntary, earnings related part which imposes the additional requirement of one year's membership in an unemployment insurance fund. In combination with the basic amount, this is to replace 80% of the income from work lost, with the basic amount nearly 30% higher than the present KAS. In addition to the tougher qualifying requirements already decided on (but which have yet to be implemented), these proposals would most likely result in a growth in the number of unemployed people with only basic security.

The future

At present there is no political stability in any of the social insurance schemes. Individuals want to protect themselves from loss of income as a result of sickness, old age, etc. When the rules and regulations of social insurance constantly change, and governments are reluctant to make long-term decisions, uncertainty will be the result, undermining the legitimacy of the system. Consequently, people try to cover themselves against loss of income and the demand for private insurance can be expected to increase. Indeed, a rise in the take-up of private pensions is observable. A second factor promoting uncertainty is strong group interests. As discussed, the present pension system chiefly favours intermediate level white collar workers, largely the middle class. How will this group respond to losing some of its advantages? Among the political parties, the Centre Party, which is in a partnership of cooperation with the Social Democratic government, and the Moderate Party, which is the largest party in opposition, have indicated a strong commitment to the view that the state should limit its involvement in social protection and provide only basic security.

This chapter however has emphasised arguments in support of the view that reform policies may have been intended to safeguard continued, earnings related public insurance coverage. Changes implemented in the 1990s do not need to be interpreted as a strategy for conversion from standard security to a limited basic security. Instead, they can be interpreted as an attempt to overcome fundamental structural problems in social insurance and to make existing schemes more sustainable in the long term.

Notes

[1] When contributions are paid directly by employers, the actual cost is decided by indirect adjustments which take place in the economy, that is, by opportunities for passing on the cost. The burden might be shifted on to employees if their real wages progress less favourably than they would have done without the contribution on employers. The burden might be shifted on to consumers via higher commodity prices. Generally it is thought that, in the long run, contributions imposed on employers are borne by employees in the form of lower wages. In Sweden's small open economy, neither profits nor commodity prices are affected by the introduction or raising of contributions on employers, at least not after a certain period of adjustment.

[2] See note 1.

[3] See note 1.

four

Social insurance in Germany – dismantling or reconstruction?[*]
Jochen Clasen

Introduction

Incorporating principles that were characteristic of German social policy one hundred years ago and have remained so since, social insurance is, as Alber (1988) puts it, the "core institutional principle of the German welfare state". The five branches of the current social insurance system represent close to two thirds of overall expenditure within the so-called 'social budget', which is the total sum of social spending in cash and kind excluding education and capital spending on housing. By comparison, the most important means tested benefits (social assistance and housing benefit) represent less than 5% of the social budget, which in 1993 was 34% of GDP for Germany as a whole (BMAS, 1994).

This chapter begins with a brief sketch of the five social insurance branches in Germany: pensions, accident, unemployment, health and long-term care. This is followed with a brief historical account of the origins and development of the systems until the mid-1970s when a long period of expansion after the Second World War came to a halt and gave way to early cutbacks. Economic crises, mass unemployment and German unification put considerable pressure on social insurance during the following two

[*] I would like to thank Angus Erskine, Karl Hinrichs and Fiona Milburn for helpful comments on an earlier draft of this chapter.

decades and led to a mixture of selective retrenchment which some regard as the beginning of a dismantling (*Abbau*) of welfare structures rather than their reconstruction (*Umbau*). After a discussion of current pressures, and suggestions for policy change, the chapter concludes with a general assessment of the future for social insurance in Germany.

Some characteristics of social insurance in Germany

There are some features that apply to all five branches of social insurance, such as their mandatory character, their categorical orientation, the principle of equivalence that they adopt and self-administration. Although funds receive some tax subsidies, the system as a whole is largely financed on a pay-as-you-go basis by employees and their employers. Each pays half of a fixed proportion of employees' earnings into separate funds, apart from work related accident insurance, which is entirely funded by employers. These earmarked contributions are mandatory for all employees. However, excluded are tenured public sector employees (*Beamte*), who rely on their own entirely tax-funded social security system, and those who in 1996 regularly worked for less than 15 hours per week with earnings below DM590 (in 1996 about £240) per month in the region of the former Federal Republic (the old *Länder*); in the new *Länder* (the territory of the former GDR) the equivalent threshold was DM500. Minimum earnings and contribution ceilings differ somewhat between the two parts of the country because of lower average earnings in the east. In the following, unless specified, figures will apply to the old *Länder* only.

German social insurance has always been focused on wage earners (Clasen and Freeman, 1994) and in that sense remains selective or 'categorical' (Döring, 1995a). However, other groups, such as the self-employed, have the option of voluntary membership. Like contributions, benefits are related to earnings, underlining the relevance of the so-called 'equivalence principle', with benefits reflecting contributions. The predominant principle is one of *Lebensstandardsicherung* or status maintenance, that is, the provision of an income that compensates for lost earnings by preserving, at least to some extent, the standard of living that individuals enjoyed prior to receiving benefits.

Social insurance is self-administered in the sense that employees and employers are jointly in control of semi-autonomous agencies which run separate funds outside of state funds. However, except for health insurance funds (see below), the government determines contribution and benefit rates. Furthermore, employers and employees are joined by representatives of public authorities on the board of the Federal Labour Office, which is responsible for the unemployment insurance system.

Pension, unemployment and accident insurance

With a volume of transfers representing about 10% of GDP, the pension insurance system is financially the most important part of the German social insurance system. Separate mandatory pension schemes cover blue and white collar workers and minors. Joint contributions from employers and employees represented 19.2% of gross earnings in 1996 and were payable on income up to a ceiling of roughly one-and-a-half times average white collar earnings, or DM8,000 per month. The level of old age and invalidity pensions are determined by a formula based on the number of years spent in insured employment, the amount of lifetime earnings and the average earnings of those currently in work. Thus, pension insurance is often regarded as the system that is most strictly oriented towards the principle of equivalence, status maintenance and horizontal (intertemporal) redistribution.

While occupational pension schemes are widespread (Hauser, 1995a), public pensions have remained the main income source for those in retirement. A person with an average wage can expect a statutory pension of 70% of previous net earnings, provided 45 'insurance' years have been credited (see below). In fact, only about 80% of male pensioners and less than a quarter of female pensioners were credited with 35 years or more in 1993, which means that average pension were lower, amounting to about DM1,250 per month (£500) in 1996 (*Sozialpolitische Umschau*, no 6, 1996). However, there are wide variations, and for some pension levels may even be below the social assistance level. Döring (1995b) argues that 80% of older, married women would have incomes of less than 40% of average earnings if they had to rely on their individual pension entitlements alone. In fact, only a very small number of elderly women receive means tested social assistance as a way of financial support. This is because most either live with a partner and have a sufficient joint income or, as widows, rely solely or additionally on a 'survivor's' pension (*Hinterbliebenenrente*), representing 60% of their deceased spouse's pension. In fact, it could be argued that the pension system has become more effective over time, since in 1975 about 3.4% of women (1.6% of men) over 65 claimed social assistance, compared with 2.4% (1.4% of men) in 1992 (Hauser, 1995b).

The 'survivor's' pension, which applies to widowers as well as widows, indicates that interpersonal redistribution is not entirely absent within pension insurance. Other elements to that effect include certain types of non-waged activities, which are treated as 'substitute' or 'fictitious' contribution periods and therefore are credited towards pension entitlement. These include time spent in higher education, military service and childrearing. Three 'baby years' per child are credited to mothers. In 1996, this increased pensions by about DM30 per month for each year of childrearing (*Sozialpolitische Umschau*, no 51, 1995). Time spent caring for relatives as well as other non-contributing periods arising from illness, pregnancy, rehabilitation or unemployment are also credited.

Thus, while the principle of *Lebenstandardsicherung* is paramount within pension insurance, it is not applied exclusively but is softened by what the government refers to as elements of 'solidarity'. In fact, when it comes to defending the current system against suggestions for reform, the government tends to stress the importance of the mixture of principles of 'equivalence' (higher rewards for better contribution records) with those of 'solidarity' (some degree of social compensation) (BMAS, 1996, p 21). These elements are also used to legitimise tax subsidies to pension insurance, which amount to about 20% of total expenditure. The 'survivor's' pension or compensation for 'baby years', for example, are generally portrayed as a burden that should fall on society as a whole and are therefore financed out of general taxation rather than earmarked contributions. Another expression applied to such types of expenditure is *versicherungsfremde Leistungen* (literally, 'insurance alien' benefits). While it is not always clear which types of expenditure can unambiguously be subsumed under this category, the term serves as a rhetorical device, helping, for example, to legitimise benefit reductions at times of fiscal pressure, as will be discussed later.

Unlike pension insurance, unemployment insurance benefits and labour market programmes are both jointly funded out of earmarked contributions to one single body, the Federal Labour Office. In 1996 the combined contribution rate was equivalent to 6.5% of gross wages for earnings up to the same contribution ceiling as in pension insurance. Unemployment compensation is a two-tier system. Provided contributions have been paid for at least 12 months, claimants are entitled to unemployment benefit (*Arbeitslosengeld*) equivalent to 67% of previous 'adjusted' net earnings (60% for claimants without children). Earnings are adjusted by disregarding certain components, such as overtime or holiday pay, so that actual levels of benefit are normally lower than nominal ones (Bäcker, 1995). The standard benefit duration is one year but can reach 32 months for older claimants with longer contribution records (Clasen, 1994a).

Unemployment assistance (*Arbeitslosenhilfe*), which in principle can be paid for an indefinite period, may be granted to those who have exhausted their entitlement to *Arbeitslosengeld* and to claimants who have been in insured employment for at least six months prior to becoming unemployed, that is, those who have insufficient contribution records for receiving *Arbeitslosengeld*. For the latter group, however, *Arbeitslosenhilfe* is restricted to one year. The level too is based on former net earnings (57% for claimants with children, 53% for others). However, eligibility to unemployment assistance is subject to a means test. What is more, unlike unemployment benefit, unemployment assistance is paid out of general taxation.

In April 1995 about 42% of all registered unemployed received *Arbeitslosengeld* and 24% *Arbeitslosenhilfe* (ISA, 1995). Because of their earnings related character, benefits are not always sufficient to prevent the need to apply for additional benefits. About 3% of unemployment benefit recipients and about one in seven unemployment assistance claimants received additional means tested social assistance in 1995 (ISA, 1995) and the number of unemployed who rely solely on social assistance has grown over the last decade, indicating one of the problems of the insurance system which will be discussed below.

As with pension insurance, the unemployment insurance system is clearly oriented towards paid employees with a strong adherence to the equivalence principle. However, apart from a redistribution between those in work to those outside, there are other redistributive elements. For example, claimants with dependent children receive slightly higher benefits than those without. Furthermore, in principle, unemployment assistance can be paid indefinitely.

Finally, the mandatory accident insurance scheme is entirely funded by employers who contribute to one of a multitude of funds which are organised largely along occupational lines (see Lampert and Bossert, 1992). Apart from wage earners, other social groups are automatically covered such as schoolchildren and students, as well as some groups of self-employed. Others have the option to join the system. Companies are obliged to continue to pay full wages for the first six weeks after a work related accident; thereafter, an injury benefit is paid for the period of recuperation by the appropriate fund which represents 80% of previous gross earnings. The fund might subsequently pay an earnings related 'bridging benefit' for the duration of a vocational rehabilitation programme, and a partial or full 'injury pension' will be paid if a rehabilitation programme is impossible or the claimant remains unemployed afterwards.

Health and long-term care insurance

Health and long-term care insurance differ from the other three insurance branches in many respects. After pension insurance, expenditure on health insurance is the second largest single item within the social budget with DM210 billion spent in 1993, or 6.7% of GDP (BMAS, 1994). German employees who work for more than 15 hours per week are automatically members in one of more than 1,100 autonomous, para-public health insurance funds (Hinrichs, 1994). Membership is also compulsory for other groups, such as students, pensioners and unemployed claimants. Thus, more than 90% of the population is covered. Funds are administered by representatives of the insured or by an equal number of board members representing employees and employers. They are responsible for their receipts and expenditure and are free to fix contribution rates necessary to cover current outlays and also to decide on the level of provision over and above the state's prescriptions on the scope of covered medical treatment and services.

Thus, there are differences in contribution rates between funds. In 1996 the average rate was 13.4% of gross earnings, with the lowest rate just below 10% and the highest 14% (*Sozialpolitische Umschau*, no 19, 1996). Contributions are paid up to a ceiling of DM6,000 per month, which is lower than that for pension and unemployment insurance. What is more, health insurance allows employees with regular earnings above this ceiling to 'opt out' of public health insurance funds and to choose private insurance instead.

Health insurance provides a sickness benefit which represents 80% of previous net earnings and is granted for a maximum of 78 weeks. It begins after six weeks of illness. During the first six weeks employers are obliged to continue to pay normal wages. (A change to this regulation became a focal point in the opposition to government's savings plans in 1996; see below.) However, the largest part of healthcare is taken up by benefits in kind (medical treatment, hospital care, dental care, home help for parents in hospital, preventative programmes, etc), the level of which is not determined by contributions, previous earnings or individual risk categories. Another important redistributive element within health insurance is the free-of-charge inclusion of family members with no or low earnings. Thus, the health insurance system involves strong elements of vertical redistribution, even though the contribution ceiling and the 'opting out' of better earners reduces the extent of their overall effect.

In principle, membership guarantees free healthcare treatment at the point of delivery. However, frequent attempts to contain costs have led to an increase of so-called 'co-payments', which are charges on a range of items such as prescriptions, spectacles, treatment for the first two weeks in hospital, dental work, rehabilitation measures, etc. In fact, while children under the age of 18, recipients of social assistance, unemployment assistance or student grants and low income earners are exempt, 'co-payments' nowadays apply to all types of provision except ambulatory care.

Health insurance funds are not the providers of healthcare. Instead, members receive sickness certificates from their particular fund which are submitted to private agencies, such as GPs, who in turn invoice the respective fund for the treatment. Remuneration is negotiated between the Association of Insurance Funds on the one hand and associations of providers on the other. Other divisions exist between ambulatory care provided by GPs, institutional care received in hospitals, and institutional divisions within a federal framework (Alber, 1992; Moran, 1994). Consequently, healthcare policy making involves a multitude of collective actors pursuing special interests, such as healthcare providers, the pharmaceutical industry, insurance funds and public authorities. As a consequence, attempts to contain rising costs have frequently been watered down or blocked by healthcare providers (Rosewitz and Webber, 1990).

While most social insurance schemes date back to the last century, the long-term care insurance scheme was introduced as recently as 1995 after a long process of political negotiation and compromise (Götting et al, 1994). Before then, persons in need of long-term care frequently had to turn to means tested social assistance in order to cover costs. The scheme provides benefits in kind or cash for both community and institutional care. As in other social insurance branches, the funding is based on compulsory contributions, evenly split between employees and their employers. The rate is 1.7%, up to a ceiling of DM6,000 per month. As with health insurance, the long-term care insurance scheme allows employees with earnings above this ceiling to opt out and join a private fund.

In addition to the provision of care or remuneration for carers, the long-term care insurance fund also pays pension contributions for relatives or other non-professional care providers. However, benefit ceilings mean that people in nursing homes are not always able to cover the entire cost of care, which means that social assistance, as an additional source for payment, has not become superfluous. In fact, while improving the situation of many in need of long-term care, financially the scheme implied a 'large scale reshuffling' of resources (Götting et al, 1994, p 304). Local authorities and *Länder* have thereby been somewhat relieved from ever increasing social assistance expenditure; better-off patients will be able to retain their savings, while employees and employers have become the main source of care funding with the latter being compensated by the abolition of one paid public holiday.

In sum, the role of social insurance within the German welfare state is paramount. On its margins it is complemented and supplemented by programmes supporting particular social groups (eg, tenured public sector employees, families with children, young people) or assisting those with low or no earnings with particular costs (eg, housing benefit, social assistance) (Clasen, 1994b). The predominance of intertemporal redistribution and the orientation towards 'individual equity' (status maintenance and equivalence principle) bear some resemblance to private insurance. However, it would be misleading to characterise social insurance in Germany as private because of the existence of tax subsidies and built-in elements of 'solidarity' or interpersonal redistribution which, as described above, is most explicit in health insurance.   In other branches redistributive effects occur because of benefit additions for those with children and the accreditation of certain types of non-paid activities.   Thus, while the German type of social insurance remains 'wage labour centred' (Vobruba, 1990), it also involves elements of redistribution, subsidising mainly marriage and families.   The subsequent sections will show that the combination and balance between these principles is not a stable one but is subject to political conflict and compromise.

Origins and expansion

Over time, the financial resources of social insurance in Germany have acquired the status of 'collective private property' (Offe, 1990, p 184) owing to the nexus between contribution and benefits, their 'wage replacement' character and the strong legal codification of the system.   Contributors trust that they will receive benefits as of right and that those not contributing are excluded from entitlement.   It has often been argued that this, in addition to the separation of funds that are controlled by agencies outside the state, has contributed to the system's remarkable resilience since the inception of early schemes during the end of the last century (Alber, 1989).   However, these principles, which are often referred to as 'Bismarckian' in origin, are not the result of a single consistent notion of welfare policy, but rather are the outcome of compromises and negotiations between social groups with different interests, political ideologies and values.

   In fact, to describe the German social insurance principles as 'Bismarckian', and to contrast them with a 'Beveridge' type national insurance system is somewhat misleading, since the Reich Chancellor's original plans envisaged a much greater role for the state in the finance, control and administration of the system (see Hennock, 1987; Ritter, 1983).   As in other countries, initial benefit levels remained moderate and systems covered only a fraction of the labour force.   Yet in the first two decades of this century coverage expanded significantly, and unemployment insurance was introduced in 1927 (Clasen, 1994a) before the repercussions of the economic crisis put the social insurance branches under severe financial pressure in the early 1930s. The system survived only because of massive tax subsidies and reduced expenditure before the Nazis decided to abolish its self-administration. After the Second World War, the Allied Forces envisaged the establishment of a more comprehensive system in line with Beveridge's principles in Great Britain (Baldwin, 1990). However, the victory of the conservative Christian Democratic Union (CDU) in the first general election of West Germany in 1949, which had "nailed the defence of the traditional social insurance system to its mast" (Hockerts, 1981, p 320), led to the reintroduction of old structures and principles, complemented by limited housing and child benefits (Schmidt, 1988).

The period from 1950 to the mid-1970s can be characterised as a time of expansion, inclusion and the assertion of the equivalence and status maintenance principles. In the context of high economic growth rates and low unemployment, social insurance became more inclusive and more generous, and within health insurance direct charges were almost entirely removed. In the early 1970s, access to unemployment benefit was granted to groups with less stable and continuous work records and was opened up to non-contributors by substituting paid work as the qualifying criterion with 'equivalent' activities such as military service or self-employment.

Previously, the equivalence principle had been strengthened and had become paramount. The 1957 Pension Reform Act removed previous elements of basic pensions compensated with a significant increase of average pensions. With the explicit aim of linking benefits more to individual earnings, pensions became more differentiated and almost entirely dependent on individual contributory records (Hockerts, 1980). Driven by the conservative –liberal coalition government, but within a largely consensual policy context, other changes too accentuated elements of reciprocity and restitution at the expense of interpersonal redistribution; examples include changes to sickness benefit and unemployment benefits introduced in the 1960s (Clasen, 1994a).

Reforms made social insurance attractive to the expanding middle classes and functioned as a 'work incentive' since participation in insured employment became the key to social protection. Because West German society was seen as becoming increasingly an 'employee society', it was widely believed that social insurance would become more and more effective. Also, while the insurance system became more geared towards those in paid work, social security schemes for specific groups (eg, tenured public sector employees), as well as complementary benefits supporting families with children, became more generous. A social assistance system was introduced in 1961 as a last resort for, it was believed, an ever decreasing minority of the population who, for transitory periods, were in need of means tested benefits.

Cost containment: the 1970s and 1980s

The two oil price shocks in the mid-1970s and early 1980s, each leading to a significant decline in economic growth followed by steep increases in unemployment, put social insurance under particular pressure because of its pay-as-you-go and wage related funding basis. The scissors movement between receipts and expenditure worsened the longer mass unemployment persisted, the volume of employment stagnated and wages rose only moderately or not at all. The extent of fiscal difficulties was somewhat mitigated owing to the rise in the volume of employment during the 1980s, increasing revenue. Nevertheless, successive governments were reluctant to increase either tax subsidies or contribution rates, since both were believed to affect private investments adversely. As a consequence, cautious and selective rounds of cost containment in the mid 1970s led to more severe cuts during the 1980s, initiated by Helmut Schmidt's centre–left coalition government and continued under Helmut Kohl's centre–right coalition after 1982.

The unemployment insurance fund was most affected. Since the government is legally obliged to balance it when deficits occur, the fund was singled out as the area where cuts had to be most substantial, affecting benefit rights by lengthening both the qualifying and suspension periods and cutting rates for claimants without children and for those leaving vocational training (Clasen, 1994a). In the second half of the 1980s, a healthier financial basis in the unemployment insurance fund allowed the government to shift some of the costs of tax-funded unemployment assistance to the unemployment insurance fund by lengthening benefit entitlement for older claimants with longer contribution records.

As far as the pension insurance system was concerned, the decline of the birth rate and projections of an increasingly adverse dependency ratio started to become a matter of debate in the 1980s. The 1989 Pension Reform Act, which came into force in 1992, aimed at reducing the need to increase contribution rates by curbing costs in the medium and longer term. Measures included a gradual increase in the average pensionable age to 65 for both men and women, the introduction of a partial pension and a shift in the pension uprating method from the increase in gross wages to net wages, resulting in a slower growth in existing pension levels (Leisering, 1992; Schmähl, 1993).

Within healthcare, charges for prescriptions and other items were increased in the first half of the 1980s while some items were removed from the list of drugs and medicine available through the health insurance fund. Recipients of sickness benefit were made to contribute to their unemployment and pension insurance schemes. A major reform of the healthcare system in 1989, which would have affected incomes of some providers, was watered down through successful lobbying. However, the level of 'co-payments' for a number of items and for dental care was increased.

There were some improvements also, aimed largely at families and those with longer contribution records. Limited credits for pensions were introduced for women not in paid work because of rearing children. Parental leave and childrearing benefits were implemented and the receipt of sickness benefit in case of illness of children was extended, as was unemployment benefit for older claimants. Overall, however, the period between 1975 and 1990 was one of consolidation marked by attempts to cut costs as a response to growing expenditure and deficits in insurance funds. Cost saving programmes were "successful attempts at containing conflict" since cuts "came in small doses, and carefully avoided vehement assaults upon large powerful groups" (Hinrichs, 1994, p 5), while for marginal labour market groups the system became more restrictive. At times of low unemployment and high economic growth rates in the 1950s and 1960s, social insurance 'opened up'; at times of tight finance, the system tended to contract by focusing resources more exclusively on contributors. Thus, there was a reversal of policies towards 'inclusion', and the period after the mid-1970s was largely one of 'exclusion'. However, policies implemented during the 1980s did not represent a departure from traditional social insurance structures or principles.

Retrenchment or reconstruction? The 1990s

Since 1990, social insurance has been under severe pressure. The costs of German unification soon became evident. Massive transfers were, and continue to be, needed to cushion the collapse of the labour market and rebuild the economy in the east. Almost 40% (3.9 million) of all jobs in the former GDR were eliminated between 1990 and 1993. Registered unemployment climbed to 16% and would have been far higher but for early retirement schemes, people migrating to the west and a battery of labour market measures.

Social insurance in the former GDR was in many ways a more comprehensive and inclusive model than the West German system (Manow-Borgwardt, 1994). However, after 1990 the latter was simply extended to what are now called the 'new' *Länder*. The only exceptions were temporary social supplements in pension and unemployment insurance, which acted as benefit minimum 'floors' in order to prevent claimants having to resort to social assistance. The government's decision to raise most of the revenue for transfers to the east by increasing contributions more than taxes was widely criticised as a blatant misuse of social insurance, since it shouldered a disproportionate burden of unification on low and middle income earners while groups not contributing to social insurance were largely left out (Ganßmann, 1993a).

The fact that public deficits were increasing as a result of the economic downturn in 1992 was used as the justification of a first wave of cost saving measures in 1993, amounting to DM28 billion over the subsequent four years. It affected non-insurance areas such as child benefits, student grants and housing benefits but also social insurance spending (Bäcker and am Orde, 1993). For example, unemployment benefit rates were cut by 1% for claimants with and 3% for claimants without dependent children. For claimants who had not previously been on unemployment benefit, unemployment assistance was reduced to a maximum period of one year.

The changed economic environment from 1992 onwards heightened the government's resolve to enact more severe measures in health insurance, and this time more substantial changes were achieved, affecting providers' remuneration and forcing the pharmaceutical industry to lower the prices of certain prescription drugs and exposing it to more competition (Hinrichs,

1994). Two organisational changes were introduced: a cross-subsidisation between health insurance funds in favour of those funds with a higher risk membership and more free-of-charge insured family members, and the introduction of a free choice of health insurance funds. 'Co-payments' for hospital stay, prescriptions and certain dental treatment were increased as well (Steffen, 1994).

A further slump in economic growth and a further rise in unemployment to an unprecedented postwar level of over four million led to the announcement of the 'programme for growth and employment' in April 1996 (*Sozialpolitische Umschau*, no 17, 1996). The government intended to save expenditure by the unprecedented amount of DM75 billion (£30 billion), a third of which was to affect social insurance spending. It was hoped that this would allow the combined social insurance contribution level to be pushed below 40% (BMAS, 1996).

Not all plans were fully implemented, owing to the influence or even veto power of collective actors within the legislative process in Germany, which affects some policy areas more than others (see below). For example, the government's repeated ideas to abolish any right to unemployment assistance for claimants without prior receipt of unemployment benefit (*Sozialpolitische Umschau*, no 44, 1995) has so far been successfully blocked in the Upper House.

Moreover, there are other ways of watering down or avoiding some types of benefit restriction. For example, at the heart of mass demonstrations against the government's plans was a proposed cut in the level of employers' wage continuation for up to six weeks' sickness leave, from 100% to 80% of previous earnings. This change has since been implemented but with little effect, since in many cases employers and unions have circumvented new regulations in collective regional agreements which, according to existing labour laws, give social partners the last say in these matters. Thus, many employees continue to receive the full wage compensation in case of sickness.

Nevertheless, a number of cost saving programmes were introduced. For example, the statutory retirement age is to be brought forward, and pension levels will be reduced for each year of retirement before pensionable age. Time spent in higher education is credited for a maximum of only three rather than seven years, and students with earnings above a certain limit are now obliged to pay pension insurance contributions. Benefits for people on training and rehabilitation courses were reduced. Statutory sickness benefit was reduced by 10%, prescription charges went up and subsidies for spectacle frames were abolished. Changes affecting unemployed benefit claimants are currently under review in parliament.

As in the 1980s, there were improvements too, mainly aimed at families.   Tax-funded child benefit levels were increased in 1995, and within pension insurance the crediting of childrearing was increased to three years per child. Within health insurance, the entitlement to sickness benefit when looking after sick children was extended and, most importantly, a new long-term care insurance scheme was implemented in 1995 (see below). However, despite these selective improvements, the severity of cuts in social insurance programmes implemented and planned in the 1990s goes far beyond those in the 1980s.

While the cost of unification and mass unemployment are the two major factors behind these, and possible future, saving plans, it should be noted that some of the fiscal pressure was of an internal rather than external nature.   For example, the encouragement of ethnic Germans from former Eastern Bloc countries to immigrate put a significant strain on pension and unemployment insurance funds.   These two funds were also affected by generous early retirement schemes which allowed companies to shed older workers on an unprecedented scale in the mid-1990s (Wagner, 1996).   As a consequence, the combined contribution rate to all social insurance branches rose from 32.4% in 1980 to 40.8% in early 1996. While the latter is regarded by many as stifling companies' international competitiveness, it should be noted that social expenditure as a percentage of GNP increased by a much lesser margin, from 32.5% in 1980 to 34% in 1993. Moreover, rising social expenditure has affected employees more than employers.   Contributions made by the former saw their share of the funding of social budget climb from 25% in 1980 to 28.6% in 1993. During the same period, the employers' share actually declined, from 37.3% to 35.3% (Hauser, 1995a).

Nevertheless, the social insurance system has become a focus in the current debate about the viability of Germany as a location for production and investment in a changing world economy. The views of those who have long regarded the system as too costly and existing contribution rates as an excessive burden on employers have been strengthened, and the government has responded by deliberately creating an atmosphere which suggests that, unlike during the 1980s, almost every item of the welfare state is under close scrutiny. The question is whether such a scrutiny would lead to a radical rethink of traditional social insurance principles and structures.

Suggestions for change and party politics

As outlined earlier, while potentially increasing the system's volatility, the mixture of social insurance characteristics and principles might actually have contributed to its historical robustness, since different elements have appealed to different political ideologies during the postwar period (Offe, 1991, p 127). However, while a political consensus and support for social insurance was stable for a long time, the system is currently faced with pressures that are doubtlessly stronger than in previous decades. In addition to economic and labour market difficulties, the share of the elderly in Germany is predicted to grow over the next decades, while the birth rate remains low. At present, for every 100 people aged between 20 and 65 there are 24 people over the age of 65; as a combined result of an increasing life expectancy and a low number of births, this number is predicted to rise to 36 by the year 2020 and to 56 by 2040 (*Sozialpolitische Umschau*, no 6, 1996). Changes in family and household structures have led to further problems for a system reliant upon a high level of employment and marriage as the two prime access points to social protection.

Suggestions for change can be divided into three camps. Left-wing and ecological groups in particular regard social insurance as inefficient and outdated owing to the adherence to assumptions about work and family life. In their view, large groups in society are increasingly excluded from adequate social protection because more people are living outside the traditional nuclear family, and because of an increase in long-term unemployment and a decline in the number of full-time, continuous types of work or "standard employment relationships" (Hinrichs, 1991). The increase in the number of social assistance claimants is seen as a sign of a dysfunctional social insurance system. Since the allocation of waged work to all those who want it has ceased to be a viable option, a solution has to be found in a 'non-productivist' design of income distribution (Offe, 1994). The possibility of topping up a non-means tested, tax-funded basic income would allow people to reduce their working hours and free up employment opportunities for those who have remained outside the labour market (Wolf, 1991).

The compulsory character of social insurance is being criticised by the libertarian right as infringing personal choice and as unjustified in the light of rising household earnings which would allow people to make private provision. Individuals should be encouraged to take responsibility for their own social protection through savings and private insurance. Such plans have frequently been made, especially in the field of pensions (Miegel and Wahl, 1985). They would imply a break with the so-called 'generational contract' (*Generationenvertrag*), which refers to its pay-as-you-go funding basis and the fact that the current workforce provides resources for current pensioners. Such a system, it is argued, cannot be maintained in the long run since future contribution rates would need to be raised far in excess of current levels, which would undermine Germany's competitiveness. The state should therefore resume a much more residual role, providing a tax-funded minimum pension only, while encouraging private provision.

A third set of proposals aims to maintain existing arrangements but to fill gaps by inserting minimum elements, especially within unemployment and pension insurance. Unlike a basic income, these elements would have a subsidiary character and would be means tested, functioning as a 'benefit floor'. Pensioners or unemployed people would remain within their respective social insurance branch without having to apply for social assistance, which is widely seen as discriminatory and stigmatising (Adamy and Bäcker, 1993). Furthermore, the degree of inclusion of social insurance should be increased by, for example, allowing access to unemployment benefit to those completing vocational training or improving the crediting of non-waged activities such as caring and childrearing. The overall effect would be to maintain existing social insurance but to shift the balance within it, putting more emphasis on redistributive elements at the expense of the equivalence principle. The financial implications of such a move would be less substantial than basic income proposals owing to the means testing of the 'benefit floor'.

None of these demands for structural change have so far influenced actual policy making. This is partly due to institutional barriers to radical policy reform in Germany, such as the bicameral legislature, the role of the Constitutional Court, the legal codification of social insurance rights and the disparate financial implications any benefit changes would have on the three tiers of public authorities as well as social insurance funds (see Clasen and Gould, 1995). Even if these restrictions could be overcome, suggestions for structural reform would have to find a majority within a centre–right or centre–left coalition government.

The introduction of the long-term care insurance scheme in 1995 is a good illustration of the continuing strength of the traditional social insurance principle in party politics vis-à-vis alternative options. Once a decision had been reached in favour of reform, a number of options were open, including a fixed tax subsidy to local authorities which pay social assistance to many people in need of long-term care, the introduction of compulsory private insurance, the incorporation of the risk of needing long-term care into existing sickness insurance schemes or the implementation of a new and separate branch of social insurance (see Götting et al, 1994). From the start, the 'social policy' wing of the ruling CDU/CSU favoured the latter solution. However, ministers had to skilfully negotiate a difficult path between coalition partners and the opposition. Both the FDP, the junior coalition partner in government, and the business wing of CDU/CSU advocated a private solution which would enable them to 'shake off the Bismarck legacy' (Götting et al, 1994). The SPD, however, not only was the biggest party in opposition but also was able to veto proposals because of its majority in the Upper House. Initially it favoured a 'solidaristic' tax-funded solution in which all citizens would be entitled to benefits. However, after a compromise over funding arrangements had been reached in negotiations, separate long-term care insurance succeeded eventually and was unanimously agreed upon in parliament. Perhaps as the lowest common denominator, this solution nevertheless indicates the continuing strength of traditional social insurance principles.

An assessment of the new scheme at this time would be premature. However, in the context of this chapter it is interesting to note, that while the government heralded the new scheme as the 'fifth pillar' of social insurance in Germany, critics pointed out that some elements, such as benefit ceilings and the compensation for employers, indicated a break with the past and the beginning of a new 'lean' and more residual welfare state (Priester, 1993). A similar division of opinion has accompanied the recent round of planned cuts. For some critics, the reductions in benefit rights demonstrate the beginning of a wholesale dismantling (*Abbau*) of the welfare state. The government itself prefers to use the term 'reconstruction' (*Umbau*) as a justification for what it portrays as a mere adaptation of social insurance in a changed economic climate.

In fact, there are many similarities between current and previous cost saving programmes. Then and now, the driving force is fiscal. Increased social insurance spending and lower revenues have led to policies aimed primarily at reducing public deficits without having to raise contribution rates. Separate insurance budgets assist in spreading the load and allow for 'hidden' cuts through changes in cross-subsidisation between funds. Cost saving measures have been justified as targeting resources on those who 'deserve' them, not because they are in need but because they have contributed to the system more than others (Clasen, 1992). 'Genuine' insurance benefits will be targeted for cuts only when redistributive 'insurance alien' elements have been abolished or minimised. For example, within the unemployment insurance system, unemployment benefit levels are less likely to be subjected to cutbacks than either labour market programmes or tax-funded unemployment assistance. There is a financial rationale for this. Since many are tax-financed, cuts in 'insurance alien elements' have a direct effect on government expenditure. What is more, singling out certain types of expenditure for cutbacks has a legimatory function. Reductions of 'insurance alien' elements are portrayed as necessary and even beneficial for 'genuine' social insurance members since they avoid having to put too heavy a burden on contributors or, applying the government's rhetoric, the 'community of solidarity' (*Solidargemeinschaft*) .

Of course, a clearcut distinction between 'genuine' and 'insurance alien' elements is impossible (Rehfeld and Luckert, 1989) and, in principle, any type of expenditure can be curbed. However, emphasising differences allows the government to portray decisions almost as non-political, or at least to minimise political repercussions. Core benefits are most directly linked to, and seen as a 'reward' for, contributions. Codified in constitutional law, they are strongly defended by unions. 'Insurance alien' types of benefits may be introduced or extended at times of healthy revenues, but are legitimately cut back at times of economic and financial difficulties. This strategy has frequently been used, and not only by the current government. It even allows political elites to proclaim that they are strengthening rather than weakening the social insurance system.

A future for social insurance?

Opinion polls show that social insurance arrangements have consistently been very popular. A fundamental restructuring, giving individual provision a greater role, is apparently not in accordance with the view of the majority of the population (Dehlinger and Brennecke, 1992). The most recent wave of cost saving led to a demonstration of 350,000 people in Bonn in June 1996, surpassing the size of any previous public opposition to cuts in public spending. It is also well established that a rise in social insurance contributions is less resisted than a rise in taxation (Hinrichs, 1994). Additional factors indicating stability rather than change are the above mentioned support for current principles within both major parties and institutional barriers inhibiting structural reform. Does that mean that substantial reforms in the long run are unlikely or, from a normative perspective, are not necessary?

To a large extent, the answer to the first question depends on the continuing trust in the system. Describing the mix between compensatory and equivalence principles on the one hand and norms of participation and solidarity on the other, Hinrichs (1994; 1996) refers to the 'moral infrastructure' of social insurance and the way in which it contributes to social integration. With regard to pension insurance, Nullmeier and Rüb (1994) point out that social insurance does more than merely constitute a contractual relationship between premiums and risk compensation based on contractual principles. Instead, it can be argued that the system has acquired a degree of social acceptance by guaranteeing statutory rights and obligations based on a mechanism that allows participation in the increasing national wealth, guided by the principle of rewards according to contributions and also by 'communitarian ideas' and a degree of social solidarity (Nullmeier and Rüb, 1994).

In a similar vein, Leisering (1996) emphasises the 'societal value' of social insurance vis-à-vis other types of social protection with regard to its impact on social integration, its legitimatory role for income redistribution and the allocation of national resources. Social insurance has contributed to a homogenisation of society, not by adhering to egalitarian principles but by 'differentiated integration' (Leisering, 1996). It gives the middle classes a 'stake in the system' and therefore can rely much more on their support for its preservation than in countries such as the USA or the UK, where low insurance benefits tend to contribute to a dualistic social structure, with poorer social groups relying on state support while the better-off are encouraged to provide for themselves. Moreover, because of its inherent mix of potentially conflicting principles, social insurance increases the legitimacy of income redistribution. Pension levels in particular are associated with the notion of a 'fair' reward for individual contributions made during one's working life. At the same time, the pension system strengthens the collectivist notion of what is referred to as 'generational contract', ie, the solidarity between those in work and those receiving pensions. The pay-as-you-go basis and the organisational separation of funds makes the necessity to finance current pensions out of the current national product much more transparent than in systems that rely on investment funds. Any socioeconomic changes have a direct effect on the level of receipts and expenditure and regularly require policy decisions about the appropriate way to adapt, and also about underlying values of the allocation of national resources. In sum, the integrative, legitimatory and allocative functions of German social insurance contribute to the system's public acceptance.

However, is it possible that the system's 'moral infrastructure' might be gradually undermined as a result of deliberate campaigns by those preferring a more residual welfare state? Current funding difficulties can easily be exploited by those hoping to discredit social insurance by claiming that the system is financially not viable in the long run owing to demographic and economic change, or by singling out and dramatising elements of solidarity and redistribution as 'insurance alien' and thus unjustified.

The health insurance system, as the most redistributive insurance branch, is most likely to be heading towards 'lean welfare' and beyond incremental change (Hinrichs, 1994; Hauser, 1995c). In some respects this is surprising, given that cost containment has as yet been difficult to achieve in a crowded policy terrain; on the other hand, it is the insurance branch least determined by the 'equivalence' principle. In any case, the government seems determined not to allow contributions to rise further and to press on with cost containment measures. Consumers of healthcare will be faced with further restrictions of covered benefits and increased 'co-payments', and structural changes could be the outcome of ongoing organisational reforms (Hinrichs, 1994).

Pressure for change in other social insurance branches could increase also. As discussed earlier, while the inclusion of middle classes is a stabilising factor within social insurance, the tendency to exclude groups that are not, or are only marginally, involved in paid employment is a problem. The larger the size of this group, it could be argued, the more inadequate social insurance could become, since either a growing section of the population would be ineligible for insurance benefits or transfers would remain below means tested social assistance levels.

The substantial increase in social assistance recipients from 1.6% of the population in 1970 to 4.7% in 1992 in the old *Länder* (Hauser, 1995b) to a large extent can be attributed to the effect of continuous mass and long-term unemployment. Only about two thirds of all registered unemployed receive either unemployment benefit or unemployment assistance, and by the end of the 1980s 8% of unemployed social assistance claimants also received unemployment benefit and 21% unemployment assistance (Jacobs, 1995). 'Loss of employment' was the main cause for turning to social assistance for almost 600,000 claimants in 1993 (Wagner, 1995). While recent longitudinal research shows that many of those are only temporarily in need of social assistance (Leibfried et al, 1995), it could be argued that social insurance fails a significant section of the unemployed.

Those in work might also be failed by social insurance, especially if they work on a part-time basis. In spring 1991, 15% of the labour force, mostly women, worked part-time (Blackwell, 1992); by 1995 this figure had risen to 16.3%, or 5.3 million people (*Sozialpolitische Umschau*, no 23, 1996). However, the majority of part-timers work a sufficient number of hours to be included in the social insurance net. In the old *Länder*, only 10%

of all part-time workers were ineligible for unemployment insurance benefits in 1991 and 20% (about one million people) were not directly covered by any social insurance scheme (BMAS, 1993). Other sources estimate this figure to be closer to 1.5 million, or 6% of the labour force (Keller and Seifert, 1993). While this is not an insignificant number, it has to be recognised that some of those working part-time will be only temporarily outside social insurance cover, since at some later stage they will increase their hours worked.

Nevertheless, the numbers working part-time and in other potentially precarious types of work is likely to increase at the expense of lengthy, uninterrupted work careers. Also, for other groups such as lone parents or ethnic minorities, the social insurance system remains inefficient. Thus, while the system is likely to remain both a crucial and popular form of social protection for a large section of the labour force, some type of reform is needed in order to adapt social insurance to a changing environment. A 'needs-oriented basic security', as advocated by the SPD and the Green Party, would indeed go some way towards preventing insurance claimants having to seek support from local authorities. Apparently incompatible with the equivalence principle within German social insurance, it has already been tested when pensioners and registered unemployed in the new *Länder* were provided with a 'social addition', lifting them above social assistance. Moreover, coverage by social insurance could be widened by treating socially useful activities as 'fictitious' contribution periods. Not long ago this was introduced for childrearing and periods of caring for relatives; it could be improved further and other non-paid activities might be considered, while sabbaticals from paid work could equally be construed as being equivalent to contributory periods. Of course, there are limits in so far as those who contribute directly to the system by way of deductions from their wages are unlikely to acquiesce to a definition of 'contributors' and beneficiaries that stretches too far (Offe, 1991). However, the degree of solidarity that goes beyond intertemporal redistribution is not predetermined, but a matter of public acceptance and political will.

The introduction of a levy on all non-contributors to pay for some types of expenditure, say labour market programmes, and an increase, or even abolition, of contribution ceilings would add resources for these reforms and create a more progressive social insurance funding. However, owing to current economic and labour market pressures, the level of transfers to the east and the self-imposed adherence to convergence criteria for joining the European Monetary Union, the financial scope for improvements is relatively narrow at the moment. Rather than additional funding, resources might therefore have to be found through a reshuffling of public spending. The generous provision for tenured civil servants, and tax relief for higher income earners, married couples in particular, are areas that could be explored. As Bäcker (1995, p 357) points out, these issues seem to be technical details and yet they are crucial in the debate about the future of social insurance and the degree of solidarity within the system.

five

A 'liberal' dynamic in the transformation of the French social welfare system*

Bruno Palier

Introduction

The French social welfare system (*la sécurité sociale*), built up from 1945 to the 1970s, has often been presented as the final stage of an evolution from social assistance to social insurance. After the Second World War social assistance was seen as residual, and it was assumed that, through the expansion of social insurance, assistance would eventually become redundant once the whole population was integrated into the social insurance system (Renard, 1995). However, despite a significant expansion during this period, French welfare has never managed to shed its assistance component.

Nevertheless, *la sécurité sociale* is usually seen as belonging to the family of social insurance systems. Indeed, its main component reflects the Bismarckian tradition. Most benefits are earnings related, entitlement is conditional upon a contribution record, and funding is based largely on contributions paid by

*This chapter is partly based on a collaboration with Giuliano Bonoli for V. George and P. Taylor-Gooby (1996). Results have been published in English (Bonoli and Palier, 1996) and in French (Palier and Bonoli, 1995). I would like to thank Jochen Clasen for his useful remarks and advice.

employers and employees (*cotisations sociales*). The system is divided into a number of separate schemes (healthcare, old age, family benefit) covering different occupational groups.

If the French system shares the main characteristics of the 'corporatist–conservative model' (Espıng-Andersen, 1990), social insurance in France centres on three main specificities: the importance of contribution funding, the focus on 'workers' (*travailleurs*), employees and their families, and the management of funds by representatives of employers and employees.

From a French perspective, these would be the three aspects of the system that make it outdated, as the crisis of the welfare state in France is analysed in terms of problems of financing, coverage and management. This chapter will argue that the main pressures and changes within the French system over the last 20 years are linked to these three characteristics, and that the progressive evolution of the system is transforming French social protection into a more liberal welfare state.

In order to demonstrate this, the chapter will first describe the main characteristics of the French social insurance system and then go on to examine its three different points of crisis, in order to put into context significant policy changes which have taken place since the early 1980s. Finally, it will outline the principal components of the recent Plan Juppé, which provoked mass demonstrations in France in December 1995 and which remains the context for reforms in the coming years.

Characteristics of social insurance in France[1]

Social insurance principles dominate the financing, coverage, benefits and organisation of the French social protection system. As Korpi (1995, p 28) put it,

> together with most continental European countries, the social insurance system in France shares the basic characteristics of the corporatist income security model. Social insurance is thus directed to the economically active parts of the population with separate programmes for different occupational groups, income ceilings for coverage and employer–employee participation in the adminis-

tration of social insurance. France has however combined the corporatist model with strong elements for the voluntary mutual organisations remaining in the system.

What follows is a brief illustration of this characterisation.

The French social welfare system is organised as a system of insurance schemes covering diverse 'social risks' which, when they occur, confer the right to benefits. Sickness, maternity, invalidity, death, industrial injury and occupational diseases, widowhood, old age and children are 'risks' or 'contingencies' covered by *sécurité sociale*. In addition, the unemployment insurance system stands out as will be discussed below. Finally, there are complementary schemes for healthcare and pensions.

Social insurance in France is very fragmented. It consists of several so-called *régimes*, a term that is applied to embrace both a specific organisation and the coverage of a risk. A set of compulsory basic *régimes*, to which anyone in work must be affiliated, is complemented by a number of *régimes complémentaires* which improve the level of coverage and may or may not be compulsory. From among the numerous *régimes*, the five major types will be dealt with here.

Most important is the *régime général*, which covers employees in the area of industry and trade. It is the largest basic scheme as it protects two thirds of the working population and is considered a model for the functioning and development of the other schemes. The *régime général* is divided into three different sectors:

- health or sickness insurance (*santé et accidents du travail*), delivering benefits for sickness, maternity, invalidity, death, industrial injury and occupational diseases;

- pensions (*retraites*), old age;

- family (*familles*), family benefits.

For people covered by the *régime général*, basic levels of benefits are increased by complementary schemes, especially in the areas of health and pensions. These are also compulsory, insurance based schemes, run by private, non-profit making organisations (such as *mutuelles*). They are organised by economic sectors (agriculture, trade and industry, etc) but also in relation to status. Supervisory and managerial employees (*les cadres*) are covered by different complementary schemes from other employees.

Nearly 20% of the population is insured by a total of 120 special or particular schemes (*régimes spéciaux* and *régimes particuliers*) which are separate from the *régime général*. The *régimes spéciaux* cover employees in certain public sector areas, such as the SNCF (the national railway), the RATP (Parisian Underground), the Banque de France, the Chambre de Commerce, the military, notary, clerks and miners. *Régimes particuliers* cover national civil servants, local civil servants and employees of companies in the public sector such as electricity, war widows, orphans, etc.

Unlike the *régimes spéciaux*, the *régimes particuliers* do not cover all risks but are dependent upon organisations belonging to the *régime général* for benefits in kind for healthcare and maternity services. For other risks, there are separate management organisations (*caisses autonomes* or *groupements mutualistes*) in charge of delivering benefits which, in certain cases, may be more generous than those provided by the *régime général*, such as pensions.

Approximately another 10% of the population is covered by 19 *régimes non-non* for *les professions non salariées non agricoles*, ie, self-employed groups such as shopkeepers, artisans, independent professions and employers, but not farmers. Wishing to remain separate from the *régime général*, these groups decide for themselves the scope of coverage and the level of contribution paid. Currently, all *régimes non-non* cover the same risks as the *régime général*, with different levels of contribution. Health and maternity insurance policies are managed by local *caisses mutuelles*, organised according to professional categories (shopkeepers, artisans, industrials). For old age pensions, there is a national *caisse* for each professional category. Finally, there are separate *régimes* for people employed in the agricultural sector and farmers. Its institutional framework is the *mutualité sociale agricole*, supervised by the Ministry of Agriculture.

The *régime général* can be considered as the most important scheme, as it includes two thirds of the working population, and all types of risks. It pays out approximately 60% of the benefits delivered by all the compulsory *régimes*. Other *régimes* cover only some of the risks, with various levels of contributions and benefits. The *régimes spéciaux* and the *régimes particuliers* are generally more generous for healthcare and pensions. The *régimes non-non* and agricultural schemes deliver less generous benefits, but require a lower level of contribution. Family benefits are the most unified area, all falling under the responsibility of the *régime général*. Even though they are contribution-financed, it has been argued that they should be regarded as universal rather than insurance based social welfare provision because of their scope of coverage (Dupeyroux, 1993).

Administration

All schemes are administered by different funds (*caisses*) at national, regional and local level, and staff are neither paid by the state, nor under its authority. Each *caisse* is headed by a governing board comprising representatives of employers and employees. Employee representatives used to be in a majority, but this has recently been changed (see below). *Caisses* are headed by a president elected from the ranks of employees or employers, and a director who is appointed by the government. Since the organisation of the different schemes is similar to that of the *régime général*, only the latter will be discussed here.

As mentioned above, the *régime général* is organised into different risk sectors. The CNAMTS (*Caisse Nationale d'Assurance Maladie des Travailleurs Salariés*: National Health Insurance Fund for Salaried Employees) is the national organisation responsible for health, including maternity, invalidity and death, as well as industrial injuries and occupational diseases. At regional level, the 16 CRAMs (*Caisse Regionale d'Assurance Maladie*: Regional Health Insurance Funds) deal with safety at work, coordinate efforts to prevent accidents and ensure uniform contribution rates for insurance against industrial injuries and occupational diseases. These regional *caisses* are also responsible for retirement pensions for those covered by the *régime général*. Benefits are delivered at the local level by the 133 CPAMS (*Caisses Primaires d'Assurances Maladie*: Primary Health Insurance Offices).

The CNAVTS (*Caisse Nationale d'Assurance Vieillesse des Travailleurs Salariés*: National Pension Fund for Salaried Employees) is responsible for the management of pension plans and has some responsibilities in social assistance for older people (home care, management of the assistance funds for the elderly), while the CNAF (*Caisse Nationale d'Allocations Familiales*) is responsible for the management of family benefits for all salaried persons of any category, except farmers. At the local level, the 125 CAFs (*Caisses d'Allocations Familiales*) deliver 25 different family benefits, and are also responsible for some other types of family assistance.

As far as the management of the budget of the *régime général* as a whole is concerned, the ACOSS (*Agence Centrale des Organismes de Sécurité Sociale*: Central Agency of Social Security Organisations) is responsible. It is run by UCANSS (*Union des Caisses Nationales de Sécurité Sociale*), which is a board comprising representatives of the three *caisses nationales* described above. At the local level, the 105 URSSAF (*Unions Locales de Recouvrement des Cotisations*) are responsible for collecting the social contributions.

Finally, on a basis of parity between trade unions and employers' associations, the unemployment insurance scheme is managed by UNEDIC (*Union Nationale pour l'Emploi dans l'Industrie et le Commerce*: National Union for Employment in Industry and Commerce). It is funded by contributions and a state-financed solidarity fund (see below). All benefits are paid through ASSEDICs (*Association pour l'Emploi dans l'Industrie et le Commerce*: Associations for Employment in Industry and Trade) at local level.

Management and finance

Espousing the principle of 'social democracy', social insurance schemes were originally intended to have some degree of independence from the state and to be managed by the social partners. Subject to only limited public supervision, the intention was to have a system run by those who pay for it, and therefore have an interest in it, in a decentralised fashion with small, local offices which are easily accessible to the public (Kerschen, 1995).

However, the state has a crucial supervisory role, laying down the basic principles of *sécurité sociale*, setting benefit and contribution levels and attempting to ensure the system's financial balance. Nevertheless, the responsibility for *sécurité sociale* has never been entirely clear. Under more or less visible pressure exerted by the state, many decisions are actually taken through negotiations between trade unions and employers' representatives. As a result, until recently the problems faced by *sécurité sociale* have not been seen as implicating government policy. This perception is evident in the fact that the social insurance budget is still considered to be separate from the general government budget.

The different social insurance schemes are financially autonomous and have several sources of financing, although the bulk of their funds stems from contributions of those insured. Indeed, within the European Union the French benefit system is the one where contribution financing plays the biggest role, accounting for 80% of the total revenue of all the schemes and 90% in the case of the *régime général*. Based on wages and paid both by employers and employees, the proportion of total contributions paid by employers has decreased from 82% in 1970 to 55% in 1992. Contributions are proportional to earnings, and rates are different for each risk. For example, within the *régime général* employers paid 12.8% of employee's salary for sickness insurance in 1996, and employees 6.8%. For old age insurance, there is a contribution ceiling equivalent to about 2.2 times the minimum salary, equivalent to 13,330FF (about £1,600) per month in April 1996. Employers paid 8.2% of earnings below the ceiling and 1.6% for earnings over and above it, while employees paid 6.55% up to the ceiling. When considering all the social contributions paid by employers and salaried employees, about half of a person's gross wage is transferred to the social insurance system.

The state's subsidy to the financing of the *régime général* has increased over time and there are social assistance benefits delivered by the *régime général* which are entirely tax-funded. However, the distinction between social insurance and social assistance is a very strong one in France. Revenue from contributions cannot be used to finance assistance expenses such as lone-parent benefits. Indeed, the two forms of financing are seen as reflecting the two different types of social protection that coexist in the French welfare system: contributory social insurance and tax-financed, non-contributory provision (*Aide Sociale* or *Solidarité Nationale*).

While the French social protection system can largely be characterised as adhering to social insurance principles, it has traditionally been supplemented by a locally administered *Aide Sociale*, which is part of the realm of *Solidarité Nationale*. The latter consists increasingly of non-contributory, usually means tested benefits, such as the minimum old age benefit, disability benefits, lone-parenthood benefit, sickness insurance for the unemployed, other minima and benefits in kind (such as RMI – see below). *Solidarité Nationale* is administered by the government and covers those without access to the social insurance system who need basic help.

The balance between social insurance and *Solidarité Nationale* is strongly tilted towards the former, which means that the French social welfare system is directed mainly at income maintenance rather than at prevention of poverty. Indeed, almost 85% of overall expenditure on social protection is paid out through contributory social insurance benefits. During the 1980s, retirement pensions accounted for half of social spending expenditure, and healthcare expenses for 28%. The proportion of family expenditures has constantly decreased since the 1950s, to 13% in 1994. By contrast, unemployment insurance benefits became increasingly important. Their share of total spending increased from below 2% before 1970 to 9% in 1994. Today, 75% of social expenditure is cash benefits (Bouget, 1996).

Social insurance benefits: access and coverage

What follows is a brief overview of the main social insurance benefits within the French welfare state.

Sickness insurance benefits (prestations d'assurance maladie)

Sickness insurance covers the insured and his or her dependants (spouse or common-law partner and children under 16, or 20 if they are still in full-time education or are disabled). To qualify for sickness insurance, the insured person must have worked a minimum number of hours in salaried employment during the period preceding the illness. The coverage has also been extended to groups not in active employment such as the unemployed, disabled, prisoners and recipients of RMI (see below).

Cash benefits (*prestations en espèces* or *indemnités journalières*), intended to compensate for loss of earnings, are paid as from the third day of sick leave for a maximum period of three years. The sickness cash benefit within the *régime général* amounts to 50% of employees' gross wages up to the so-called social security ceiling of about two-and-a-half times the minimum salary. Benefit levels are regularly uprated and complementary schemes (*mutuelles*) improve the level of wage replacement.

Sickness insurance schemes also reimburse costs incurred for medical expenses and prescriptions, dental treatment, dentures, prostheses and so on, and pay hospital expenses directly. Health-care provision is delivered on a fee-for-service principle. For prescriptions, insured persons initially pay themselves and are subsequently reimbursed in part. The remainder, known as the *ticket modérateur*, which varies between 20 and 60% of the total cost, has to be paid by the patient. This system is supposed to encourage people to moderate expenses. However, complement-ary insurance schemes often reimburse *ticket modérateur*.

Fees for medical care and treatment are decided in negotiations between social insurance agencies and medical practitioners' professional organisations. Costs are reimbursed at up to 75% of the charge. When inpatient care is required, the insured person pays a daily amount to cover the cost of food and accommodation (*forfait hospitalier*). This was 70FF (about £8) per day in 1996, and increased after 90 days in hospital. Public hospitals receive a global allowance (*enveloppe*) from the state to cover their medical expenses.

Maternity insurance benefits (assurance maternité)

Eligibility rules for maternity insurance benefits in kind and cash are the same as for sickness insurance, except that cash benefits are paid only to women who have been registered under an insurance scheme for at least 10 months at the expected date of confinement. Cash benefits amount to 84% of gross salary up to the social security ceiling. They are generally paid for 6 weeks before the confinement and 10 weeks after but are increased to respectively 8 and 18 weeks for the third child onwards. Benefits in kind are pre- and postnatal examinations, the costs of which are reimbursed in full.

Invalidity insurance benefits (prestations d'assurance invalidité)

Designed to compensate in part for the loss of income suffered by an insured person, invalidity insurance grants three categories of invalidity pension according to the degree of disablement: people capable of paid work, people incapable of any job at all and people incapable of any job and who are in need of care. Invalidity pensions are paid at 30% of former salary for people who can do some work and 50% for those who are unable to work at all. A supplementary benefit is paid to those needing help. Payment stops at retirement age. Those not fulfilling the required contribution record may turn to the assistance benefit, the minimum invalidity benefit (*allocation pour adulte handicapé*).

Industrial injury and occupational illness benefits (prestations d'accident du travail et maladie professionnelle)

Special protection is provided to victims of industrial injuries including accidents taking place on the way to and from work, and to people with an occupational illness. Treatment relating to the accident or illness is free of charge and cash benefits are delivered from the first day of sick leave. Daily allowances represent 50% of the relevant daily wage for the first 28 days, and two thirds thereafter. In the event of a fatal accident, spouses and children under 16 years of age (or 20 if in full-time education) receive a pension.

Old age insurance pensions (pensions de retraites)

France has both statutory basic and compulsory supplementary pension schemes which operate on a pay-as-you-go basis. Within the *régime général* employees contribute and receive only a basic pension. They must have paid contributions on earnings up to the social security ceiling. This scheme ensures that anyone who is at least 60 years old and has contributed for 40 years receives a pension equal to 50% of the average gross salary of the 25 years with the highest earnings; the pension is paid on a pro rata basis if the contribution period is shorter. A surviving spouse receives a 'reversion' pension equal to 52% of the basic pension.

In order to improve the level of wage replacement, retired people receive complementary pensions from compulsory complementary Funds, resulting in combined levels of wage replacement of between 75% and 80% of the average gross salary of the 10 best years. For people who, prior to retirement age, did not contribute, or contributed only for a very short period, or were on a very low income, there is a minimum (non-contributory) old age allowance (*minimum vieillesse*).

Family benefits (prestations familiales)

Family benefits in France are also financed mainly through insurance contributions, albeit paid by employers only. However, eligibility is not tied to insured employment. Instead, there are both universal and means tested benefits, except for the parental education allowance (*allocation d'éducation parentale*), where entitlement is dependent upon an employment record and the benefit is aimed at compensating for the loss of income resulting from the reduction or interruption of a parent's paid employment at the birth of a third child or subsequent children. As far as other benefits are concerned, any family living legally in France with one or more dependent children is entitled to a family allowance.

There are five categories:

- benefits linked to birth and infancy, such as allowances for young children (*allocation pour jeune enfant*);

- maintenance benefits, such as family allowances (*allocations familiales*) which are granted, without a means test, for families with second and subsequent children, and which account for almost half of total family benefit expenditures;

- targeted benefits such as the 'new school year' allowance (*allocation de rentrée scolaire*) to cover costs for books etc, the lone-parent allowance (*allocation de parent isolé*) and family support (*soutien familial*);

- an allowance for mothers' helps or nannies (*allocation de garde d'enfant à domicile*);

- housing benefits (*allocations logement*), such as housing benefit given to families (*allocation logement*), social housing allowance (*allocation sociale de logement*) and personalised housing aid (*aide personnalisée au logement*);

- unemployment insurance benefits (*allocations chômage*).

The main unemployment insurance benefit (*allocation unique dégressive*) is payable only for a certain period, which varies according to contribution record, and the level of benefit decreases over time. For example, in 1996 a person who within the previous two years had worked at least 14 months would receive a full benefit for nine months, then lose 17% of the benefit at four-monthly intervals. Claimants with shorter contribution records might be awarded benefits for a shorter period. While entitlement to the main unemployment insurance benefits runs out after 30 months, a variety of benefits exist to extend the cover. Most important of these is the *allocation de solidarité spécifique*, a type of unemployment assistance which is subject to a means test. For those who do not qualify, or whose insurance benefit is insufficient to live on, it is possible to claim the tax-funded RMI (see below) either on its own or as a supplement to unemployment benefit.

The crises of the French welfare state: social insurance in question

Until the late 1970s, French social security policy was oriented towards expansion and improvement. Since then, it has gone through a phase of major restructuring. Reforms have incorporated measures with two main objectives: decreasing expenditure and raising revenue, and modifying the structure of the system.

Several attempts have been made to restore the financial viability of the system, which is affected by the twin pressures of rising demands and insufficient growth of revenue. Since 1974 the deficit of *sécurité sociale* has been a major preoccupation of successive governments. In 1995 the deficit of the social security budget as a whole was 67.3 billion FF (which was equivalent to about 2% of total social expenditure, and less than 1% of GDP). The accumulated deficit, including an estimate for 1996, was evaluated at 250 billion FF by the then Prime Minister Alain Juppé in the summer of 1995.

In this context, cost saving measures have included raising user charges in healthcare and decreasing the level of reimbursement of medical expenses. A reform introduced in 1993 reduced the generosity of pensions by lowering benefit levels and increasing contribution requirements. Other reforms affected unemployment benefits (creation of the *allocation unique dégressive* in 1992) and family benefits (no increase in the level of family benefits in 1996).

Governments have also aimed at increasing revenue by creating new forms of taxes on alcohol and tobacco, as well as the *contribution sociale généralisée* in 1989 (see below) and by raising social insurance contributions paid by employees. On average, every 18 months since the mid-1970s, a new programme for 'rescuing the social welfare system' has been announced. These programmes share several characteristics, ie, increases in social insurance contributions, coupled with cost saving measures primarily within the *régime général* and often focused on sickness insurance in particular. These programmes have usually led to temporary breaks in the increase of social expenditure (Oudin, 1992).

More importantly, several attempts have been made to modify the structure of the French welfare state, without altering, in principle, the overall level of provision. Since the early 1990s, the nature of these reforms has changed as a result of the introduction of a 'liberal dynamic' (see below). The different dimensions of the current crisis of French social policy are all linked with social insurance. They are threefold: the system faces an economic crisis, as a result of the problems created by the pivotal role of contributions in the financing of social insurance; a social crisis, arising from the increasing number of non-traditional salaried workers who are excluded from the system; and a political crisis, regarding the management of social insurance.

From social insurance contributions to taxation

Beyond the current deficit, the structure of financing of the French system is problematic. As mentioned earlier, in principle social insurance schemes are supposed to be financed solely by employers' and employees' contributions, without government subsidies. This is fairly central to the French debate, since the high level of employer contribution is seen to have an overall negative impact on the country's economic competitiveness and thus, at least in part, to be responsible for the high level of unemployment. Accordingly, social insurance contributions are often referred to as a 'social burden' (*charges sociales*). Since they have a direct impact on the cost of labour, contributions are believed to inhibit job creation. This claim is made in the light of international comparisons. Between 1983 and 1991, total employment in France increased on average by 0.5%, whereas in the EU as a whole it grew by 1.7%, in Japan by 1.3% and in the USA by 1.9% (OECD, 1994c).

The overall cost of labour is not significantly higher in France than in similar countries (Euzéby, 1994). However, it has been argued that the negative impact of social insurance contributions on employment is greater in the case of low wages. Because of the existence of a contribution ceiling within old age pension schemes, the proportion of gross salary paid in contributions is actually higher for low wages than for high wages. For example, total contributions paid on a minimum wage (SMIC) amount to 48% of gross salary; the equivalent figure for a salary three times as high is only 41.6% (Join-Lambert, 1994, p 334). As a consequence, and also because of the existence of a minimum wage, the cost of labour for low wages is artificially inflated.

The existence of a minimum wage (raised by 4% to 6,249FF by the Juppé government in July 1995), is strongly supported by French public opinion (Rosanvallon, 1995), and it would be detrimental for any government to try to reduce it. This reflects the overall French scepticism of the Anglo-American low wage approach to job creation (Esping-Andersen, 1996b), which, though more successful in numerical terms, creates problems such as poverty traps and the creation of a social group which might be categorised as the 'working poor' (Albert, 1991). Thus, in France the only viable option left to policy makers intending to lower the cost of labour lies in the reduction of social insurance contributions.

Changes in contribution rates have affected employers and employees differently. The share of social insurance contributions paid by employers has decreased while the share of contributions (below the ceiling) paid by employees within the *régime général* rose, from 17.2% in 1970 to 44.4% in 1992 (Join-Lambert, 1994). Meanwhile, since the late 1970s governments of different political orientations have adopted different types of contribution exemption for employers in order to encourage job creation. These are targeted at employers taking on particularly disadvantaged groups, such as the long-term and young unemployed, or at small companies, which are most adversely affected by the relatively high cost of unskilled labour.

This shift from contributions paid by employers to contribution paid by employees signifies a structural change in the French welfare system. As Ewald (1986) explains, the historical emergence of compulsory social insurance implied a type of collective protection, in which employers were also responsible for the social situation of their employees; yet the shift described above undermines this collective aspect of social insurance and implies a progressive move towards a type of social insurance where employees are more directly 'paying for welfare' (Glennerster, 1992). For example, as illustrated earlier, certain expenses in healthcare (*ticket modérateur, forfait hospitalier,* some medical fees) are no longer reimbursed by the basic schemes, but only by complementary types of insurance. A similar phenomenon is occurring within retirement pensions, where benefits within the basic schemes have become less generous after the reform in 1993, increasing the dependency on complementary schemes. This implies that the degree of social protection is becoming progressively dependent on individual premiums, while the degree of interpersonal redistribution is diminishing. This development could be characterised as a tendency towards a re-commodification of welfare in health and old age.

This trend is accompanied by another change linked with the problem of finance. Since lowering unemployment is seen as conditional upon a reduction in the level of insurance contributions, governments have tried to compensate for a decrease in the latter with the introduction of new types of taxation, such as the *Contribution Sociale Généralisée* (CSG) in December 1990. Unlike social insurance contributions (*cotisation*), this tax is levied on even the lowest wages and also on some forms of other income such as capital revenues and welfare benefits. Unlike the progressive income tax system in France, the CSG is strictly proportional and serves as earmarked revenue to fund non-contributory welfare programmes. What is more, while income tax in France is paid three times a year by households themselves, this new tax is deducted at source. Initially levied at 1.1% of all incomes, the Balladur government increased it to 2.4% in 1993.

Replacing part of the employers' contribution to family benefits, the CSG has enabled a shift in the funding structure of social insurance. Indeed, it can be argued that a series of measures aimed either at reducing the financial burden on employers (contribution exemptions) or at shifting the burden (CSG) indicate at least a partial shift from contribution towards tax-financing (Pellet, 1995).

From salaried workers to the socially excluded

The second crisis is linked to the limited coverage offered by social insurance. The predominantly contributory social insurance system is regarded as unable to deal with those who do not have access to the system, such as the long-term unemployed and others excluded from the labour market. The size of these groups has grown in recent years. In November 1996, 3.5 million people were unemployed and about one million households were in receipt of the minimum income scheme, RMI. These groups represent the most pressing social issue in France. For them, the social insurance system, which is the main provider of welfare, is of very little use. A two-tiered system seems to emerge which exacerbates social divisions and inequalities between those with full entitlement to generous social insurance protection, and those with no or insufficient connection to the labour market, and thus to social insurance, and who have to rely on minimum income or social assistance programmes (Fitoussi and Rosanvallon, 1996).

In this context, a new perception of social problems has emerged. The inadequacy of a social protection system based on contributory social insurance has become increasingly evident. As a result, pressures to develop new policies to combat poverty and exclusion have built up. The *question sociale* (Castel, 1995; Rosanvallon, 1995) is no longer about protecting people from the occurrence of social risks such as sickness, old age or raising children, but about protecting them from poverty and exclusion.

Since the early 1980s, policies of social reinsertion have been introduced, underlining the inadequacy of the social insurance system which is geared towards 'workers' (*travailleurs*). By contrast, these new policies have targeted the most disadvantaged. Rather than delivering uniform benefits, social insertion policies offer provision designed to suit local and individual needs. Insertion policies are thus characterised by a high degree of devolution to local authorities. In addition, and unlike the social insurance system, which treats social risks separately, insertion policies address a whole range of relevant social problems in an integrated manner.

In this context, the creation of the *Revenu Minimum d'Insertion* (RMI: Minimum Income of Reinsertion) is certainly the most significant development. Accepted unanimously by the French parliament at the end of 1988, the RMI's main feature is to guarantee a means tested minimum income to each individual resident in France who is over 25 years of age (2,375FF per month for a single person in April 1996). In addition, the RMI has a reinsertion element in the form of a 'contract' with society. Claimants must commit themselves to take part in a reinsertion programme, as stated in a contract signed by the recipient and a social worker. Programmes include job seeking activities, vocational training or activities designed to enhance a recipient's 'social autonomy'.

The RMI, as well as other social reinsertion policies, belongs to the realm of state provision and should be seen in the context of an ongoing process of structural change within the French social welfare system, following the recognition of the inadequacy of a system predominantly based on social insurance. Overall, these changes are characterised by a re-commodification of social insurance, an increased significance of taxation in the financing of social welfare, and the development of non-contributory, means tested and targeted benefits. Indeed, it can be argued that a 'liberal' dynamic has been introduced to the system with the implementation of reinsertion policies and a greater degree of tax-financing, both of which are characteristic of a 'liberal' rather than a 'corporatist-conservative' welfare state regime (Esping-Andersen, 1990). As mentioned above, the tendency towards individualisation within the funding of social insurance points in the same direction of re-commodification. In addition, there is also a new role for the state.

From social insurance to state welfare?

The third dimension of the crisis in the French welfare system is a political one: the explicit empowerment of the state within the system (Bonoli and Palier, 1996). Central to the current debate on welfare is the question whether the tendencies described above should go deeper and further and, more specifically, whether sickness benefits and family benefits should be taken out of the social insurance system and become tax-financed, non-contributory transfers. The latter is a crucial point in the debate between different actors involved in the social welfare system, and in particular between governmental, political and administrative actors on the one hand and certain employees' representatives on the other (Palier and Bonoli, 1995).

Some of the trade unions have a strong attachment to the original structure of French welfare.[2] Defending social insurance principles, they are calling for an even stricter distinction between insurance and assistance. The social insurance system should continue to be financed through contributions, should cover employees only and should continue to be managed by represent-

atives of trade unions and employers; conversely, the state tax-
financed sector should continue to fulfil its function as 'last resort'
or safety net for those without access to the insurance system.

By contrast, in 1996 the government, supported by the
socialist opposition and by the civil service (among which most of
the so-called 'experts' are to be found), advocated a move away
from original social insurance structures towards a system in which
the balance between tax and contribution funding is shifting
towards the former, which covers the entire population with non-
contributory, yet mainly means tested, benefits and in which the
state plays a much larger role. Such a shift would permit a
decrease in the rate of social insurance contributions paid by
employers and thus would help to reduce the cost of labour. It
would also be fairer than the present system because of its
'universal' scope, covering everybody. In addition to these
economic and social justifications, there is a political rationale. An
expansion in the relative importance of tax-funding would justify a
more substantive involvement of the government in the
management of the system, which, it is argued, is in need of more
control than is currently exercised by the social partners.

In order to understand the political implications of these
arguments, one needs to consider the changes in terms of the
distribution of power and management responsibilities that a shift
towards a non-contributory state-centred welfare system would
imply. As discussed earlier, in France the type of benefit is
supposed to determine the funding mechanism. In turn, the
financing determines the responsibility regarding management. In
other words, an insurance based system should be run by social
partners, whereas the state is responsible for non-contributory
(universal or means tested) transfers. A shift towards more tax-
financing would therefore justify greater control being conferred
to the state.

Traditionally managed by social partners, social insurance in
France was supposed to represent a type of 'social democracy'
which is distinctly different and in contrast to the bureaucratic
power of the state (Kerschen, 1995). Thus, the trade unions'
defence of social insurance principles has to be seen as a defence of
their own position within the system. However, commentators
have stressed the fact that trade unions have been reluctant to take
a lead role in controlling and reforming the French system. In
fact, except for unemployment insurance and complementary

schemes, difficult and unpopular decisions such as increases in contribution rates and lowering the level of provision have always been taken by governments.

Existing ambiguities of management responsibilities, and the lack of leadership on the part of social partners at the head of the social security funds, have provoked criticism, particularly among civil servants, of the social partners and also of the social insurance system, which gives the latter such importance because of their management responsibility. As a senior civil servant put it:

> "The financing system based on social contributions has generated a system of discussion between people who *believe* they are the representatives of employees and employers. Such a system has resulted in much abuse. The CSG (*Contribution Sociale Généralisée*) can remove the legitimacy, or false legitimacy, from the trade unions, which have not done much for the social security system, and will allow parliament to examine the social budget.... The social security system is locked by lobbies who do not want the system to change." (Interview, Ministry of Social Affairs, 1994)

By contrast, trade unions explain why they resent reforms of funding:

> "In general, we oppose the tendency towards shifting financing from contribution to taxation. The transfer of financial obligations to the state will imply the transfer of decision-making power, and we are against that." (Interview with representative of the FO, 1994)

However, trade unions are not unanimous in their position towards welfare reforms.[3] Still, resistance to reforms has been supported by a majority of the population. Social insurance is very popular, and the trade unions are regarded as defending it against the government's retrenchment plans. This resistance manifested itself most clearly in mass demonstrations towards the end of 1995.

Le Plan Juppé

Social policy reforms proposed by the former Prime Minister Juppé in 1996 may be the framework within which social welfare systems will develop in the coming years. Juppé presented his ambitious plan as being based on three 'forceful ideas': 'justice', 'responsibility' and 'urgency' (Juppé, 1996).

The latter concerns the 'deficit' of social security funds. A new tax was created to pay off the accumulated debts of the system, calculated at 250 billion FF, which included the provisional deficit for 1996. This tax, called RDS (*Remboursement de la Dette Sociale*), is levied at a rate of 0.5% on all types of income for 13 years. A number of complementary measures have been taken in order to increase revenue of the social insurance system, including increases in the rates of sickness insurance contributions payable by pensioners and the unemployed. A contribution of five billion FF to be paid by doctors and the pharmaceutical industry was initially planned but was later reduced to one billion FF. This money will be returned to doctors as earmarked funds to finance computer equipment in consulting rooms. Despite Juppé's promise not to decrease the level of provision, family allowances were frozen for 1996.

Long-term measures, intended to improve both justice and economic efficiency, have not yet been implemented. They correspond to the economic analysis of the weight of social insurance contributions on labour costs, identified by the government as the major economic failure of social insurance in France. In order to expand its financial base, currently seen as too restricted on wages, the government intends to widen the scope of CSG by progressively replacing contributions for sickness insurance with CSG resources. What is more, the level of employers' contributions to social insurance is to be based on companies' 'value added' as well as wages. The implementation of these measures would clearly accelerate the development of the tax-financing of the French social welfare system. However, after demonstrations and strikes in November and December 1995, these plans, as well as a much broader reform of the entire French fiscal system, were postponed.

Justice, the first of Juppé's 'ideas', concerns problems of fragmentation, benefit disparities and coverage associated with the French social insurance system. "In the name of justice, we want a social security for all" (Juppé, 1996, p 221). As far as healthcare is concerned, the introduction of a universal health insurance scheme was planned in which contributions would be harmonised and everyone would receive the same benefits in kind. Plans were still in discussion in late 1996. As far as family benefits were concerned, family lobbies successfully opposed the introduction of means testing the universal general family allowances and a proposition to tax family benefit has also been abandoned. Although defeated, these plans illustrate that social welfare in France might be moving away from the social insurance model. Albeit contribution funded, family benefits are considered universal because of their scope. However, the new orientation is towards targeted, means tested benefits, usually associated with a residual welfare state, identifying the transformation of social protection in France as basically a 'liberal' rather than a 'universal' dynamic.

Juppé also planned to reform pension schemes within the *régimes spéciaux* and the *régimes particuliers* by imposing the same method of calculation of pension rights as the one applicable within the *régime général*. Thus, 40 (rather than 37.5) contribution years would be needed in order to qualify for a full pension, and the best 25 (rather than 10) years of salary would become the basis for calculating individual pension levels. This was vehemently opposed by employees and their representatives and triggered off the mass protests at the end of 1995, which included strikes in the public sector and eventually forced the government to back down. This could be interpreted as evidence of the continuing popularity of the 'conservative–corporatist' French social insurance system, since the strikes occurred partially in order to defend advantages of particular occupational and status groups (Esping-Andersen, 1990).

An interpretation of the political crisis of November–December 1995 would be incomplete without a reference to 'responsibility', the third dimension of the Juppé Plan, which was directed at trade unions. As a new 'architecture' for the whole system, a new 'chain of responsibilities' was proposed, as well as a new organisation of the healthcare system in particular. However, what was described as a clarification of responsibilities in fact meant a stronger role for parliament and more state control over the social insurance system.

In February 1996 the French Constitution was amended, allowing parliament to formulate guidelines and political objectives for the social insurance system. In future, parliament will fix 'expenditure targets' for each *caisse*, and will have more power over sickness insurance *caisses* in particular, which will be overseen by supervising councils answerable to parliament. Within healthcare, new regional organisations (*Union Régionale des Caisses d'Assurances Maladie*) will be created to harmonise health policies of the different sickness insurance schemes at regional level, and ambulatory and hospital care will be more closely controlled. What is more, on the basis of 'expenditure targets' established by parliament, the government will negotiate with the different social insurance *caisses* so-called 'agreements on objectives and management'. Thus, while social partners will remain responsible for the management of the social insurance funds, they will have to act within a framework negotiated with the government.

The composition of the governing boards of *caisses* have changed also. Instead of an employees' majority, there will be parity between employers and employees on each board. In addition, new members have been appointed by the government and 'mutualities' and family associations will also be represented on boards. Directors of each *caisse*, even at regional and local level, will be appointed by the government. Overall, these changes represent a reduction in trade union influence within the system and an increase in the power of employers' representatives and government. As a result, the system has lost what is characteristic of social insurance in many countries, the management of social insurance funds by contributors, that is, social partners.

All these reforms are continuing and enforcing the dynamics of the evolution of the French welfare system analysed in this chapter. Even though the replacement of contributions by CSG has yet to materialise, the degree of tax-funding has increased and a greater diversity of financial resources is diminishing a traditional characteristic of French social insurance. Changes in managing structures reinforce the role of the state within the system. Overall, it can be argued that the general design of reforms that were officially aimed to 'combat deficits and unemployment' (Juppé, 1996, p 226) is in fact fostering the 'liberal' dynamic of the transformation of the French welfare state which is progressively leaving the realm of social insurance.

Notes

[1] For a more detailed presentation of the French welfare system, see Dupeyroux (1993) and Join-Lambert (1994). See also documents in English produced by the Ministry of Social Affairs, especially a leaflet written by the Social Affairs Council of the French Embassy in London; *Social welfare in France*, as well as a text distributed within the Ministry; *France's social security system*, and a document distributed by Mutualité Française, *The French mutualité and social welfare in France*. Unless otherwise stated, the data for this chapter have been provided by the statistical service of the Ministry of Social Affairs.

[2] There are five main trade unions, or 'confederation of employees' representatives', in France. The communist Confédération Générale du Travail (CGT) and the socialist and Trotskyist Force Ouvrière (FO) are strong defenders of the current welfare system. The socialist Confédération Française Démocratique du Travail (CFDT) is divided over welfare reforms. The two other main trade unions have been less categorical in their opposition to reforms: they are the catholic Confédération Française des Travailleurs Chrétiens (CFTC) and the white collar Confédération Générale des Cadres (CGC). The rate of unionised employees is currently estimated at between 10% and 15% in France.

[3] See note 1 above.

six

Switzerland: institutions, reforms and the politics of consensual retrenchment

Giuliano Bonoli

Introduction

The development of the Swiss welfare state was influenced to a large extent by what was happening in neighbouring countries. Given the small size of the country and the common languages with France and Germany, this is not surprising; in fact, it is a typical feature in areas other than social policy. Swiss policy makers, mainly German speakers, tended to look at developments in Germany. The introduction of social insurance by Bismarck in the 1880s was widely seen as an example to be followed. The choice between contributory social insurance and alternative forms of welfare provision, such as tax-financed universal schemes, was never seriously debated, the former being seen almost as the 'natural' solution for social problems. The construction of the Swiss welfare state, thus, started with a strong inclination towards the social insurance model (Gilliand, 1988).

However, while Swiss reformers were keen to follow the German example, they were operating in a substantially different institutional environment which imposed some important constraints. Swiss federalism made it difficult to enforce centrally decided and uniform policies right across the country, since cantons have the power to intervene effectively in the law making process. In general, cantons were reluctant to give up their sovereignty to the central government in the area of social policy. The biggest constraint on policy, however, was (and is) the particular and frequent use of referendums (see Table 2).   For instance, constitutional change, typically the starting point of welfare reforms, is automatically subject to referendum.   In addition, Swiss voters can call a referendum on any law passed by parliament, provided they are able to produce 50,000 valid signatures.

Table 2: Use of referendums (including constitutional and optional referendums) and their outcomes (1848-1994)

Period	Number of referendums	Number accepted	Number rejected
1848-1873	11	2	9
1874-1880	11	5	6
1881-1890	12	5	7
1891-1900	19	9	10
1901-1910	9	7	2
1911-1920	12	10	2
1921-1930	15	9	6
1931-1940	17	10	7
1941-1950	14	8	6
1951-1960	33	18	15
1961-1970	22	16	6
1971-1980	65	47	18
1981-1990	37	24	13
1991-1994	37	30	7

Source: Kriesi (1995, p 99)

This particular institutional environment affected the shape of social policies by limiting the realm of what was feasible and by channelling the preferences of different actors in certain directions. The impact of institutions on (social) policy has recently been recognised more fully in several studies by authors of the 'neo-institutionalist' school (Hall, 1986; Skocpol and Amenta, 1986; Merrien, 1990; Stone, 1992; Immergut, 1992; 1996; Pierson, 1994).   Hall, for example, points out that law making institutions determine the way in which preferences of relevant actors are aggregated and can also prompt actors to define their interests in certain ways (1986, p 19). Pierson claims that "these institutions establish the rules of the game for political struggles, shaping group identities and their coalitional choices, enhancing the bargaining power of some groups while devaluing that of others" (1994, p 31). In sum, while it is accepted that social and political forces are the motor behind policy change, it is argued that their actual impact on policy outcomes is significantly mediated by the institutional environment in which they operate. Perhaps the impact of institutions on policy is nowhere clearer than in the case of Switzerland .

Political scientists have long regarded the availability of referendums to dissatisfied minorities as a major determinant of policy making practices. The consensual style of politics, which is considered as a key feature of the Swiss political system, originated as a result of the use made of referendums by minorities (Neidhart, 1970; Kriesi, 1995). In order to be able to rule effectively, the majority was forced to recognise influential minorities in the law making process. Rather than trying to impose a controversial bill, with the risk of seeing it defeated in a referendum, governmental majorities have frequently opted for concertation with external and generally unsympathetic interests. These would then refrain from calling referendums on bills, having been involved in drafting them.

Referendums, however, are not the only force behind consensual politics. As Lijphart (1984) and Katzenstein (1984; 1985) have shown, consensual patterns of policy making emerged also in countries such as Austria, The Netherlands and to some extent Nordic countries without the presence of a referendum system. In particular, Lijphart (1984) has found a correlation between the degree of societal segmentation and the presence of consensual practices. Countries characterised by a high degree of segmentation (ethnic, religious or ideological) have tended to integrate dissent, so as to avoid centrifugal reactions. Katzenstein (1985), in contrast, argues that the size of a country, or of its economy, is the main determinant behind consensual policy making practices. Small countries, having very little control over their economic environment, were forced to develop such practices in order to compete successfully in the world economy.

In practice, consensual politics in Switzerland means that legislative change is negotiated by the social partners and other relevant organised interests even before reaching parliament. Until very recently, parliament had relatively little impact on legislation and its role was limited largely to ratifying what had been decided by the social partners. The most remarkable feature of consensual politics, however, is arguably the composition of the federal government. Initially (1848-90) there was a one-party government of the Liberal Democrats who progressively incorporated other parties to form grand coalitions: in 1890 the Christian Democrats, in 1928 the Farmers' Party and in 1956 the Social Democrats. Since then, these four parties together have ruled the country, sharing ministerial posts between them. Government policies thus tend to be moderate in order to be acceptable to all coalition partners. This approach, however, is not always accepted by parliament, where right-wing parties have a majority and occasionally try to impose controversial measures.

The overall impact of referendums and consensual politics on the development of social insurance was to delay the adoption of programmes that had already been agreed upon by parliament and to limit their scope, sometimes to minimal schemes by European standards (Immergut, 1992). Typically, compromises were possible only on a minimum level of provision, and even so this approach was not always successful in satisfying all affected groups who were able, occasionally, to block the adoption of reform through referendums.

Since the early 1990s, however, the direction of welfare reform has changed. With the emergence of mass unemployment, virtually unknown before the 1990s, and with rising healthcare costs and with predicted population ageing, social insurance programmes are increasingly under pressure. Institutions, however, have remained unchanged, and the available option of referendums might prove a formidable obstacle to retrenchment. What is more, given the general unpopularity of retrenchment policies, a consensual approach is more difficult to achieve than in the past, when reforms led to improved provision

This chapter looks at current issues and the transformation of social insurance in Switzerland. First, it briefly describes the key features of the main social insurance programmes of a country, which regrettably is rarely included in international comparisons. Second, it focuses on recent socioeconomic change and on reforms that have affected the shape of these programmes. An interpretation is put forward which attempts to link the direction of current policy change with the peculiar institutional environment in

Switzerland. The chapter concludes with a look at likely developments for the near future.

Social insurance in Switzerland: an overview

This section concentrates on the three main social insurance programmes run by the federal government: health insurance, the basic pension insurance scheme and unemployment insurance. Smaller social insurance programmes not considered here include the invalidity insurance scheme, which operates along the same lines as the basic pension scheme, a scheme for replacing earnings lost by construction workers and farmers because of bad weather conditions and one that compensates people serving in the country's militia for loss of income. Other areas, such as maternity insurance and family benefits, despite the fact that they are constitutionally treated as areas of federal competence, are still managed by the cantons, which means that there are 26 different legislative codes. As in Germany, social insurance schemes are supplemented by a last resort social assistance scheme, which is administered by local authorities and grants means tested benefits.

Health insurance

Switzerland remains an exception in Europe in not having a public health insurance scheme, although, influenced by developments in Germany, Swiss reformers started debating the introduction of a public health insurance scheme as early as the end of last century. A law (the so-called Forrer law) modelled on the German scheme and leading to the establishment of a health insurance scheme was presented in parliament in 1899. It provided a centralised fund covering a large number of waged workers. Accepted by parliament, this law was subsequently subjected to a referendum in which it was defeated by a coalition of the medical profession, the anti-welfarist right and existing mutual societies, which would have become redundant as a result of the introduction of the new scheme (see Immergut, 1992). As a consequence, Swiss policy makers had to abandon the Bismarckian model for health insurance and search for alternatives that would be able to survive a referendum challenge.

In 1910 a law establishing the basis of the current healthcare system was adopted. It was a rather minimalist arrangement, in the sense that it provided only for subsidies for mutual societies which complied with given requirements. Affiliation was not compulsory and financing was based on premiums, unrelated to earnings. Since then several attempts have been made to introduce a Bismarckian type contribution financed health insurance scheme. So far, all have failed, including the latest attempt through a referendum initiative sponsored by the Social Democratic Party in 1994. Thus, while the early system has been reformed several times, many features still reflect the 1910 scheme.

The Swiss health insurance system consists of a number of mutual societies (*Krankenkassen/caisses maladie*) to which people are affiliated. Before 1994 membership was not compulsory by federal law, but a majority of cantons had already introduced this requirement. The law prescribes a minimum level of coverage in terms of reimbursed treatments and drugs (basic insurance), which must be granted by mutual societies in order to qualify for public subsidies. Premiums paid by insured persons are their main source of funding, however. These premiums are unrelated to earnings or income, and are uniform for members of the same fund and in the same canton. As a result, they affect in particular large families and those on low income, though there are income tested subsidies. In addition, premiums can vary between funds, and, until 1994, between insured persons within the same fund. For example, premiums for women could be up to 10% higher than for men and age could justify a 100% difference. However, the most significant variation is between cantons. Mutual funds operate at the cantonal level, and differences in health expenditure are directly reflected in levels of premium which tend to be higher in French and Italian speaking cantons and in urban areas.

Pressure for change in this system intensified towards the late 1980s when healthcare costs increased dramatically, leading to rising health insurance premiums. To a large extent, the significant rise in healthcare costs, from below 8.5% of GDP in 1990 to more than 10% in 1994 (*Sécurité Sociale*, 1995), has been due to the low degree of regulation within the system and to the lack of incentives for either providers or mutual funds to keep costs down. Switzerland is second only to the USA as far as per capita health expenditure is concerned. Recently, a number of measures have been adopted in order to tackle these problems. These are discussed below.

Old age pensions

As with health insurance, legislation of old age pensions was hampered by the use of referendums. A basic pension scheme was accepted by Swiss voters only in 1948. The scheme (AHV/AVS), which has been amended a number of times since then, is universal in its coverage. It is financed through contributions (4.2% of salary each for employees and employers; up to 7.8% for the self-employed), and receives a state subsidy equal to 19% of outlays. Some groups not in work, such as students, can be required to pay flat-rate contributions or, as carers for example, are entitled to contribution credits. There is no ceiling on contributions, but pension levels can vary between a floor and a ceiling, the upper limit being twice as high as the lower limit. Within these limits, the amount of the benefit is related to both the value and the number of years contributions have been paid while in work. Because of the existence of a lower and an upper limit benefit level, replacement rates vary between 100% for someone on a very low income and 40% for someone on an average income and further decreases for higher incomes. The scheme is thus fairly redistributive, and is considered by many to be one of the most progressive components within the Swiss welfare state.

The lower limit applies only to those with a complete contribution record (currently 45 years for men and 42 for women). For others the pension is reduced correspondingly. What is more, the lower limit does not represent a sufficient standard of living since it is even below the social assistance level. For this reason, a tax-funded, income tested pension supplement which is slightly higher than social assistance, was introduced at the federal level in 1965. While it is administered by cantons, it is financed by the federal government, and unlike social assistance the pension supplement is not regarded as stigmatising. In addition, in 1982 occupational pensions, as a second tier of pension provision, became compulsory for employees with earnings above a certain limit (about 50% of average earnings). Occupational pensions, however, had been fairly widespread before.

Unemployment insurance

A compulsory unemployment insurance scheme was introduced only in the late 1970s. Previously, the trade unions had developed a patchy system of unemployment insurance which received subsidies from the federal government. Its coverage, however, remained low. In 1975 only 22% of employees were covered by unemployment insurance (Gilliand 1988). In 1976 the Constitution was amended in order to allow federal authorities to legislate in the area of unemployment benefits. A compulsory scheme was adopted in 1977 by decree, and the current unemployment insurance scheme was finally introduced in 1984. The scheme is financed by employment-related contributions and government subsidies. Before the recession of the 1990s unemployment levels were rather low, with official unemployment rates of less than 1%. This allowed contributions to be fixed at below 1% each for employers and employees. The replacement rate is 80% or 70% of gross earnings (see below), with a benefit ceiling equal to about 150% of average earnings .

Unlike in Germany or France, the Swiss unemployment insurance scheme provides only insurance, with no subsequent assistance benefits. Thus, once the entitlement period is exhausted, unemployed people have to rely on social assistance, which is regarded as highly stigmatising and does not favour reinsertion. Social assistance benefits are treated as loans which theoretically should be repaid once recipients get back to work. However, such a system seems inadequate in the emerging context of mass unemployment, which is why a number of cantons are currently reviewing provision for unemployed people who have used up their entitlement to insurance benefits (Cattacin, 1996). Measures introduced include a French style minimum income with a reinsertion component. However, it seems unlikely that a new income maintenance scheme will be introduced at federal level. In fact, since there are significant differences in unemployment rates between cantons, it is likely that those with low levels of unemployment will resist such proposals.

Changing the rules: policy reforms in the 1990s

Unlike in other European countries, unemployment in Switzerland remained extremely low throughout the 1980s. Consequently, there was little pressure for reforming social insurance schemes. The situation, however, changed dramatically in the early 1990s when unemployment rose to unprecedented levels in Swiss post-war history with a rate of 4.6% in March 1996. While this might be low by European standards, there are higher peaks in some regions, namely in the Italian and French speaking parts. In addition, as described earlier, there was the problem of increasing healthcare costs in the early 1990s which led the government to adopt cost containment measures by emergency decrees, the standard legislative process being too lengthy.

Overall, the recession of the 1990s marked a watershed in the development of the Swiss welfare state which until then was in a phase of expansion, albeit in part still catching up with its European counterparts. The change in attitude towards welfare is particularly obvious if one looks at the 1995 pension reform. The debate on new pension legislation started in the late 1970s with the overall aim of improving the situation of women. By 1993 proposals included provision for raising the retirement age for women from 62 to 64. Since then, significant reforms have been adopted in all three major social insurance programmes.

The 1994 health insurance reform

The dramatic increase in health expenditure of the late 1980s and early 1990s has generally been explained as a consequence of a healthcare system that does not provide incentives to limit consumption and to contain cost. Providers (such as self-employed doctors) have no interest in limiting expenditure since their earnings are proportionally related to outlays. Mutual funds, which negotiate fees for treatment with healthcare providers, adjust their premiums in order to meet current expenditure; thus, additional expenses arising from higher providers' fees and higher consumption are simply passed on. Even though the insurance holders might have regarded increases in premiums as excessive, there was no opportunity to sanction their mutual funds until 1994. Unless someone was young and healthy, a move to another mutual fund could prove to be a difficult and costly operation. As a result, there were no incentives within the healthcare system to exert a downward pressure on cost.

It was to a large extent this situation that has led health expenditure to rise dramatically over the past few years, with health insurance premiums increasing correspondingly. Since premiums are flat-rate and not income related, they constitute a substantial burden for those on low incomes. In response to public dissatisfaction with increases in insurance premiums, the federal government enacted emergency legislation aimed at containing healthcare costs in 1991 and in 1992. Such legislation cannot be delayed by a referendum. The main measures included a freeze of doctors' and hospitals' fees for 1993 and 1994, the equalisation of premiums between men and women and between individuals of different ages, a compensation system between mutual funds with different age and gender structures and a charge of 10Sfr per day (£5.40) for hospital stays. The measures were relatively successful, as they managed to contain quite substantially the increased rate of healthcare costs. Per capita health insurance expenditure rose by 19.2% in 1991, by 10% in 1992 and by 3.6% in 1993 (*Sécurité Sociale*, 1993, p 23).

Both decrees were temporary, and were enacted because the standard legislative process was regarded as too lengthy to cope with the situation. However, some of these measures were incorporated in the health insurance reform of 1994 which had been presented to parliament in 1991. Its main aims were to introduce a greater degree of 'solidarity' (according to the official terminology) and mechanisms that would counter the upward trend in expenditure, and to adapt coverage to the changing needs of the population, in particular by including long-term care and home care for older people. Parliamentary debates lasted until March 1994, which is a relatively short period by Swiss standards, especially if one considers the potential for controversy involved in the subject matter.

Perhaps the most remarkable innovation of the new law is the attempt to create a competitive markct between mutual funds. Competition, it was thought, would provide an incentive for mutual funds to keep premiums low and to negotiate lower fees with healthcare providers. This was not possible under the previous legislation, which included a number of obstacles to free competition. First, fees for services were negotiated collectively between the associations representing providers on the one hand

and mutual funds on the other. With the new legislation, individual funds are able to negotiate with providers directly, and thus, it is hoped, to negotiate lower fees by introducing competition between providers as well. Second, the previous legislation did not oblige mutual funds to accept new customers. Thus, affiliation could be refused if applicants were considered as 'bad risks'. The new law also includes provision which allows customers to switch between different mutual funds without risking being left without coverage. Finally, it introduced a mechanism for inter-fund compensation in order to equalise the competitive position of mutual funds with different age and gender structures. This system implies actuarially determined cash transfers from funds with a lower proportion of 'bad risks' to funds with a higher proportion. This is intended to rule out competition in terms of risk selection and instead to promote competition in efficiency and degree of customer choice.

A second important change that was introduced concerned the targeting of subsidies at those on low incomes. Under the old legislation, the federal government and cantons subsidised mutual funds, which consequently were able to offer lower premiums than their market price, thus benefiting insured persons regardless of their income. In the new law subsidies are increased and targeted at those on low incomes. In practical terms, this change implied the withdrawal of subsidies to mutual funds and the introduction of individual means tested health insurance grants.

The new health insurance legislation came into force at the beginning of 1996. Since then, it has been severely criticised for being ineffective. During 1996 premiums increased on average between 6% and 7% which was far above the rate of inflation. For 1997, an increase of about the same amount was announced by the country's largest mutual fund. A major problem seems to be the fact that plans to set up a competitive market have been undermined in a number of ways by a majority of mutual funds which were largely against the introduction of the new law. First, instead of increased competition there has been a massive wave of mergers of mutual funds over the last few years. Second, for effective competition to be set in place, it is essential for customers to have access to adequate information with regard to the options for choice; however, it seems that mutual funds have been rather reluctant to disseminate information with regard to new opportunities available to customers (*Sécurité Sociale*, 1996).

Third, the new law concerns only the basic compulsory insurance. Mutual funds can, against a premium supplement, offer additional coverage, which might include a single room in a hospital, dental care or alternative medicine. Additional provision of this sort is treated differently from basic compulsory insurance, allowing mutual funds scope for manoeuvre in order to retain customers. For example, funds can still refuse affiliation for additional provision to those representing 'bad risks'. Finally, the new provision has to deal with the problem of 'customer inertia', whereby insured people simply might not be used to taking the initiative, and therefore might be reluctant to 'shop around for the best deal'.

The government has acknowledged that the new legislation is not producing the expected outcomes in terms of either the creation of a competitive market or cost containment. However, it maintains that it is too early to assess the effectiveness of the 1994 health insurance reform and so far has refused to take corrective action (*Sécurité Sociale*, 1996).

In areas where insurance premiums were high, the reform was welcomed. French speaking cantons, for example, mainly regarded it as progressive, since much emphasis was put on the increased level of 'solidarity', a notion that referred to the obligation not to charge different premiums on the basis of sex, age or health condition. Nevertheless, in the long term the 1994 reform might open the way towards a two-tiered system of healthcare. Under the new legislation, mutual funds are able to offer 'discount' health insurance policies which allow access to a number of selected providers, such as in-house surgeries, or require patients to meet a larger proportion of cost.

The 1994 Swiss healthcare reform shows quite powerfully the impressive level of difficulty involved in regulating a complex market such as healthcare. There seems to be an inevitable contradiction between the government's objectives in terms of social policy, ie to guarantee both universal coverage at affordable costs and a significant degree of economic freedom to the different actors involved. Moreover, the fact that funding is not related to income constitutes an important limitation on the financing capacity of the scheme. Premiums cannot be increased above a certain limit because they become unbearable for those on low incomes. The introduction of means tested grants for healthcare attempts to deal with this problem, but only at the lower end of the income distribution. Those just above the means test cutoff point are likely to be hit particularly hard by future premium increases.

Interestingly, a similar contradiction between social policy objectives and economic freedom has been central to debates in France. However, French policy makers seem to be trying to deal with this problem in exactly the opposite way. Instead of encouraging more market mechanisms, stricter controls on the activity of healthcare providers have been introduced, such as limited budgets for hospitals or prescriptions of appropriate treatments for practitioners (*Références Médicales Opposables*). Such an 'interventionist' solution has not been given serious consideration in Switzerland, despite the fact that it could provide an effective response to the problems the country is currently facing. However, given the likely opposition of providers and the opportunity the latter have to challenge legislative change in a referendum, an interventionist solution does not seem politically feasible in the Swiss context.

The 1995 pension reform

The overall aim of the 1995 pension reform (known in Switzerland as the 10th AHV/AVS revision) was to introduce gender equality in the basic pension scheme, particularly with regard to women. Under previous legislation, a married man would receive a 'couple pension' corresponding to 150% of his pension entitlement, regardless of the contribution record of his wife. In other words, a married woman would lose her entitlement to a pension, this being replaced by a supplement on her husband's benefit. In addition, there were no contribution credits for raising children or taking care of relatives, which is common practice in many European countries. This existence of gender-based discrimination was widely regarded as inadequate, especially after the adoption of a constitutional article on gender equality in 1981. As a result, a significant amount of pressure had mounted and this led the government to amend pension legislation.

Preliminary work on the reform started in 1979, but it was only in 1990 that a bill was finally presented in parliament. Despite the, not exceptionally, lengthy legislative process, the 1990 pension bill was seen by many as disappointing. The proposal adopted only the minimum requirements needed in order to comply with the constitutional article on gender equality. Basically, the bill removed any reference to gender as entitlement criterion and in the calculation formula of the benefit. It was intended that married couples would continue to receive a 'couple pension' as before, except that it would be possible to draw it separately; that is, on request each partner could receive half of the total pension. Maintaining the 'couple pension', it was argued, was justifiable since marriage remained the predominant type of cohabitation.   The bill did not include provision for the equalisation of retirement age (then at 65/62), which was also regarded as unconstitutional after the adoption of the 1981 amendment on gender equality. The government argued against equalisation on the basis that equality in the labour market in terms of wages, career patterns, access to occupational pensions, etc, was far from being achieved; thus, equalisation would have to be dealt with in a later reform.

The 1990 pension bill soon came under attack from women's organisations and progressive groups for failing to take a more far reaching approach to gender equality.   In fact, in the political debate prior to 1990 a number of organisations and political parties had published reports which advocated a system of individual pensions, to be granted regardless of gender and marital status, and the abolition of the 'couple pension'. Such proposals were put forward by the Social Democrats, jointly with the Federation of Swiss trade unions (PSS/USS, 1987), by a working group of the Liberal Democratic Party (PRD, 1988), and by the Federal Commission for Women's Issues (CFQF, 1988), a consultative body which includes MPs and representatives of other relevant interest groups.

The different proposals were in fact remarkably similar.   In general, it was suggested that individual contributions paid by partners should be added, divided by two, and counted separately for each of the two spouses. Such a system became known by the name of 'splitting'. All the proposals argued for the introduction of contribution credits for couples with children, and for those with other caring responsibilities. This was also needed in order to offset possible losses in the amount of the pension for one-earner couples once a contribution splitting system became operationable. In fact, even in the case of one spouse with a complete contribution record, the sum of the two individual pensions could have been lower than the previous couple pension because of the loss of the former 'couple supplement'.

These proposals became extremely influential. In fact, the original bill was substantially modified by parliament precisely by adopting these measures. In its amended version, the pension bill included the notion of an individual entitlement to a pension regardless of gender or marital status, and the abolition of 'couple pensions'. Contributions paid by the two spouses while married were to be added, divided by two, and counted half each. In order not to penalise one-earner couples, a contribution credit for couples with children was introduced. Couples with children below the age of 16 receive a credit equal to the amount of contributions payable on a salary of three times the minimum pension (or 56% of average earnings); this credit is counted half for each partner, with single parents receiving the full amount. However, because of the existence of a benefit ceiling, the incidence of the contribution credit on the actual pension is higher for low earners and can be negligible or non-existent if both spouses are in work and earn enough to be entitled to the maximum pension.

The bill as modified by parliament also included the controversial measure of raising the retirement age for women from 62 to 64. The proposal was made by a right-wing dominated parliamentary commission, allegedly in order to comply with the constitutional requirement of gender equality as well as to achieve some savings in view of the predicted ageing of Swiss society over the next decades. The measure was eventually pushed through by a coalition of right-wing parties, against the opposition of the Social Democrats and also some Christian Democrats. Outside parliament, trade unions and some women's organisations attacked the proposed increase in retirement age for women. In response, the Federation of Swiss Trade Unions organised the collection of the 50,000 signatures needed in order to call a referendum. The move was successful and the referendum on the pension bill was held in June 1995.

According to the constitution, referendums decide between the adoption or rejection, but not the content, of a bill. Therefore the referendum called had to cover clauses concerning the increased retirement age as well as provisions for gender equality, which, as discussed above, had long been advocated by the Left in general. This situation therefore presented a dilemma, since the question whether or not to support the referendum depended on what was seen as more important: improved gender equality, or an increase in women's retirement age.   In the end, the Social Democrats declined to join the unions in the referendum against the pension bill, thereby reducing its chances of success.   Indeed, the bill survived the referendum and has become law.   The division within the left obviously played an important role in bringing this result about.   The way the bill was designed inevitably led to divisions, as it combined elements of expansion and of retrenchment within a single legislative package.

The 1995 unemployment insurance reform

The sharp rise in the unemployment rate in Switzerland in 1990-91 led to a steep increase in outlays and a growing deficit in the unemployment insurance scheme (Table 3).   As a consequence, the scheme was unable to meet its liabilities and had to borrow funds from the general government budget.   As in the case of healthcare, the perceived gravity of the problem persuaded the federal government to act with an emergency decree in 1993.   For those without dependent children, the replacement rate was reduced from 80% to 70% of insured salary and the entitlement period was extended from 250 working days to 400.   A stricter definition of 'adequate work' was also introduced, whereby unemployed persons could be required to accept jobs with salaries lower than insurance benefits.   These emergency measures lasted until December 1995 in order to allow policy makers time to introduce a more substantial legislative change.

The 1995 unemployment insurance reform was drafted by a joint group of representatives of employers and trade unionists, and was accepted by parliament without major changes.   As a clear compromise between different conceptions, it included measures aimed in diverging directions.   On the one hand, the financial base of the scheme was strengthened and more funds were made available for labour market programmes, such as vocational training and job creation schemes.   On the other hand, the maximum entitlement period was reduced to two years, whereas under the previous legislation benefits could be drawn practically indefinitely, provided the recipient was prepared to participate in labour market programmes.

Table 3: Level of unemployment in Switzerland and receipts, outlays and balance of the unemployment insurance fund (1988-96)*

	1988	1989	1990	1991	1992	1993	1994	1995	1996
Unemployment rate (% of active population)	0.5	0.5	0.6	1.2	2.6	4.6	4.8	4.3	4.6
Receipts (m Sfr)	907	976	787	866	805	3556	3680	na	na
Outlays (m Sfr)	551	442	503	1340	3462	5986	5921	na	na
Balance (m Sfr)	+356	+534	+283	-474	-2657	-2430	-2241	na	na

*1996 figures from March

Source: *Sécurité Sociale*, various issues

The joint contribution rate was raised to 3% (1.5% each for employers and employees), payable on earnings of up to 160% of average salary. An additional contribution of a joint rate of 1% is charged on earnings between 160% and 400% of average salary. This measure is temporary, in principle at least, until the debt accumulated by the scheme with the government is repaid. In addition, 5% of current expenditure will be financed by a federal subsidy. With these measures, it is hoped to repay the debt before the year 2000.

As far as benefits were concerned, the changes introduced with the emergency decree were maintained. The entitlement period was fixed at two years, and during this period unemployed persons are required to undertake retraining, to take part in a job creation scheme or to take up temporary work. Failure to do so will result in sanctions which can lead to a 60 day benefit suspension period. Cantons are required to set up job creation programmes, although 85% of the costs are met by the unemployment insurance scheme. If a canton fails to offer a job or another relevant activity to an unemployed person, the latter is entitled to 80 working days' extension of his or her entitlement period, partly paid for by the canton. Unemployed persons must agree to take up an 'adequate job offer', which is defined in terms of salary (at least equal to benefit level), distance (two hours' travel time per day is regarded as justifiable) and compatibility with the skills of the recipient.

What is more, during the two-year entitlement period an unemployed person may be required to take up a job with a salary lower than his or her benefit, the difference being compensated by the insurance scheme.

It is too early for an assessment of these changes, which came into force in January 1996. However, a major problem seems to be the fact that its success depends to a large extent on the cantons' willingness and ability to set up job creation schemes. Altogether, 25,000 (temporary) jobs are expected to be created in this way. A second, and possibly rather serious, problem lies with the fact that after the two-year period an unemployed person is excluded from the insurance scheme and, if unable to find work, is forced to rely on social assistance. This was not the case under previous legislation, since participation in labour market programmes was considered as a contribution period. As a result, unemployed people were able to remain in the system virtually indefinitely as they regained entitlement to insurance benefits. This is ruled out under the new law. The consequences can be expected from 1998 onwards in the form of increasing dependency on social assistance.

The politics of welfare retrenchment in Switzerland

The debate on welfare retrenchment and restructuring is fairly new in the Swiss political arena. Until the recession of the 1990s there was an overall consensus on the desirability of maintaining the existing arrangements and structures. Given the low rate of unemployment and the overall economic performance, social insurance programmes did not constitute a problem. However, with the recession and increasing government and social insurance deficits, political pressure in favour of welfare changes has mounted. The three major reforms of 1994-95 are rather novelties, in the sense that for the first time legislative change was adopted with the explicit aim of achieving savings. The reforms however cannot be qualified purely as retrenchment policies. Instead, while savings are central to all of them, each also includes elements of expansion and improvement such as the introduction of pension credits for carers, the increase in funds available for active labour market policies and the introduction of a new income tested 'health insurance grant'.

This combination of retrenchment and expansion within a single piece of legislation can be seen as a strategy developed by the right-wing parliamentary majority in order to make cutbacks more acceptable to the electorate. Obviously, retrenchment measures combined with improvements of existing programmes stand a much higher chance of being accepted in a referendum than cuts alone. Arguably, this is not only a Swiss peculiarity. As Pierson (1994) has noted, governments in the UK and the USA have frequently combined retrenchment and expansion elements in welfare reforms as a political strategy aimed at making cuts politically more acceptable.

However, it seems that in Switzerland the combination of divergent measures is further encouraged by the use of referendums. Indeed, referendum politics is significantly different from parliamentary politics. Although political parties issue voting recommendations, a recent study has estimated, that on average, 12.5% of voters do not respect them in referendums (Y. Papadopoulos, 1996). This means that a parliamentary majority in favour of a bill might not be sufficient to receive acceptance at the polls. Yet, a defeat in a referendum is regarded as a major setback by the government, as it implies a considerable waste of effort, given the fact that the law making processes can last more than a decade, and the likelihood of being unable to legislate in that particular area for some time to come. Hence the need to secure wider approval by introducing elements in a majority sponsored bill demanded by other groups.

This approach proved particularly effective in the 1995 pension reform, which combined in a single reform package measures for gender equality, which were accepted by virtually all relevant actors and the electorate as a whole, and an increase in retirement age for women, which was advocated merely by the right-wing majority. Since the constitution does not provide the opportunity to challenge only parts of a bill, voters were forced to choose between accepting or rejecting both sets of measures in a referendum. This proved an important advantage for the right-wing parliamentary majority, since the left was divided on the question whether the positive elements of the bill outweighed the negative ones. What is more, during the referendum campaign, the right-wing majority and the government tended to emphasise the improvements for women and to downplay the increase in retirement age for women as something perhaps less desirable, but which, since it was part of the bill, could not be avoided without losing improvements as well. Interestingly, the organisers of a television debate on the referendum were unable to find a speaker who would argue in favour of raising the retirement age for women per se (TSR, 1995). Those who had previously supported the introduction of this measure were now able to portray it as perhaps less desirable, but as part and parcel of a wider reform which, in contrast, was described as highly positive and needed.

From the point of view of those who advocate retrenchment, such a strategy can secure the adoption of cutbacks to a wider extent than would be possible otherwise within the context of a standard consensual approach. Reductions in provision do not have to be agreed upon, but can be enforced and combined with compensation measures for dissatisfied groups. The outcome is not necessarily a compromise between different conceptions of policy. Instead, political actors with different priorities focus primarily on the inclusion of their main concerns in legislation, without paying much attention to the overall coherence of a bill. Often, the result is legislation incorporating elements that can attract support from very different sections of the electorate, which is essential in order to minimise the risk of defeat at the polls.

In addition, the combination of divergent measures in a single reform provides advocates of retrenchment with relatively large scope for blame avoidance for unpopular cuts. Typically, media exposure of welfare reforms is highest during the referendum phase of the law making process. It is usually then that the general public becomes aware of the content of legislative proposals. At that stage, however, the reform package has already been designed, and cannot be modified by voters. As a result, those responsible for the inclusion of retrenchment measures in the bill are not forced to disclose their approval of possibly unpopular cuts, but can focus their support on the more widely accepted parts of the reform. In other words, they can advocate the adoption of a bill which includes cuts without being identified as favouring retrenchment.

The impact of formal institutions on policy making in the area of social policy has somewhat changed since the early 1990s. In the past, the availability of referendums encouraged the majority in parliament to adopt a consensual approach to policy in order to minimise the risk of being defeated at the polls. However, possibly because of a stronger polarisation in the political debate and increasing financial constraints, consensus building seems to have become a more difficult exercise in recent years. As a consequence, more than in the past, welfare reforms have tended to combine elements demanded by groups with different political orientations. While such a strategy appears to produce legislative changes which can lack coherency, it has proved rather successful as far as overcoming the vulnerability to referendum challenges is concerned.

Implications for the future of social insurance

It has been argued that the standard decision making procedures in Switzerland are inadequate for dealing with the challenges the country is currently facing. Above all, this critique has been directed at Swiss elites who are regarded as incapable of leading the country to join the European Union (Kriesi, 1995). However, as Cattacin (1996) points out, there are problems also in the area of welfare reform. He argues that the standard law making process suffers from two main shortcomings. First, because it requires the establishment of a compromise, it tends to be too slow to be able to confront rapidly emerging and changing problems. Second, given the vulnerability of the government in relation to organised interests, it is difficult to legitimise more interventionist programmes unless socioeconomic pressures are extremely strong. As a consequence, the Swiss government is forced in general to adopt a reactive stance in social policy reform.

This analysis suggests that radical change in the Swiss welfare state is rather unlikely. Basic structures will remain to a large extent untouched since compromises have to be reached, implying incremental rather than major change. Even the three reforms discussed above, which in Switzerland are regarded as major changes, are perhaps not that substantial by European standards. However, the analysis of these reforms has indicated that the traditional consensual pattern of policy making is increasingly under pressure. Two of the three reforms (healthcare and pension) have been subjected to referendums, which shows a weakness of well established consensus building mechanisms within government and parliament. The 1995 pension reform in particular demonstrated that the right-wing parliamentary majority is able to force the adoption of controversial elements within an overall consensual context, while still standing a good chance of success in a referendum challenge. To some extent, the Swiss political system is characterised by the presence of two different policy making mechanisms. The traditional consensus building approach is still alive, and takes place somewhat behind the scenes within the various commissions and between the social partners. At the same time, decisions in parliament are occasionally taken in a purely majoritarian way. The three main right-of-centre parties, all of which have a similar orientation in socioeconomic policy, can impose the adoption of controversial measures, but then have to provide compensation if legislation is to survive the referendum challenge.

The two decision making mechanisms bear different consequences for the future of social insurance. As long as decisions are taken consensually, a radical change of current structures is unlikely. However, if the parliamentary right-wing majority favours a departure from the social insurance model, it stands some chance of succeeding, as long as sufficient 'compensation' is provided. If this were the case, the direction of reform would almost certainly be towards a more liberal welfare state, since this would match the orientation of the right-wing parliamentary majority. The compensation might take the form of means tested provision targeted at those who are likely to be the main losers of welfare reform. This is precisely what has happened in the health insurance reform, when the introduction of more market mechanisms has been supplemented with the creation of an income tested health insurance voucher.

In this respect, it is interesting to compare the Swiss health insurance reform with recent changes in France (see Chapter five in this volume). In both countries, healthcare systems are faced with similar problems of rising expenditure resulting from a lack of regulation or incentives to moderate medical consumption. The strategies adopted, however, were quite different. In France the inadequacy of the health insurance model has been responded to with stronger state intervention (budget holding, prescription of appropriate treatment for doctors), with the aim of containing expenditure directly. In Switzerland policy makers have opted for a supposedly self-regulating, market based system. Given the institutional context and the availability of a referendum to dissatisfied minorities in particular, such an interventionist solution seems unthinkable in Switzerland.

In sum, formal institutions are a major factor affecting the shape of welfare reform in Switzerland. Given the existence of socioeconomic pressures, Swiss policy makers have to find politically feasible ways of implementing change in the context of a political system that allows legislation to be challenged at the polls and is used to operating within an overall consensual framework. From the point of view of those who favour a reduction in the role of state welfare, combining retrenchment with improvements is the most rational path to welfare reform. Although the right-wing majority does have the parliamentary power to impose more radical cuts, such a strategy would significantly increase the risk of being defeated by voters, and thus to be left with the status quo. In that sense, the three social insurance reforms of the early 1990s might be the standard pattern for future change.

seven

The withering of social insurance in Britain[*]

Angus Erskine

Introduction

In this chapter I argue that in Britain the principle of social insurance has become undermined by restrictions on entitlement and generosity of insurance benefits and the extension of means tested benefits. This has meant that the insurance principle plays a decreasing role in British income maintenance. The chapter is divided into four sections. In the first part, the characteristics of social insurance in Great Britain, that is, of the National Insurance scheme, are examined. For a British audience these features will be well known, but I expand upon them to allow for the comparison which this volume is seeking to achieve. I do not propose to discuss some of the advantages and disadvantages of social insurance in Great Britain which are well covered elsewhere (Alcock, 1996; Bennett, 1993). The second part points to some of the relevant policy changes which have been shaping the current system. This section briefly addresses five issues: the piecemeal way in which change has been taking place and the residualisation of National Insurance in the British income maintenance system through the extension of means testing and the increase in private insurance.

[*] I wish to thank Jochen Clasen and anonymous reviewers of this chapter for their very helpful advice.

The third part examines the current pressures on the system which are giving rise to debates about the role of social insurance. In examining these pressures, I first address those that are part of the context within which social insurance operates, in particular labour market changes, demographic change and changes in family structure; and second those that are part of the system itself, such as funding and benefit levels. The fourth part is more speculative and looks ahead to the future of social insurance in Britain. I suggest that there are a number of possible future scenarios which can be grouped under three general headings: the continuing withering of the insurance principle, the strengthening of social insurance, and radical reforms. I suggest that the general message from Britain is pessimistic – social insurance does seem to be a policy design that has seen its time.

The characteristics of social insurance in Britain

The structure of income maintenance

For the purposes of this chapter, I define social insurance (see Silburn, 1995, and Atkinson, 1995, for a discussion of the nature of social insurance) as cash benefits, eligibility for which is based upon compulsory contributions (or credited contributions for certain groups) into the National Insurance Fund. It is a characteristic of the British system that there is one single fund into which employees and employers contribute (although there is a separate fund for Northern Ireland). These funds are entirely administered and controlled by central government. They operate on a pay-as-you-go basis; contributions are paid out to current beneficiaries and the fund is balanced on an annual basis. The system is therefore more akin to a hypothecated tax than an insurance fund.

Social insurance benefits are only one element of a complex pattern of social security transfers in the British system. Social security includes benefits that are not dependent upon past contributions but are based either on a means test, such as income support, or are non-contributory and non-means tested and based upon residence as well as category. However, the system is complicated by anomalies such as the guardian's allowance (a benefit paid to those looking after children who are effectively orphans), which is paid out of the National Insurance Fund but is not dependent upon contribution conditions. National Insurance contributions also partly fund the National Health Service (about 12% of National Health Service funding comes from National Insurance contributions), although receipt of healthcare is not dependent upon past contributions. The most complex area of income maintenance is support for long-term sick and disabled people, where there may be entitlement to insurance benefits, non-contributory benefits or means tested benefits and where entitlement may be based upon extent of disability, past contributions and level of income.

The administration of the National Insurance scheme

The main areas of income maintenance covered by social insurance in Britain are pensions, sickness and unemployment. However, in all of these areas National Insurance provides a restricted and minimal coverage. Insurance contributions are collected by the Contributions Agency, which receives income related contributions from employees and employers. The payment of benefits is the responsibility of the Benefits Agency. These government agencies, staffed by civil servants, are directly responsible for their operations to the Department of Social Security which determines the policies that they are to implement.

The funding of the National Insurance scheme

Contributions are collected through employers and are calculated as a proportion of employee's earnings above and below certain levels of income. In 1996/97, employed earners were liable to contribute if their weekly income exceeded the lower earning limit of £61 up to the upper earnings limit of £455. In 1994 this upper earnings limit was at 120% of average male earnings (Hills, 1995a). Rather than contracting out their pension to a private or occupational scheme, employees who have chosen to stay in the State Earnings Related Pension Scheme (SERPS) paid 2% on earnings below the lower earning limit and 10% on earnings between the lower and upper limits; employers paid 10.2% on employees' earnings above £210 per week and a reducing percentage on earnings below this figure.

From its beginnings in 1911 until the late 1980s, the British system involved a threefold contribution from employers, employees and general taxation. In the late 1980s the government ceased making contributions to the fund, which then had to rely entirely upon employer and employee contributions. However, this was reversed in the early 1990s under financial pressure caused by rising unemployment. Currently the Treasury can make a grant of up to 17% of the National Insurance Fund's expenditure on benefits in any one year. This is a ceiling, not a floor – the Chancellor can set the contribution at a lower level. In addition, the fund receives payment from general taxation to recompense it for contributions withheld by employers to pay statutory maternity pay. The National Insurance Fund also forgoes income deducted at source from contributions by employers in respect of contributions to occupational and personal pension plans. In 1995/96 this amounted to £7.4 billion (HC132, 1995). This is not compensated for by the Treasury. The income from investments of the Fund in 1993/94 was £0.5 billion representing 1.1% of receipts (DSS, 1995, Table H1.01). These investments are restricted to government securities therefore surpluses in any one year are effectively lent to the Treasury.

The level of both National Insurance contributions and benefits were flat-rate until 1966, when earnings related contributions for both employers and employees and also earnings related supplements to some benefits were introduced – but abolished again in 1982, except for SERPS, which is therefore the only earnings related insurance benefit in Britain today. However, as indicated earlier, it is not a compulsory pension scheme. Contributors can opt to pay a reduced contribution rate if they join an alternative occupational or personal pensions scheme.

The scale of National Insurance

There are two ways of looking at the size of the National Insurance scheme. One is to look at the levels of expenditure and the extent of its coverage of the population; the other is to look at National Insurance from the contributor's and beneficiary's view. The two provide a stark contrast. The expenditure on National Insurance represented just over a half of all social security expenditure at £46 billion in 1993/94 (Cm 2813, 1995). Of this, in 1993/94, 17% (£7.6 billion) derived from general taxation, and about 78% represented a direct transfer from contributors to beneficiaries. About two thirds of social security expenditure (£29 billion) went to about ten-and-a-half million pensioners and war widows; the two other main groups of beneficiaries were sick and disabled people (£7 billion) and unemployed people (£1.6 billion). Only a very small proportion went to families through maternity allowance and statutory maternity pay.   A majority (83%) of pensioners received only the state retirement pension without any means tested addition, which implied that they therefore had an income that was above the social assistance level, or below it but not claiming.   Less than a quarter of unemployed claimants were in receipt of only the National Insurance unemployment benefit. The position regarding the sick and disabled is more complex because of the existence of additional non-contributory benefits, and therefore it is not possible to estimate the numbers in receipt of no other form of state income maintenance benefits except the insurance benefit – incapacity benefit.

The significance of the preponderance of expenditure on pensions and the proportion of pensioners solely in receipt of the state retirement pension for the future becomes more apparent when we examine the trends.   The proportion of pensioners who have incomes from occupational pension schemes increased from 43% in 1979 to 62% in 1993 (DSS, 1995, Table B2.06).   Most of these pensions are very small.   At the same time, Townsend and Walker (1995) point out that membership of occupational schemes among the employed population reached its peak in 1967 at 53% and declined to 48% in 1991.   Whatever the future of occupational pensions, as the SERPS matures and more pensioners have occupational or personal pensions, the proportion of pensioners in receipt of social assistance in the form of income support will decrease.   Therefore, while the state retirement pension is declining in terms of its value relative to earnings, reliance upon it alone will decrease.

As far as income maintenance for the unemployed is concerned the value of unemployment benefit between 1979 and 1994 fell by one third against average earnings for a single person (Convery, 1994).   At the same time there has been a dramatic reduction in the proportion who are solely in receipt of National Insurance unemployment benefit, from 30% in 1983/84 to 18% in 1993/94 (Cm 615, 1989, and Cm 2813, 1995).   This is likely to continue to decline further due to the introduction of the Job Seekers Allowance (JSA) in 1996, which represented the culmination of a series of measures to restrict eligibility for benefit to unemployed people (see below).   Finally, incapacity benefit, which replaced invalidity benefit and long-term sickness benefit in 1995, also will restrain future levels of expenditure and limit the numbers of beneficiaries.

For the majority of non-pensioner claimants, National Insurance benefits represent a small and invisible element of their income. The retirement pension is an exception in terms of its visibility in that the majority of pensioners receive only this benefit. Yet the amount is relatively small, at £61.15 per week for a single pensioner in 1996/97, and its value has fallen from 20% of male average earnings in 1977/78 to about 15% in the early 1990s (Commission on Social Justice, 1994). For pensioners and others who are in receipt of social assistance in the form of income support, their National Insurance benefit is deducted pound for pound from their entitlement to social assistance.

Recent policy changes

Piecemeal changes to social insurance in Britain

A number of significant changes in the National Insurance scheme have already been referred to. In this section I want to bring them together to form a background to the following section, which examines pressures for change.

Looking back to the mid-1970s, there are two features of social insurance in Britain which stand out. First is the essential continuity in its structure, and second is the extent of the changes that have taken place. These changes have meant that the place of social insurance within the income package of those in receipt of income maintenance has become increasingly marginal. However, this outcome is not due to any coherent attempt by successive governments to review the relevance and nature of social insurance in Britain. Instead, in the British tradition, changes have been incremental and small scale and only a look back over the past twenty years allows us to grasp their extent.

The shift away from the basic social insurance scheme as conceived by William Beveridge in the 1940s took place in Britain in two stages. The first began with the introduction of earnings related contributions and benefits in the 1960s, and the second with the shift in income maintenance policy towards means testing in the 1980s. In the first period, policy on benefits for the unemployed through National Insurance represented a tentative shift towards the linking of a more active labour market policy to benefits policy.   Earnings related benefits, combined with improved provision for redundancy, were designed to encourage workers to accept some of the temporary unemployment that industrial restructuring would require.   This use of National Insurance diverged from the minimalist objectives of Beveridge. Also in this early period, the development of provision for a second-tier pension represented a move away from Beveridge's belief in the role of the state being only to ensure a minimum standard for pensioners and that beyond this individual provision would ensure that living standards were protected through private provision.

The 1980s saw a shift in another direction.   The so-called Fowler Reviews of Social Security (after the then Secretary of State for Social Security) were central to this shift (Cmnd 9517, 1985; Cmnd 9691, 1985).   The Green Paper that resulted from these reviews began with a quote from Beveridge, claiming a popular paternity for the proposals for change, but went on to outline a different vision for social security.   Two of the three key objectives it identified were that social security expenditure should be determined by what the economy could afford, and that benefits should be concentrated upon those most in need.   These two objectives marked an explicit shift towards a concern with restraining expenditure on social security and developing more means testing within the system (Piachaud, 1996).   Consequent policy changes involved encouraging people to opt out of SERPS through preferential treatment for personal and occupational pension contributions, and reducing the basis upon which benefits from SERPS were calculated.   While the 1986 Social Security Act introduced a new structure for social assistance and a restructuring of benefits for people with dependent children in low paid work, it did not introduce significant changes to the National Insurance scheme.

The residualisation of National Insurance

One of the effects of this lack of any overview of the role of social insurance within the British income maintenance system has been its gradual withering away, mainly because of the growing importance of elements of social assistance in the overall structure of social security.   Since the 1970s, as subsidies to public sector housing have shifted from holding rents down to subsidising individual tenants' rents, rising housing costs and the increase in owner-occupation has meant that more households have become dependent upon means tested benefits to supplement their National Insurance benefits.

As far as pensions were concerned the 1986 Act altered the basis of the calculation of SERPS entitlement from the best 20 years to lifetime average earnings, and encouraged (through tax reliefs and National Insurance contribution rebates) contracting out of the state scheme and contributing instead to private and occupational pensions. This has meant that social insurance for retirement is returning to Beveridge's conception of a minimum pension, albeit a pension that is now at such a low level that many pensioners without any additional source of income require means tested benefits to top it up. Since pension levels rise in line with prices rather than wages, those solely dependent upon a retirement pension will see their relative living standards fall as living standards of the employed population improve. Hills (1993) points out that, relative to average disposable incomes, the value of the basic state pension reached its peak in 1983, and by 1992 was lower than in 1948. Those who are contributing to occupational and private pensions schemes are in the anomalous position of having government income invested in funded pension schemes (through insurance contribution rebates). If this situation continues, their future pensions will have been paid for by today's workers and they are effectively paying less towards today's pensioners. Those who have not opted out of SERPS are paying for today's pensioners and will rely upon tomorrow's workers to meet their pension obligations.

For the unemployed, the combined effect of the abolition of child additions to unemployment benefit in 1984, the more stringent application of eligibility conditions and the rise in long-term unemployment accompanied by increasing casualisation of employment have forced more claimants to rely upon means tested social assistance. Yet, the biggest change in the insurance system for the unemployed was the introduction of the Job Seekers Allowance (JSA) in 1996 which replaced income support and National Insurance unemployment benefit. Expenditure on support for the unemployed has been cut by reducing the period for which contribution-based JSA is payable from one year to a maximum of six months. This measure, which represents the first major structural change to the benefits system for unemployed people since the 1930s, will have important implications for claimants.

Overall, the JSA will reduce the total cost of benefit expenditure for the unemployed. Savings of £140 million were anticipated for 1996/97 and of £270 million for 1997/98. Much of these savings will come from the reduction of entitlement to contributory unemployment benefit (£70 million in 1996/97 and £220 million in 1997/98) (Hansard, 1994). This will potentially affect the majority of unemployed claimants. Of the 2.4 million people claiming benefit as unemployed in October 1994, 44% had been unemployed for less than six months. Overall, it is estimated that a quarter of a million people will be worse off under the JSA (Unemployment Unit, 1995), 70,000 of whom will receive no benefit at all and 95,000 of whom will be switched from insurance benefit to means tested JSA. This residualisation of insurance benefits can also be illustrated in terms of finance. The latest estimates suggest that only 5% of benefit expenditure for those who are unemployed will come from the National Insurance Fund in 1997/98 (Cm 2813, Table 1).

Yet, the JSA is not only an important benefit reform but also a labour market change. It has always been the case that duties are placed upon the unemployed as a condition of benefit. Beveridge proposed that anyone unemployed for more than six months should be required to attend a work or training centre as a condition of benefit (Deacon, 1992), and some suggest that motivating the long-term unemployed is important to ensure that they remain in contact with the labour market. However, since the 1970s governments have abandoned full employment as a central feature of economic policy, and what the JSA does is to shift the onus further on to the unemployed person. It narrows the definition of 'actively seeking work' which was imposed upon claimants in the 1989 Social Security Act. Under the JSA a person is required to 'be available for any work which they can reasonably be expected to do' (Cm 2687, 1994, para 4.3). Under the Act, claimants are required to complete and sign a so-called 'job seeker's agreement' which details the steps they will take to find work. One of the most contentious element of the Act is the power given to the Secretary of State to determine by regulation whether or not a person has a good cause for leaving employment or failing to take up a job or a place on a training or employment scheme. According to the government of the day, these measures were designed to prevent people from behaving in ways that guarantee that they will not get a job. In addition, under the Act, benefit can be withdrawn if the claimant fails to carry out a written direction issued by an employment officer based on the 'job seeker's agreement'. Claimants may be required to attend courses to improve their 'job seeking skills or motivation' or to 'present themselves acceptably to employers' (Cm 2687, 1994, para 4.18).

As part of the former government's objective to promote a flexible, low wage labour market, employment protection was weakened and unemployment benefits were reduced to encourage employers to create, and the unemployed to accept, low paid jobs. The argument was that a low paid job is better than no job, and that it is easier to get into a better job from employment than from unemployment. Thus, the JSA was not just a way of reducing the bill for benefits for the unemployed, but part of a labour market policy designed to create jobs through deregulation.

Pressures for change

The reduction in the significance of social insurance has had the effect of reducing the salience of the social insurance principle in the policy debate over income maintenance. Whether the incremental withering away of social insurance was part of an overall project to minimise its importance as a prelude to a full scale switch to income maintenance policies based entirely upon means tested state benefits and private insurance can only be guessed at. If current trends continue, the place of social insurance within the income maintenance system, and therefore the debate over its role, will become increasingly marginal.

The political debate is about the funding of National Insurance and the ability (or willingness) of taxpayers to fund retirement pensions. As has already been pointed out, by far the largest proportion of expenditure from the National Insurance Fund goes on paying the basic retirement pension, and the income comes mainly from employer and employee contributions. As insurance benefits to unemployed people and people who are ill become further reduced, the fund becomes a means of paying state pensions, and because of the upper earnings limit on employee contributions, National Insurance becomes largely a transfer from lower and middle earners to today's pensioners. The absence of a fixed government contribution to the fund reduces the potentially progressive element of the transfer.

In identifying the pressures that may be leading to changes in the system of social insurance in Britain, those that are exogenous and those that are endogenous should be distinguished. Social and economic changes lead to the questioning of the relevance of social insurance today, while the place of social insurance within the British income maintenance system is being affected by changes taking place in the system as a whole.

Exogenous influences

There are three main external changes which are affecting the place of social insurance within the income maintenance system: changes in the labour market, demographic changes and the growth of private insurance. In the labour market, in contrast to the position in the years immediately following the Second World War, we are seeing sustained high levels of unemployment and high levels of long-term unemployment affecting particular groups such as young workers, older workers and the unskilled; a growth in the number of families with two earners and, more recently, the expansion of insecure employment, often part-time and low paid (Walker, 1995).

That the British system of social insurance was designed to sustain a very different labour market and different patterns of household from those existing in the 1990s is now well recognised (Land, 1994). It was meant to deal with short-term un-employment between jobs in a full-employment economy. It was also assumed that households had one breadwinner, whose income in work would be sufficient to meet the ordinary needs of the household. The insurance scheme was intended to protect the household from poverty through the entitlements built up by the contributions of the male breadwinner. Since the mid-1970s, the labour market and household arrangements have changed dramatically, and even if there were to be a return to full employment it would not be the form of full employment envisaged for the postwar years. High levels of unemployment place the finances of the system under immediate pressure. In 1995/96, an increase in unemployment of 100,000 would have increased expenditure on National Insurance unemployment benefit by £55 million (Cm 2813, 1995). Because unemployment falls unequally on certain sections of the working population, it leads to longer periods of unemployment for those most at risk (Walker, 1995). Previously, consistent high levels of unemployment meant that people became dependent on social assistance when they ran out of entitlement to National Insurance benefit after 12 months; with the restriction of benefit to 6 months under the JSA, this dependence upon social assistance will increase.

However, not only does this unemployment fall upon particular individuals, but also, because of the interaction between social insurance and social assistance, it falls upon particular households. Webb (1995) points out that, whereas three decades ago two households in every three contained a married couple with just one breadwinner, in the 1990s that proportion has halved with only one in three couples having a single breadwinner. This increase in two-earner households makes National Insurance unemployment benefit more important, because when one person becomes unemployed the earnings of the partner are taken into account when calculating their entitlement to social assistance. However, as Webb (1995) points out, the use of the family or the household as the basis for calculating entitlement to means tested benefits can result in making low paid or part time jobs attractive only to those whose partners are in work. High levels of unemployment, combined with restrictions to insurance benefit for the unemployed, impacts on two-earner households by reducing the incentive of one partner to continue working if the other partner becomes unemployed. The level of insurance benefit is not sufficient to take the household above the social assistance threshold. The growth in low paid and part-time employment (Blackwell, 1994), alongside high levels of unemployment, is producing a division between what have been called 'work-rich', two-earner households and 'work-poor' households with no earners (Commission on Social Justice, 1994; Gregg and Wandsworth, 1994; Webb, 1995; Hills, 1995b).

Because of the gender segregation that exists in the labour market and the way in which unemployment arising from industrial restructuring has been falling upon traditionally male jobs while traditionally female employment has been increasing, the effect of the interaction between a changing labour market and the benefits system disadvantages women in particular, because the woman in a couple is more likely to be in employment which provides no net benefit to household income if the male partner becomes unemployed. If the woman leaves the labour market to maximise the household income from social assistance benefits and to reduce work related expenditure, in addition to losing her independent income, she shares with her partner the disadvantages created by unemployment when they try to re-enter the labour market (Walker, 1995). Where the employed partner does not give up their employment on the unemployment of their partner, then the unemployed partner will lose their income when their entitlement to unemployment insurance benefit ends.

Changes in the labour market reflect, and reinforce, the changes that have been taking place within the household. National Insurance unemployment benefit was available on the basis of individual contributions, while social assistance entitlement has always been based upon the resources of the household or family. Increased participation of women in the labour market, at the same time as the availability of National Insurance benefit is being restricted, has meant, that while working patterns are leading to the financial independence of couples from each other, the social assistance scheme acts to reinforce dependence within the household.

In addition to the participation of women in the labour market, there are two other changes that are putting pressure upon the effectiveness of the current arrangements of social insurance. First, there is the growth in the numbers of lone-parent households; and second, there is the ageing of the population. Lone parenthood was not a 'risk' that was covered by social insurance; therefore lone parents are now dependent upon means tested social assistance for a large part of their income. Lone parents today comprise a significant and growing proportion of the population who live in poverty (Bradshaw and Millar, 1991) and social insurance, for which they paid during their periods of employment, provides them with no protection.

The ageing of the population and the rising numbers in receipt of the state pension is producing a different problem. As pensioner incomes are increasing and the sources of their income are becoming more diverse, there is an increasing divide between pensioners who are relatively affluent and those who are living in poverty. The rise in pensioner incomes means that a smaller proportion of pensioners are living in poverty (Dilnot et al, 1994; Goodman and Webb, 1994), but the state retirement pension provides those who rely on it alone with minimal protection. To increase the state retirement pension across the board would be a relatively inefficient way of reducing pensioner poverty, because the increase would be received also by all those pensioners not in poverty (Commission on Social Justice, 1994). National Insurance in Britain has not managed to achieve one of its primary objectives of protecting pensioners, and it is among pensioners that the take up of means tested assistance tends to be lowest (Barr and Coulter, 1990), partly because of the stigma and partly because the amounts of assistance to which pensioners are entitled tends to be small because receipt of the basic pension places many of them on the margins of social assistance entitlement. Estimates suggest that as many as 10% of pensioners have incomes below the social assistance level but are not claiming (Atkinson, 1995, p 166).

A final external pressure for change in the National Insurance system comes from the growth in private insurance, the development of new products by the insurance companies and the development of new markets for these products. This growth in private insurance is not surprising, given the minimal coverage of social insurance. One area where private insurance is making major inroads into state provision is in the field of dentistry. While dental care is not dependent upon contributions, it is part of the National Health Service and partly financed through National Insurance. With restrictions on expenditure in the dental service and increases in patient contributions to meet the costs of dental treatment, more dentists are offering forms of private insurance to cover treatment (Clark et al, 1995).

Another developing private insurance product is unemployment insurance protection, available on credit cards and on bank loans to allow for continued repayment. This product has been extended by the limitation on mortgage repayment protection through social assistance and the consequent requirement to take out private mortgage protection for new housing loans. Current proposals for the development of private insurance (Cm3242, 1996) against the costs of long-term care represent another step along the road to individual private insurance against risks that traditionally might have been covered through a social insurance scheme. It is clear that private insurers are looking for new markets (Boleat, 1995) and that there is also a political momentum developing, as is discussed below, advocating an increase in private cover. Whether private insurance will be able to respond is yet to be seen, but for private companies to produce a product that appears as attractive as social insurance requires first, as the example of dentistry illustrates, the continuing residualisation of cover from the state scheme.

Endogenous influences

Turning to internal pressures for change, three key elements can be identified: structure; financing and level of coverage. In the first place, there is the relationship between social insurance and social assistance in Britain. It had been the intention of Beveridge that dependence upon social assistance would reduce as entitlement to insurance was built up, but the reverse has happened. Low levels of insurance benefits, rising unemployment and the inability of a universal insurance scheme to provide cover against particular and special needs has meant that social assistance has become the main form of income maintenance for people of working age. For many people the existence of social insurance becomes a technicality rather than a reality.

For example, the Job Seekers Allowance combines the administration of means tested and insurance benefits, which means that as far as claimants are concerned it may be of no significance whether their entitlement derives from past contributions or not, except for those who are excluded from benefit because of the imposition of a means test when entitlement to contributory JSA ends. The blurring of the boundaries between social assistance and social insurance undermines the basis of social insurance benefit as an entitlement based upon contributions. It will be a minority of the unemployed who will be entitled only to contributory JSA and therefore will be aware of its significance.

It could be argued that this blurring of the boundaries is likely to have an effect upon the finances of social insurance. The legitimacy of National Insurance contributions relies upon people being aware that they pay in when they are working to protect themselves against future risks. While much of the political debate about income maintenance is couched in terms of the country's ability to afford it, it is clear that the issue is more one of willingness to pay (Dilnot, 1995; Hills, 1993; Hills, 1995a). As insurance benefits for the working population become invisible, contributions become more of a hypothecated tax going to support current pensions. The question that this raises is whether, as current workers are encouraged or compelled to take out their own protection for their old age as well as other forms of insurance, they will remain politically willing to continue to pay to support today's pensioners with a benefit that goes to all pensioners, irrespective of income. Arguments for increasing insurance contributions may be met with resistance from contributors based on the perceived unfairness of having to protect themselves against old age while also being asked to enhance the incomes of today's pensioners, many of whom may have a higher income than low paid workers who are paying the contributions into National Insurance. There are already signs of this fracturing of what is an implicit contract between generations (Walker, 1996).

The third part of these internal pressures is closely connected to the previous two. The low level of National Insurance benefit and the restricted nature of its coverage means that social insurance in Britain is at risk of neither protecting living standards nor ensuring an adequate minimum for those in receipt of benefit. While benefits remain limited, it is difficult to see where the political support for increasing funding will come from. Instead, as is discussed below, both of the major political parties are proposing greater reliance on alternative forms of insurance against old age. The National Insurance scheme appears to be becoming increasingly vulnerable to political attacks and further deterioration.

Finally, because of the structure of National Insurance in Britain, there are no organised interests which take part in the administration of the scheme and are institutionally involved in the debate about its future. Employers are involved only in the collection of contributions and the push towards deregulation of business, and the arguments put forward by small employers may be influential in reducing what is seen as a burden upon business (Cabinet Office, 1995). Trade unions have no direct role in the scheme and the interests of contributors are expressed only through the wider political process. Within this structure, the future of social insurance is more likely to be determined by government policies which will be directly influenced by other actors in the insurance business. It is to the future of social insurance that I now turn in conclusion.

The future for social insurance

So far, this chapter has been fairly pessimistic about the directions being taken by social insurance in Britain. While it still performs its original role of providing a minimum income in return for contributions, its coverage is not universal and its significance within the overall system of income maintenance is being eroded as it has not adapted to deal with new patterns of labour market participation, changing family forms and an ageing population. In discussing the future of social insurance in Britain, it is useful to group likely directions around three main approaches. One would be to continue on the path already being followed – the continued erosion of insurance and the shift towards social assistance for some and private provision for others. The second is the strengthening of social insurance, and the third approach is the adoption of one of a number of more radical reforms which might replace social insurance. While I differentiate these three approaches, there are elements within them that do not make them entirely distinct and incompatible. We may see a combination of elements of some of them in the future for different types of risk and different forms of coverage.

The withering away of social insurance

As has been commented upon, the changes that have taken place in social insurance in recent years have not been the product of any explicit review of the position of social insurance within the income maintenance system as a whole. While Conservative governments' rhetoric since the mid-1980s has been about targeting benefits, no government has developed any public proposals for the wholesale replacement of social insurance. In part this might be explained by the fear of the electoral consequences of what are middle class benefits, but it also stems from of the opposition of private insurers to the proposal to abolish SERPS entirely (Atkinson, 1995, p 311), a move that would have left insurers providing compulsory second pensions and administering what in many cases would be relatively small contributions for small benefits at high administrative costs. For some on the Right, the privatisation of social insurance is an attractive option ('No Turning Back Group', 1993), ensuring, as it would, personal responsibility for protection, a new market in insurance products and a dramatic reduction in public expenditure with consequent options to cut income tax. While the possibility of cutting social security spending dramatically through a wholesale reform of social insurance has always been on the cards, the hypothecated nature of the contributions makes it less urgent in the attempt to restrain overall expenditure on social security and so reduce the politically all important rate of income tax. Recently, it has only been the impact of rises in unemployment that has required the reinstatement of a Treasury contribution to the fund.

The strategy pursued by the former government was gradualist – the coverage and generosity of insurance benefits were eroded; in some limited cases private insurance was encouraged through market disciplines; and means tested social assistance replaced insurance benefits for most who were without any income and were sick, old or unemployed. It remains to be seen what the new Labour government will do, but if these current trends continue, it is not difficult to foresee a situation in which almost all unemployed claimants receive only means tested benefits. The sick and disabled are also being edged out of the insurance system through the shifting of responsibility for the administration of sick pay on to employers, the introduction of stringent standards for incapacity benefit and the development of other forms of non-contributory or means tested provision. As the incomes of the majority of pensioners increase as a result of investments, savings and second-tier pensions, those without these sources of income will increasingly rely upon social assistance to ensure that their income meets a minimum standard. It might be that political resistance from pensioners to changes in the state pension scheme decreases, while political opposition to pension increases will become more forceful from the (smaller) working population which is paying for it through their contributions while at the same time contributing to their own future protection through personal or occupational schemes. The gradualist approach may wither social insurance away, to be replaced by means tested benefits and private provision.

The election of a Labour government does not signify a break with the withering of social insurance. It is clear that policies for the unemployed will focused upon attempting to get them back into work rather than ensure that, when unemployed, living standards are protected (Labour Party, 1996). The promise to review the operations of the JSA avoids any commitment to returning to insurance as the way to provide income when unemployed. Likewise, while in opposition, Labour's proposals in relation to second-tier pensions envisaged a mix of private, voluntary and state provision and do not suggest any enhancement of the basic state pension. Thus the Labour government is not proposing any strengthening of social insurance, and, given its clear commitment to maintain a prudent fiscal policy, it is clear that the necessary resources are not going to be available in the short term, if ever. The concentration on supply side responses to unemployment, and on developing a mix of pension provision, which is being proposed by the Labour Party suggests that, while the rate of attrition of social insurance may be slowed down, the trend will continue in the same direction.

The strengthening of social insurance

The Commission on Social Justice, set up by the late leader of the Labour Party, John Smith, argued for the creation of a new social insurance system that recognises the changes that have taken place since Beveridge. In particular, it proposed extending insurance protection against unemployment to the self-employed, the introduction of part-time unemployment benefit, improved insurance for family responsibilities and the coverage of long-term care through social insurance (Commission on Social Justice, 1994).

This proposal, and others, to strengthen social insurance has to deal with three main issues: how social insurance will operate in a new labour market; the funding of enhanced social insurance and the treatment of pensioners. A labour market in which there is high unemployment and new and more precarious forms of employment is not well suited to a social insurance scheme where entitlement is based on strict contribution conditions. Relaxing contribution conditions and moving towards wider insurance coverage (Alcock, 1992) would inevitably increase benefit expenditure, as too would any improvement in benefit levels to lift people off means tested benefits. Such strengthening of social insurance would improve the position of many households and particularly women who become unemployed but are not entitled to any benefit. But in the current political climate, it seems that there are no influential groups within the political process who can push in this direction. So, despite its advantages (Alcock, 1992;

Bennett, 1993; Commission on Social Justice, 1994), such a move is unlikely to happen in the short term, especially if unemployment remains high.

The problems associated with the costs of an improved social insurance scheme are illustrated by the Commission on Social Justice's recommendation for a 'pension guarantee', which would operate as a form of negative income tax for pensioners to raise the incomes of poorer pensioners rather than via an increase in the level of the basic state pension. The Commission is also equivocal about whether insurance for long-term care or the second-tier pension should be provided through an improved social insurance scheme or through voluntary or private provision.

Radical reforms

The third approach is the more radical set of proposals for either a negative income tax or some form of basic income (Adam Smith Institute, 1989; Parker, 1989; Pioch, 1996; Walter, 1989). The idea of one form or other of basic income attracts support all across the political spectrum, from the Right to the Greens. The extent to which such proposals would replace social insurance and social assistance vary, but their main problem has always been that, while they are superficially attractive as a way of providing a guaranteed income for all, there is a direct trade-off between the level of benefits provided and the rate of income tax at the margin. Inadequate levels of benefit can be provided at current tax rates, but high levels of tax are necessary to provide benefits that are nearer to meeting needs. Given that there is little indication that people are prepared to pay higher rates of tax to improve social insurance benefits, which are at least targeted on specific categories of people, it is difficult to conceive of the political feasibility of having higher rates of tax to achieve a larger redistribution of resources. The simple attraction of basic income schemes begins to disappear when the specific and particular needs of some groups are considered. A basic income could not cover the costs associated with many disabilities or deal with the variations in housing costs. The Right solves this problem by suggesting a greater role for charities and voluntary organisations.

Conclusion

Has social insurance in Britain seen its day? Is it an outdated policy design? For supporters of social insurance, current trends do not lead to optimism. Benefits are low, coverage is limited and there is little sign of any significant political support for the recasting of social insurance to meet the needs of the new labour market and new family patterns that have developed since the system was first developed. Instead, there is greater concentration on means testing and on alternative forms of provision within a political climate, which makes restraining or reducing public expenditure one of the major objectives of fiscal policy.

The debate in Britain has never been entirely clear about the purposes of social insurance (Atkinson, 1991). The objectives of social insurance may involve a mix of preventing want, protecting living standards, promoting income equality between different groups, promoting integration or ensuring intergenerational and life cycle transfers. Until we decide what we are trying to do with it and as long as social objectives remain subordinate to economic policy, it will be difficult to see how it can be effectively adapted to meet the new demands placed upon it today.

eight

Social protection and social insurance in Portugal

Jack Hampson

Introduction

Social policy in Portugal has to be placed in a context that differs in many ways from the situation in other, more developed, European countries. A useful indicator of the extent of the difference is the location of Portugal in a classification of social policy regimes. A well-known example of such an approach is the typology of Esping-Andersen, whose 'three worlds of welfare capitalism' include 18 advanced capitalist economies (Esping-Andersen, 1990); while the majority of those included come from Western Europe, it is significant that the Mediterranean countries of Portugal, Spain and Greece are not featured in his analysis of 'welfare state regimes'. All three of these countries, however, do appear together in the fourth type of social policy regime identified by Leibfried as the 'Latin Rim' (Leibfried, 1993). The separation of the 'Latin Rim' countries into a distinct regime is based on claims that their social policy is 'rudimentary' and that development is still taking place. In relation to Portugal, these characteristics are certainly recognisable; according to many social indicators, Portugal is the least developed of all the current members of the European Union and social provision is still clearly limited. From commentators within the country, the welfare state has been analysed as both 'incipient' (Campos, 1990) and 'weak' (Santos, 1991).

In consequence, comparisons with other European countries need to take account of these factors and especially the variation in the time scale for Portugal. When many countries were extending their welfare states during the 1950s and 1960s, Portugal was isolated from the mainstream development and was still experiencing a long period of dictatorship. Since the 1970s, while other more advanced European countries have been tackling issues of reform, Portugal has been attempting to establish basic social policies. In this period, the 'crisis of the welfare state' has led many countries towards policies of curtailing social expenditure. In Portugal, on the other hand, the process of development has brought 'Basic Laws' in healthcare (1979), social security (1984) and education (1986). Indeed, in some areas the new policies are still evident; for example, in July 1996 a guaranteed minimum income was introduced in order to tackle one aspect of social exclusion.

A further dimension to the analysis of social policy in countries such as Portugal is the extent of other sources of social provision outside the boundaries of the public sector; in addition to private sector services, there are many institutions that are not profit making in areas such as education, healthcare and social work. In addition, all kinds of informal sources of support are far more widespread in Portuguese society. Such variety lends support to the claim that Portugal might have a "weak welfare state but a strong welfare society" (Santos, 1991, p 37). Finally, it is also important to recognise the problematic role of the state in countries such as Portugal; specifically, the integrity and impartiality of policy administration cannot be taken for granted (Santos, 1991; Sapelli, 1995; Ferrera, 1996).

In the analysis of social policy in general, therefore, it is necessary to be aware of the different features of Mediterranean countries such as Portugal. Such awareness can help in assessing generalisations about 'welfare states' and can also assist in the study of the content of social policy. In the specific task of investigating the role of social insurance, the same caveats apply and there are also additional complexities which derive from different conceptual frameworks. The content of social provision can be classified in various ways, and language translations compound the difficulties. The concept of 'social insurance' can be linked in some countries with provision of cash benefits and also services such as healthcare, while in others the term 'social security' excludes the delivery of services. In the Portuguese case, social security (*segurança social*) is mostly concerned with income maintenance, but 'centres of social security' are also responsible for services of social care. The term 'social insurance' (*seguro social*) does not feature prominently in the analysis of social policy in Portugal although in practice insurance mechanisms are significant.

Within the institution of *segurança social*, contributory insurance regimes are predominant but there are also schemes of social insurance outside this institution. For income maintenance, civil servants have a separate 'regime of social protection' (Neves, 1993) while in healthcare there is a mixed system of finance and delivery. The mechanism of social insurance is used for about 25% of the population but the remaining 75% are covered by a tax-financed National Health Service (Pereirinha, 1992). Clearly, the Portuguese situation is complicated and it is necessary to take a broad view in order to appreciate the various divisions. While no single phrase can capture precisely the fragmentation in Portugal, the concept of 'social protection' is now frequently used to embrace both income maintenance and healthcare for European Union comparisons (European Commission, 1995). In consequence, this phrase will be used in the subheadings that follow. Analysis of the extent of social insurance mechanisms will be placed in this context.

Origins and development of social protection to the 1970s

Unlike Germany and a few other pioneering European countries, Portugal did not introduce any significant policies of social provision in the 19th century. Despite a rich history in the 15th and 16th centuries, Portugal was very backward in economic and social terms during the 19th century and was more dominated by political conflict. During the early part of the 20th century a weak monarchy eventually lost power, and in 1910 Portugal became the third European Republic after France and Switzerland. From 1910 to 1926, the establishment of parliamentary institutions received higher priority than social policy, but there were a few initiatives in the area of education and in 1919 there was an attempt to introduce compulsory social insurance (*seguro social obrigatório*) on a similar basis to Germany (Maia, 1985; Carreira,

1996a).   Although legislation was passed, scarcely any of the measures were implemented and the initiative has been described as an "almost absolute failure" (Maia, 1985, p 40).

The inability to implement legislation on social insurance illustrates the problems of the first Portuguese Republic, and the general instability provided a good opportunity for a military coup in 1926.   This heralded the long period of dictatorship until 1974. Dictatorial rule was soon established on a personal basis by Salazar, who created the 'New State' (*Estado Novo*) in 1933. Salazar was a devout Catholic who perceived his mission as restoring the social order in Portugal.   In terms of social policy, defence of the family was a prominent objective, and the 1933 Constitution also included aims of 'solidarity, mutuality, cooperation'.   At the level of policy, a system of social protection was introduced in 1935 under the banner of '*Previdência Social*'. The term was chosen to distinguish the policies of the New State from the failed legislation of 1919 and so *seguro social* was dropped from the vocabulary of Salazar's proposals (Maia, 1985, p 45).   In selecting the term *previdência*, Salazar was able to emphasise the new elements of his regime and the word has almost always been linked with the period of the dictatorship.

In the system of *Previdência Social*, there were various institutions with separate funds (*caixas*) for different occupational groups.   Significantly, one separate category consisted of public sector employees whose role in the dictatorship was clearly important.   Although the system was intended to cover for such contingencies as old age and unemployment, the lack of revenue prevented these ambitious aims, and overall the eventual implementation of *Previdência Social* was very limited.   Funding was based exclusively on contributions from employers and employees, so the levels and range of benefits were severely restricted.   Following a strict observance of the principle of 'subsidiarity', the state was not prepared to give financial support. Initially, coverage was low, but by 1960 the proportion of industrial, commercial and service workers included in *Previdência Social* was 70%; in the agricultural sector, however, the coverage in 1960 was only 20% (Maia, 1985).   During the 1960s, the growth of funds and some policy changes increased overall coverage to 78% of the active population by 1970 (Carreira, 1996a).

Apart from the inclusion of families in the schemes, the strategy of *Previdência Social* was based on the principle of insurance, and there was no provision of public social assistance during the period of the dictatorship. In terms of expenditure, there are no recorded figures before 1960, but the total share of 'social protection' in that year has been given as 2.76% of GDP (Carreira, 1996a). During the 1960s rates of growth of expenditure increased, and in the early 1970s the share of GDP reached 5%-6%. By this time the dictatorship was much weaker, and in 1974 a peaceful revolution gave a new direction to social policy.

Characteristics of social protection after the 1974 revolution

In the 1976 Constitution, the rights to social security were expressed in terms of citizenship with protection against a wide range of contingencies (Constituição da República Portuguesa, 1991). Even before 1976, however, initiatives were taken towards these objectives. Within one month of the 1974 revolution, a 'social pension' was introduced as the first non-contributory element of state income support. In 1975 unemployment assistance became available, and in 1977 social security began to include the self-employed. Partly as a result of these changes, but also because of an upsurge prior to the revolution, social security spending as a share of GDP increased during the decade of the 1970s from 3% to around 9% (Barreto, 1996; Carreira, 1996a; OECD, 1994b).

The full policy implementation of constitutional rights was eventually made in 1984 with the 'Basic Law of Social Security'. Following the approach taken in the 1976 Constitution, the Basic Law emphasised universalism and social democracy. Eight fundamental principles were included as the basis of the new social security system: universality, unity, equality, efficiency, decentralisation, guaranteed justice, solidarity and participation (Secretaria de Estado da Segurança Social, 1985). At this stage, the Basic Law is a very good illustration of 'the welfare state of institutionalised promise' included in Leibfried's characteristics of the 'Latin Rim' (Leibfried, 1993, p 142).

To operationalise the above principles, the system was planned to rationalise 14 existing contributory schemes into a new structure of general categories. Prior to 1984, about 90% of workers belonged to separate schemes, with each scheme operating different rates of contributions. Typically, employees paid contribution rates in the range of 7%-11%, but the rates for employers varied from 8% (religious institutions) to 23% (agricultural employers). The new system was to be financed, as before, on the basis of social insurance, but the rates of contributions were to be unified into a common system (*taxa social única*). In 1984 the total single rate was set at 29% but this was soon increased in 1986 to 35.5%. After 1986, the single rate remained at 35.5% until 1995, with employees paying 11% and employers 24.5% (Neves, 1993).

Despite the intentions to unify the rates, however, practice has not followed principle and all the pre-1984 variations have continued. Formal integration has taken place within the new 'general regime' but it is more accurate to refer to 'contributory regimes'. Unlike other countries, the contributory regimes are controlled by the government within a ministry, but in reality the fragmentation contrasts strikingly with the principles of the 1984 Basic Law. As indicated at the start of the chapter, there is also a separate regime for civil servants outside the institution of social security which covers the main contributory regimes. According to the 1984 legislation, civil servants were to be included in the unified contributory regime, but this change was not implemented (Maia, 1985). The status of the 'regime of social protection of civil servants' can be compared to the situation during the period of the dictatorship and it reflects the higher priority given to this group in society. Overall, the lack of unification after 1984 has resulted in a plurality of schemes that conflicts with the principles (Neves, 1993) and it supports recent claims that fragmented systems of social security still exist in southern Europe (Ferrera, 1996).

The creation of the non-contributory regime was clearly expressed in terms of the needs of people who would not be covered by the contributory regimes and for whom finance was to be made available by subsidies from the state. Even in the Basic Law, however, there were several variations envisaged in the range of benefits compared with the contributory regimes. While the contributory regimes cover a wide range of contingencies, people who are dependent upon the non-contributory regime cannot claim any income support for sickness, unemployment and maternity. On the other hand, the 1984 Basic Law did include a third and different method of social support consisting largely of services instead of transfer payments. The phrase 'social action' was used to embrace a variety of services to vulnerable groups of people with particular needs. Social action was designed to complement the financial regimes, with the emphasis on objectives such as prevention and integration; in practice, this came to focus most of all upon social work. Finally, the Basic Law also included a new administrative structure with a 'Regional Centre of Social Security' for each of the regions of mainland Portugal (Secretaria de Estado da Segurança Social, 1985).

As outlined above, there are several discrepancies between the 1984 legislation and the eventual implementation, particularly in relation to the contributory regimes. A further area of discrepancy concerns the finance of social security. According to the Basic Law, contributions were required to cover the contributory regimes while state transfers would pay for non-contributory benefits and also social action. In practice, the divisions of financial responsibility have not been maintained as clearly as the law expected; the distinction between insurance based finance for the contributory regimes and state finance for the non-contributory regime has been blurred. On occasions the revenue from contributions has been used to finance non-contributory benefits, while more recently there has been a trend towards larger transfers from the state to assist contributory regimes. The extent of this overlap and the reasons for such a significant change will be discussed later in the chapter.

Before moving on to a review of social security in the 1990s, it is worthwhile commenting on the overall expenditure trends in the period surrounding the 1984 Basic Law. As mentioned earlier, social security spending had increased sharply up to 1980 when the share of GDP is estimated to have been around 9%. Although each source reveals slightly different figures, the overall trend in the decade of the 1980s is clear. Steady expansion in the GDP share occurred, with estimates for 1984 indicating around 10% and then further increases up to a share in the range of 11% by 1990 (Barreto, 1996; Carreira, 1996a; OECD, 1994b). In assessing these trends, the estimates should be set against the fast rates of economic growth achieved in the late 1980s, but even so the increased expenditure on social security is fairly modest in comparison with the previous decade. Evidence of any kind of 'explosion' after the passing of the 1984 Basic Law cannot be substantiated.   When viewed in a comparative context, the 9% share of GDP in 1980 was well below the average for countries of the European Union of 16%.   By 1990 the same comparison reveals a closing of the gap – Portugal at 11% and the EU average 16.5% (OECD, 1994b).   In this broader context, therefore, Portugal has been 'catching up' from the 'rudimentary' ratios of earlier decades.

Specific policies of social protection

Before making further generalisations on the current situation in Portugal, an analysis of specific policies of social protection should help in assessing overall strategies within the country and also in broader cross-national comparisons.   As far as possible, current data and information will be given, with indications of any changes and reforms in recent times.

Sickness and health

The location of policies for sickness and healthcare is always problematic in comparative studies.   International data on social protection regularly include health services and sickness benefits with other measures of social security.   While this accords well with national strategies in countries such as Germany and France, it is only partially valid for Portugal.   For the majority of the population, healthcare is provided on a universal basis by the National Health Service (*Serviço Nacional de Saúde*, SNS), while monetary benefits for sickness are available in the contributory regimes of social security.   Unusually, however, the SNS has covered only between 75% and 80% of the people; since its inception in 1979, various subsystems of compulsory social insurance have existed for particular occupational groups.   Public sector employees, members of the armed forces, bank workers and other smaller groups are entitled to healthcare for themselves and their dependants outside the SNS.   The largest scheme, for about 14% of the population, covers civil servants (ADSE) who once again have a separate status similar to their 'regime of social protection' which remains outside the institutional framework of the social security regimes (Campos, 1990; Pereirinha, 1992).

On policy for sickness benefits, the tradition of earnings related payments is well established in Portugal for those belonging to the contributory regimes of social security. The current replacement rate is 65% of gross earnings – technically calculated as the average remuneration in the six months prior to the second month before the date of sickness. Since the entitlement is linked to gross earnings, this raises the 'net replacement rate' that is normally used for international comparisons. To illustrate the conversion, a figure of 79% of average net earnings has been given for short-term illness (European Commission, 1993). These earnings related benefits are available only for employees after three 'waiting days' and the maximum period for payment is three years. Less generous benefits are provided for the self-employed. The growth of expenditure on sickness benefits is difficult to analyse since it is frequently aggregated with spending on healthcare. In consequence, the following estimates are only tentative, as they are based on calculations from different sources. From 1980 to 1985, it appears that there was a substantial rise in expenditure on sickness benefits, but this was significantly lower in the years 1985-90. Since 1990, a high rate of growth has returned (European Commission, 1993; Barreto, 1996). As always, the underlying reasons for the estimated changes are hard to trace.

Unemployment support

Policies to provide financial compensation for unemployment were first introduced in Portugal after the 1974 revolution and, initially, only unemployment assistance on a means tested basis was available. Following the 1984 Basic Law, two forms of support were established: an 'unemployment subsidy' and a means tested 'social subsidy of unemployment'. Both are restricted to members of the regimes of employees and so are not available to the self-employed. The main form of support – the 'unemployment subsidy' – is earnings related at the same rate as sickness benefit, that is, 65% of previous gross earnings. Eligibility requires 540 days of work in the two years prior to involuntary loss of employment. The length of time for which 'unemployment subsidy' can be claimed is age related. For beneficiaries under the age of 25, the entitlement is 10 months; the period increases in age bands up to 30 months for those unemployed over the age of 54.

The 'social subsidy of unemployment' is linked to the national minimum wage of the relevant sector of the economy and also to the number of dependants. For a single person, the rate is 70% of the minimum wage; if the number of dependants is four or more, the rate becomes 100%. For the likely case of three or fewer dependants, the rate is 90%. The element of means testing restricts qualification to those unemployed members of the contributory regimes whose aggregate family per capita income does not exceed 80% of the relevant minimum wage. For those who still qualify under the means testing limit, there are two other separate eligibility requirements. First, anyone who has exhausted the period of entitlement for 'unemployment subsidy' can claim the 'social subsidy' for a further 50% of the previous time period. Second, anyone who cannot meet the 540 days of work requirement for the main 'unemployment subsidy' but who has worked more than 180 days in the previous 12 months is also eligible. For the second category of unemployed, the 'social subsidy' is available on a similar age-related basis to the main 'unemployment subsidy'.

Clearly, the details of unemployment support are complicated. The general effects of the various regulations can, however, be indicated. For those members of the contributory regimes who meet all the requirements, financial support is available at fairly high replacement rates. The 65% rate for the main scheme converts to around 80% of net previous earnings and so compares very favourably with average rates in the European Union. While the replacement rates do drop below 50% when a transfer is made to the 'social subsidy', they are clearly much higher in general than those obtained with flat-rate systems. For those unemployed who do not qualify under the requirements for the 'social subsidy', however, there is no form of unemployment assistance and, indeed, no kind of income support. Taking a narrow definition of the 'registered unemployed', it has been estimated for 1993 that 30% of this category did not receive any financial support (Barreto, 1996). On the broader definition of the ILO, it has been reported for 1994 that 75% of those available for and seeking work were not in receipt of income maintenance (European Commission, 1995). Evidence in general tends to confirm the comment that Portugal belongs to a group of Mediterranean countries giving "good protection to a small number of unemployed" (European Commission, 1993, p 48).

Maternity benefits

Maternity benefits are available to all members of contributory regimes, including the self-employed. The length of time for which benefits are paid is now 98 days (90 days prior to 1995) and the replacement rate is 100% of previous gross earnings, calculated on the same base as for sickness benefit. Since the financial compensation is again linked to gross earnings, the effect for maternity benefit is an increase in income during the period of eligibility. The equivalent net replacement rate has been reported as 124% (European Commission, 1993, p 59). The overall effects seem to be financial gain for a relatively short period of time. In some cases, it is possible to secure unpaid leave for a further period of time up to 24 months, but this has to be agreed with employers. Although maternity benefits are available only to members of the contributory regimes, it must be pointed out that the number of working mothers in Portugal is higher than might be expected. Significant increases in labour force participation have taken place since the 1970s and now the rate of employment for women is one of the highest in the European Union. For 1992 the activity rate had reached 55% of the 15-64 age group (André, 1996). Hence, this factor has increased eligibility and consequently expenditure on maternity benefits.

Old age pensions

For the contingencies of old age, invalidity and widowhood, financial support is not restricted to the contributory regimes. Since 1974 pensions have been available on a non-contributory basis, although the criteria for entitlement and the structure of benefits are both clearly different. There is no universal provision from the state for the contingencies, so once again, the specific features need to be analysed separately. Overall, though, as in other countries, the total financial burden of providing pensions is very high and constitutes by far the largest item in social security expenditure. Not surprisingly, most of the burden derives from old age pensions, and it is in this area that policy changes have been the most significant in recent years.

In financial terms, the old age pensions of the contributory regimes present the greatest challenge. Since 1993, there have been several amendments made to the requirements and the benefits given. First, the retirement age is currently changing for women. Between 1973 and 1993 the age at which women became eligible for a pension was 62, but this is being increased progressively by six months per year up to a figure of 65 years in 1999 (Barreto, 1996). At that point, the retirement age for women will be the same as the traditional retirement age for men. Second, the number of years of contributions required has also been subject to change. Prior to 1982 only 5 years were needed for an old age pension, but this was increased to 10 years between 1983 and 1993; currently, the contributions requirement is 15 years. Third, the formula for calculating the earnings related benefit has been amended. From 1973 to 1983 the pension was calculated at 2% of average earnings for the 5 highest years out of the final 10 years; in 1983 the proportion was raised to 2.2% as partial compensation for higher rates of inflation; since 1993 the rate has been restored to 2% but this is now based on the highest 10 years of earnings out of the final 15 (Carreira, 1996a). In all cases, the exact pension entitlement is multiplied by the number of years for which contributions have been made.

In addition, there are two further complicating factors in the determination of benefits. As a modification of a straightforward earnings related strategy, there have always been upper and lower limits to the formula given above. The final pension cannot exceed 80% of previous earnings and there is also a lower limit of 30%. While the lower limit has helped towards the problem of incomplete records, the value of the final pension has not been protected against inflation until recently. In a contrary direction to other changes, old age pensions are now index linked to price changes, whereas until 1993 increases were simply subject to discretionary decisions taken annually by governments. During the years of severe economic difficulties from 1980 to 1985, the real value of old age pensions was reduced by over 50%, so the recent index linking does give greater protection (Barreto, 1996).

A non-contributory pension for old age has been available since its introduction immediately after the 1974 revolution as the first non-contributory form of state income support. The 'social pension' can be claimed by anyone reaching the age of 65 whose income is not above 30% of the national minimum wage. (For a married couple, the income limit is 50%.) In January 1996 the level was 37% of the national minimum wage. In the same way as old age pensions were secured within the contributory regimes, the value of the 'social pension' has not always kept pace with inflation. Indeed, the highest value in real terms came in the first year of 1974, when the pension was worth approximately 20% more than in the 1990s (Barreto, 1996).

In a broader comparative context, pensions for old age in Portugal do not rank highly. In 1993 expenditure amounted to 7% of GDP, the second lowest in the European Union. When adjustments are made for demographic influences, a comparison of expenditure per person places Portugal as the lowest by some margin (European Commission, 1993, p 72). When comparisons for the 'social pension' are made, the provision is 'relatively modest' in Portugal; in July 1992 the 'social pension' was 21% of GDP per head and the third lowest in the European Union (European Commission, 1993, p 8).

Invalidity

Pensions for invalidity in Portugal are very similar to pensions for old age in the formulas for calculation. In the case of the contributory regimes there is a contribution requirement of five years, and for the 'social pension of invalidity' there is an age requirement of being over 18. Otherwise, the benefits are the same as for old age, both in the earnings related situation and the fixed, flat-rate non-contributory case. The number of claimants for invalidity pensions has remained more or less the same since the mid-1980s, but the overall expenditure has increased in real terms (Carreira, 1996a).

Widowhood

Pensions for widowhood differ in the regulations and also between the contributory and non-contributory regimes. In the former, only three years of contributions are required for the 60% of the member's pension to pass to a spouse or ex-spouse. A surviving spouse of a beneficiary of the 'social pension' is entitled to only 30% of the fixed sum.

Family benefits

Financial provision for family responsibilities is generally based on a strategy of universal, flat-rate benefits which are uprated each year according to the discretionary powers of government. In principle, Portugal is strongly supportive of family policy and the constitutional rights once again illustrate 'institutionalised promise' (Constituição da República Portuguesa, 1991; Leibfried, 1993). In practice, however, not all the policy instruments are available to both the contributory and the non-contributory regimes. Whereas employees and the self-employed receive a wide range of benefits, several of these are not granted on a non-contributory basis (ie, single payments for marriage, births and funerals). In addition, the levels of the flat-rate benefits are relatively low and increases in expenditure fall behind rates of inflation. As an illustration of family policy, child benefit is available on a universal basis up to the age of 15 and this can continue if the descendant remains in the education system, up to the age of 25. For the third and subsequent children, there is a higher rate granted on a means tested formula, but there is no specific help for lone parents.

When placed in a comparative context, Portugal has been listed in a group of countries with the 'least generous child benefit package' (Bradshaw et al, 1993b, p 265). While this is clearly confirmed by other evidence (European Commission, 1993, p 49), the indicators for Portugal do rank above Spain and Greece. In a similar way to trends for other elements of social protection, the real values of family benefits have fallen in comparison with 1974, but they have been generally maintained since the passing of the 1984 Basic Law (Carreira, 1996a). This factor can explain part of the total increase in expenditure on family benefits, which has been above the average of the European Union (European Commission, 1995).

Comparative assessment

In an overall review of strategies of social protection, specific policies and indicators of success, the Portuguese situation can change according to the angle of perception. On the one hand, an optimistic view based on expenditure data can treat countries such as Portugal as "full members of a family of nations in the welfare state mainstream" (Castles, 1995). Other views are less complimentary but still locate the country as a 'poor relation' of the same family. Katrougalos, for example, generalises Greece, Portugal and Spain as 'discount editions' of a more advanced continental model (Katrougalos, 1996). Within Portugal, there is strong awareness of the limitations of social security, especially for people dependent on the non-contributory regime; critical articles are frequently written on 'social insecurity' and the need for policies to uphold the original principles of 1984. The neglect of the most vulnerable people in society is also reflected in the comparative figures for relative poverty, which consistently place Portugal as the country with the highest rate in the European Union (Eurostat, 1991; Abrahamson and Hansen, 1996). From these angles, social protection in Portugal for the poorest in society is still very rudimentary, and it is this perception that has been important in recent years.

In October 1995, there was a change of government in Portugal when the Socialist Party was returned to power in a general election. Prior to this change, the Social Democratic Party had been in control for a decade under the leadership of Aníbal Cavaco e Silva. For many years, the Socialist Party had been campaigning for a minimum income policy as part of a more general strategy of social inclusion, but this was recognised as a 'maximum social challenge' for any government (Guimarães, 1991, p 15). Nevertheless, the new government of October 1995 immediately created a 'Ministry of Solidarity and Social Security', including a 'Secretary of State for Social Inclusion' (Diário da República, 1995). The rhetoric of language was not simply symbolic and an appropriate policy initiative was taken in June 1996. A guaranteed minimum income (*Rendimento Mínimo Garantido*, RMG) was introduced as an addition to the non-contributory regime of social security. For the first year of operation this was restricted to a pilot scheme, but from July 1997 the RMG was extended to become a national policy along with specific attempts to enhance social inclusion (Trabalho and Segurança Social, 1996b).

The objective is the provision of means tested income support to all eligible people resident in Portugal. The value of the minimum income is to be the same on an individual basis as the 'social pension' (ie, 20,000 escudos at the 1996 rate). For a couple, the rate is double, and there is a 50% rate for dependants under the age of 18. In all cases, the eventual payment made is the difference between the above values and the aggregate family income. In return, those receiving the RMG are required to accept certain conditions which are designed to increase 'social inclusion'. After 'social reports' have been compiled by social workers, various conditions need to be met. For example, recipients need to accept suitable work or training, and dependants of school age are required to attend classes; where relevant, drug addicts and alcoholics have to accept treatment (Trabalho and Segurança Social, 1996b).

In the pilot scheme, the government allocated a modest budget of 3.5 billion escudos in order to assist between 8,000 and 10,000 families living in a sample of 30 parishes (O Público, 1996e). When operating in full for 1997-98, the budget has been estimated by the government at 25 billion escudos, equivalent to no more than 2% of social security expenditure (O Público, 1996d). Critics, however, think that the total required could be two or three times higher and that the 'socialist programme is ambitious' (O Público, 1995b). Clearly, the total is partially dependent upon the number of claimants, for which estimates suggest around 500,000 people, close to 5% of the Portuguese population. At a time of economic and financial uncertainties, the introduction of a minimum income policy is brave and there may need to be restrictions on social protection expenditure in other areas. Alternatively, additional finance will have to be raised. Such broader questions of finance and expenditure figure prominently in the remainder of the chapter.

Financial and demographic issues in social protection

During the 1990s the funding of social protection, and more specifically the social security budget, has been much debated within Portugal. There are conflicting interpretations, often linked with different presentations of data. In addition, policy implementation in Portugal frequently departs from the principles contained in legislation. According to the 1984 Basic Law, the divisions of financial burdens for social security were clearly laid down. Following a strategy of social insurance, the contributory regimes were expected to be self-financing while the remaining expenditure on the non-contributory regime and 'social action' would be the responsibility of the state. Such simplicity is deceptive, and there have been several departures in practice.

First, strict application of self-financing is inconsistent with the principle of 'pay-as-you-go', which was adopted in 1977 to modify the traditional system of funding (Neves, 1993). Depending on the balance of contributions and expenditure in any particular situation, the adoption of 'pay-as-you-go' can require varying degrees of state subsidies. Although formally an element of capitalisation was reintroduced in 1989 with the creation of a 'Fund of Financial Stabilisation for Social Security' (FEFSS), its importance has been very limited to date (Mendes, 1995). In consequence, the mix of finance from contributions and state transfers has varied considerably. After the 1974 revolution, the distribution of income was changed considerably in favour of labour rather than capital. Huge increases in wages for most employees led to a large rise in contribution revenue. By the mid-1980s the burden of finance had shifted very much towards the state, for several reasons. The 1984 Basic Law coincided with a period of high inflation; also, the historic balance of income distribution between capital and labour was being restored. Since 1985 the financial burden has fluctuated, but most recently it has fallen more upon the state (Barreto, 1996; Mozzicafreddo, 1992).

The extent of the recent financial burden can be linked with questions of deficit or surplus for the contributory regimes of social security, and this second issue of finance is more problematic. Starting with the composition of social security expenditure, the proportions have not changed much since the 1980s. Around 85% of expenditure is normally destined for beneficiaries of the contributory regimes, including the self-employed. A further 5% is allocated to non-contributory benefits while the activities of 'social action' regularly require between 5% and 6%. The final item of administrative spending (around 4%-5%) completes the total (Carreira, 1996b; Mendes, 1995; European Commission, 1993).

The question of deficit or surplus for the contributory regimes should now be capable of resolution; if revenue from contributions falls in the range of 85%-90% of total expenditure, the conclusion of deficit is difficult to sustain. From 1988 to 1992, contributions financed between 88% and 91% of total spending (Neves, 1993), but between 1992 and 1995 the revenue from contributions has covered only 70% of the total social security budget, so transfers from the state have become more typically 30% instead of 10% (Carreira, 1996a; Barreto, 1996). In consequence, the state has been subsidising the contributory regimes.

While the increased finance required from the state is a clear change, there is a controversy over the expectations of state transfers. The issue concerns the burden of redistribution towards agricultural workers. Historically, the status of agricultural workers has been low, and in southern Portugal prior to 1974 their situation was close to serfdom. Social security provision during the period of dictatorship was minimal. Since 1974 their rights have been brought into line, but revenue from the contributions of agricultural workers has always been well below benefits received. In 1985, most agricultural workers were placed in a special regime in an attempt to overcome dependence on cross-subsidisation from other workers (Carreira, 1996a). Since this time, it has never been clear whether redistribution towards agricultural workers should come from the other contributory regimes or from the state. In 1994, expenditure on benefits for members of the special regime amounted to 12% of total social security which is a significant proportion. If the burden is perceived as one of 'national solidarity', there is an expectation that transfers from the state should cover the costs. Defenders of this perception have claimed that the state has not done so. If these costs were made an explicit subsidy, the contributory regimes would still be in surplus, even in the last few years (Carreira, 1996b; E. Rosa, 1996). At the very least, such complications obscure the precise role of insurance contributions and state finance in social security. To clarify the situation, the government has recently stated that the "general contributory regimes have yet no problems of finance" and that the 1996 budget would stand 80% of the cost of the special regime of agricultural workers (Trabalho and Segurança Social, 1996a).

Whatever line is taken over the burden of finance for agricultural workers, the increased pressures on social security are evident in the 1990s and it is now important to investigate reasons. The familiar and likely pressure from demographic change will be considered separately, but there are other factors which can be identified. On the specific contingency of unemployment benefits, expenditure in real terms increased by over 46% from 1990 to 1993 and this is a clear consequence of rising unemployment. When unemployment is excluded, the real increase on other social protection expenditure was 9.6% for the same period (European Commission, 1995). Apart from spending on old age pensions, there were substantial increases in other items such as sickness, invalidity and maternity benefits.

Explanations of these changes are less obvious. On the side of finance, pressure of a different kind has become stronger in the 1990s and has reduced the receipts of the contributory regimes.

The pressure concerns the debts of firms for the payment of social security contributions, which have increased significantly since 1992; it has been estimated that one third of all firms were in debt during 1995 (O Público, 1996b). The extent of the debt in 1995 was equivalent to 11% of total social security contributions (O Público, 1996a). While it has been suggested that recent increases in debt have been related to economic recession, the poor administration of the Centres of Social Security has also been highlighted as an important reason.

Additionally, there has been some concern over the treatment and status of social security for the self-employed (*trabalhadores independentes*). Opportunities for income from self-employment in Portugal are extensive, representing 25% of total employment in 1994 (European Commission, 1995). Among the member states of the EU, only Greece has a higher proportion. Although the regime of the self-employed was formally integrated within the 'general regime' in 1984, the rates of contributions have necessarily been different. Until 1994 there were three rates in the range 8% to 15%, but these were subject to a rare policy reform in January 1994 when substantial increases in rates were introduced, phased in over several years. The new maximum rate for the basic scheme is a unified 25.4% (Secretaria de Estado da Segurança Social, 1993). The main explanation for this reform was the lack of balance between contributions and benefits. In retrospect, it is surprising that this is virtually the only reform in the finance of social security, but it would be equally surprising if it were not followed by several more in the near future.

Demographic pressures on both the finance and the benefits of social protection have been given considerable attention throughout Europe in the 1990s. In the case of Portugal, analysis has to take account of a slightly different age structure from many other European countries and also the late development of expenditure on social protection as well as the similar trend towards an ageing population. Taking the age structure first of all, this can be assessed by examining the dependency ratios of non-working age groups to the working-age population (15-64). In 1980 the ratio in Portugal was 58.6%, above the European Union average of 55.6% (Maia, 1993, p 56). For the age group 65 and over, however, Portugal had the lowest dependency ratio in the EU at 16.1%. By 1990 the equivalent figures were 52.1% for the overall dependency ratio and 17.9% for the age group of 65 and over.   While the Portuguese population was ageing, the overall dependency ratio was reduced by the fall in the numbers below the age of 15.   Hence, a younger age structure has helped to allay immediate demographic concerns for the 1990s.   On the other hand, the later development of the social security system is creating pressures.   In 1991, for example, incomplete career records still reduced the burdens on social security expenditure. According to a study by Ribeiro Mendes, the average number of years of contributions for old age pensions was only 13.5 and, along with invalidity pensions, over 50% of the beneficiaries had less than 10 years of relevant records (Mendes, 1995, p 422). Clearly, the trend towards longer career records is probably a more important factor currently than the ageing of the population.

When predictions have been made beyond the 1990s, the trends in Portugal correspond more to the typical demographic forecasts.   Even so, comparative data give dependency ratios for the 65 and over group that are lower in Portugal than in any other European Union country for all years up to 2025 (European Commission, 1995, p 42).   In view of the continuing fall in numbers under the age of 15, the total dependency ratio has been predicted as almost the same in 2010 as in 1991 (M. Rosa, 1996, p 209).   More precisely in relation to social security, estimates of receipts and expenditure have been made by Ribeiro Mendes and the higher burden of the ageing population becomes more significant than the unchanging dependency ratio (Mendes, 1995, p 424).   While his forecast of the deficit between contributions and expenses gives reason for optimism from 1995 to 2010, there is a sharp increase thereafter, and the eventual prediction for 2020 confirms the huge problem of paying for old age pensions.   In this particular year, the balance of the dependency ratio will have shifted considerably.   Overall, therefore, longer-term forecasts do suggest problems similar to other countries, even if the degree of severity is less.

Economic and political factors related to social protection

Beyond the immediate financial issues and the pressures of demographic trends, social protection needs to be considered in the broader context of economic and political factors. Expenditure on social protection and its finance both form part of a wider budgetary framework, and this in turn is interdependent with the Portuguese economy. Equally interlinked with a range of economic factors are all kinds of political influences.

When expenditure on social protection is placed in this broader context, its significance can be measured against other elements of public spending. Taking first a breakdown of all social expenditure for 1992, the total for social security together with the separate regime for public sector employees amounted to 51%; of the remainder, healthcare accounted for 20.4% and education for 25.7% (Carreira, 1996a). When viewed as an element of all public spending, the share of social expenditure was 41.7% for the same year. All other items of resource spending formed a smaller share of 34.1%, thus leaving a large proportion of 24.2% on the servicing of the public sector debt (Carreira, 1996a). With estimates for 1993-96 of shares in the range of 39%-26%, the management of the national debt has become a most important issue in Portugal, and clearly this has implications for the capacity to finance social protection.

Until the mid-1980s the servicing of debt was not a major problem, but the burden of higher interest payments became prominent after 1985. In the 1990s, interest rates generally have varied within the range of 10%-15%, so the costs on the state have been correspondingly high (Lopes, 1996, p 317). In addition, large increases in the total of public sector debt have occurred since the 1974 revolution, with only limited repayments until recently. Bearing in mind the 60% public debt–GDP ratio recommended by the European Union, Portugal has exceeded this figure ever since 1984 and a peak figure of 75% was reached in 1988 (Lopes, 1996, p 335). In the 1990s, policies of debt repayment have further exacerbated the problems of public expenditure. The outcome in terms of the balance of the economy can be clearly traced over time. In 1975 public expenditure as a share of GDP was almost 40%; by 1985 the share was approaching 50%, and the most recent estimate for 1995 has been given as 63% (Carreira, 1996a). During 10 years of government by the Social Democratic Party, largely unintended increases in public spending have coincided with attempts to reduce the role of the state. Given the problems associated with public sector debt, it is difficult to detect much scope for expansionary social policies. If debt repayment is postponed, even more problems will accumulate in the future.

Analysis of public sector finance in Portugal parallels the trends in public expenditure. Whereas the concept of a balanced budget was almost a sacred principle during the period of the Salazar dictatorship, the public sector has been in deficit ever since 1974. The margin of deficit has exceeded 3% of GDP in every year and frequently has been in the range of 5%-10% (Lopes, 1996, p 328). On the composition of public finance from taxes and social security contributions, there have been three distinctive trends: first, the share of social security contributions increased steadily from the 1960s to 1985 when the proportion reached 33% of public finance; second, the share was more or less static throughout the 1980s; and finally, there has been a trend towards a greater proportion of tax funding in the 1990s. An estimate for public finance in 1995 gives shares of 24% from social security contributions and 76% from taxation (Carreira, 1996a, p 288). In a comparative context, this kind of balance places Portugal just below the average for members of the European Union; only three countries fall below the 24% share for social security contributions (the UK, Ireland and Denmark), but Portugal is still well short of the cluster of countries where social insurance is more dominant (Greve, 1996).

When the study of social security is linked to the wider setting of the economy as a whole, recent developments in Portugal are not encouraging. When the Portuguese economy experienced fast rates of economic growth from 1985 to 1990, the rates of increase in social expenditure were both comparable and sustainable. In the 1990s the economy as a whole has been much less successful; the average rate of growth in real terms from 1991 to 1994 was 0.7%, in contrast with an average for the previous period of 4.8% (Carreira, 1996a; Barreto, 1996). In a debate on the future of the welfare state, it has been suggested that a growth rate of only 1% would have 'catastrophic effects' on the system of social security and that average growth rates of 3% would be necessary in the future to match expectations of required expenditure (Amarel, 1996).

As a reflection of reduced rates of economic growth, unemployment has increased substantially in the 1990s. From a low point of 4% in 1991-92, the official rate of unemployment increased to 6.8% in 1994 and 8.7% in 1995 (Banco de Portugal, 1994; Barreto, 1996). As indicated earlier, spending on unemployment benefits has risen in consequence. Forecasts of recovery and future growth are less optimistic than previously. While Portugal did experience an upsurge in the late 1980s, the conditions then were more favourable. The structure of the Portuguese economy continues to display weaknesses in its lack of high technology industries and its attachment to more traditional products, so the prospects in a more global economic environment are not strong (Corkill, 1993; Lopes, 1996).

In relation to political influences, several points have already been made in the course of analysing policies of social protection. A fundamental influence, by no means restricted to any single area of policy, is the consistent gap between legislation and implementation. The limitations of the Portuguese welfare state are not simply a question of development from a rudimentary base; there are additional weaknesses in state institutions which act as barriers to progress. In elaborating these issues, Boaventura de Sousa Santos refers to the 'parallel state' and gives various reasons for the way 'reality' falls short of the original laws (Santos, 1990, pp 214-34). In the case of income transfers, there are fewer examples than in the delivery of state services but some gaps have been identified. While the principles underlying policies of social protection have been universalist and solidaristic, the plurality of regimes has allowed more fragmentation and status differentiation based on occupational groups (Neves, 1993). In the absence of major reforms, existing power structures continue to be important in Portugal. A further deviation from principles has also been evident in the pragmatism shown over the financing of social security. Strict adherence to principles of social insurance for the contributory regimes has been less important than the reality of finding ways to cover the costs of all social security expenditure.

On the issue of party political influences, the period 1974-85 was essentially dominated by the establishment of democracy (Gallagher, 1983; Birmingham, 1993), but in terms of economic and social policy, there were many signs of radical idealism. The 1976 Constitution, measures of nationalisation and the introduction of 'Basic Laws' reflect these features. After 1985, the growing power of the Social Democratic Party under Cavaco eventually brought much greater emphasis to modernisation, liberalisation and privatisation (Corkill, 1993). These strategies affected the economy more than social policy, but there were some reforms of labour law and a few inducements to privatisation in healthcare (OECD, 1994a). Reforms in social security were not given high priority by the Cavaco governments and policy changes were only marginal. Criticisms of the neglect of social policies, however, were consistently made by opposition parties and expectations of change were raised by the opportunity gained by the Socialist Party in the 1995 general election.

In all previous general elections since 1974, the Socialist Party had never managed to reach 40% of the popular vote. In October 1995 the breakthrough at 43.9% was a significant improvement, although the party was still four seats short of an overall majority (O Público, 1995a). However, while clearly gaining votes and enough seats to form a government, the Socialist Party did not present itself as radically different from the previous administration (Corkill, 1996) and so expectations of change were raised to only a small extent. Analysis of the 1995 general election results does not reveal a uniform shift to the left; indeed, the conservative Popular Party managed to double its share of the vote (O Público, 1995a). While the introduction of a guaranteed minimum income from July 1997 may seem a clear expression of change in social policy, it could prove to be exceptional when viewed against the broader political background. In addition, the economic and financial constraints discussed above may well be more important than political influences and so may give little scope for expansionary strategies in social policy (Corkill, 1996, p 403).

Conclusion

In reviewing recent changes and considering future developments in social protection, the various pressures outlined above may lead to a general consensus on the nature of the problems and even some agreement over which strategies to follow. Even so, different perspectives can be identified from the studies so far carried out. Currently, additional investigations are taking place and their reports are eagerly awaited.

Starting with a review of changes in recent years, there has been no major reform of social security in Portugal along the lines of other countries. Marginal amendments to entitlements, qualifications and rates of contributions have, however, been made since 1993. For old age pensions, several adjustments have already been reported and generally they have been intended to reduce expenditure commitments. On the other hand, the index linking to prices will have the opposite effect. On rates of contributions, there has been no change to the long established figure of 11% for employees, but the rate for the self-employed was increased in 1994. For employers, there was even a reduction in the rate of their contributions to 23.75% in January 1995 to offset increases in taxation (Direcção-Geral dos Regimes de Segurança Social, 1995). Overall, therefore, the effects of changes under the Cavaco governments can be only marginal. As indicated earlier, the predicted consequences of the new minimum income policy do vary, but total expenditure is certain to increase.

While there is a clear consensus that financial and economic difficulties in Portugal have become greater in the 1990s, perception of the problems can differ. Following a distinctively financial approach, Medina Carreira has reached pessimistic conclusions when he comments on the current 'pauperisation' of the Portuguese state (Carreira, 1996a, p 311) and on the "accentuation of the crisis in social security" (Carreira, 1996b, p 5). On the other hand, a more optimistic view has been put forward by Ilídio das Neves, who completes his study by drawing attention to the ideals of a social security system, despite demographic pressures (Neves, 1993). In between, greater realism is shown by Ribeiro Mendes in his analysis of likely reactions to future problems (Mendes, 1995). According to Mendes, there is almost an inevitability of increases in rates of contribution or reductions in entitlements by the 21st century. To alleviate these problems, he recommended that Portugal should follow the example of other countries in devising a two-tier system: a 'basic regime' with a low replacement rate, supplemented by 'complementary or professional regimes' with ceilings on the levels of incomes covered (Mendes, 1995, p 424). Since Ribeiro Mendes was appointed as Secretary of State for Social Security in October 1995, a further touch of realism has been added to his proposals.

Alongside the realistic forecasts of the future, current ambiguities remain. In the final report of the 1996 budget, statements on the importance of solidarity and redistribution precede announcements of the guaranteed minimum income and other measures of support (Trabalho and Segurança Social, 1996a). A practical illustration of these ambiguities was the creation of the Ministry of Solidarity and Social Security, with one secretary of state responsible for social inclusion and another in charge of social security.   In parallel with the initiatives on social inclusion, an official commission has been appointed to investigate and report on the reform of social security with a view to the publication of a White Paper (O Público, 1996c).   Early indications of the work of this commission suggest that radical approaches are being considered.   In addition to the Mendes proposal outlined above, the promotion of private insurance is under review and also a major strategy change from universal to selective benefits for family responsibilities (O Público, 1996c).

Finally, in relation to the financing of social protection in a broader sense, recent evidence from Portugal does not reveal an overriding attachment to mechanisms of social insurance.   A diminution in revenue from contributions in favour of transfers from the state has been noted while current proposals for reform highlight alternative strategies.   Nevertheless, the contributory regimes still feature prominently in the current system of social security, and there are additional elements of social insurance in the schemes of social protection for specific occupational groups. Although social insurance does not seem to be a design for the future in Portugal, its current importance in these ways should be recognised.

nine

Social insurance and the crisis of statism in Greece

Theodoros N. Papadopoulos

Introduction

Social security arrangements in Greece are characterised by fragmentation and complexity. In principle, one can distinguish between three sectors: social insurance, social assistance (welfare) and healthcare. In practice, however, social insurance represents the predominant element. Yet referring to a unified system of social insurance is misleading. Rather, one may talk of a fragmented 'system' consisting of a variety of schemes, characterised by significant differentiations in the quality of welfare provision.

This chapter attempts a critical presentation of this mosaic of institutional arrangements and discusses its origins, its present structure and its future development. The first section provides a brief overview of contemporary administrative arrangements and examines current levels of financing and expenditure. The second section gives an overview of a number of key sectors of the Greek social insurance 'system', namely pensions, health insurance, unemployment insurance and family allowances. The third section offers an account of the historical evolution of social insurance in Greece; references are made to the wider sociopolitical and economic environment forming the backdrop for this evolution. The chapter ends with a discussion of the challenges facing the welfare system of Greece and those of other countries of the European Union semi-periphery. Indeed, it is one of the main theses of this chapter that, with respect to their social protection systems, these countries are experiencing a structural crisis, the dimensions of which are qualitatively and quantitatively different from the crisis experienced by the welfare states of the 'core' countries of the EU. It is both the structures of their particular institutional arrangements and the potential for a political alternative to the dominant neo-liberal consensus that will determine the answer to these challenges.

The Greek 'system' of social insurance

The concept of 'social security' is absent from the 1975 Constitution of the Hellenic Republic. Nevertheless, it is widely accepted that a legal basis for contemporary social security arrangements in Greece can be found in Sections 21 and 22 of the Constitution. In particular, Section 21 consists of a series of articles establishing the obligation of the state to: protect the institutions of the family and marriage as well as motherhood and childhood (article 1); provide care for large families, orphans, war victims, invalids and persons with special physical and mental needs (article 2); provide healthcare to Greek citizens, protect the young and the elderly and provide assistance to persons in need (article 3) and provide housing for those without sufficient accommodation (article 4). Section 22 (article 1) establishes the right to employment, the obligation of the state to promote full employment and the entitlement to equal remuneration for equivalent work, irrespective of gender or any other distinctions. Further, article 4 establishes the state's responsibility for social insurance of working people.

Administration

It has been claimed that the articles of the Greek Constitution allow for "a wide discretion with regard to concrete implementation of social rights" (Pieters, 1990, p 132). In fact, the vast number of legislative texts and regulations comprising Greek social security law can be seen as reflections of the institutional legacy and dynamics of a fragmented social insurance 'system'. There are more than 300 social insurance funds corresponding to a large number of socioprofessional groups. The Institute for Social

Insurance (IKA) is by far the most important one, covering approximately 47% of the population (Stathopoulos, 1996, p 138). Providing insurance to salaried employees in the private sector and their family members, the IKA covers the contingencies of sickness, maternity, old age, invalidity and death. Insurance coverage for farmers and their families, an estimated 33% of the population, is provided by the Agricultural Insurance Organisation (OGA) (European Commission, 1993, p 28). Public sector employees, persons employed in public utilities, employees in the banking sector, self-employed people and other professional groups such as persons involved in trade, lawyers, academics and civil engineers are covered by their categorical social insurance funds.

This mosaic of funds is characterised by a multiplicity of organisational and administrative structures which result in substantial differences in the quantity and quality of coverage as well as in funding. What is more, these differences tend to reproduce in the domain of social security the inequalities that exist between and within the socioprofessional groups in the labour market.

However, despite the plurality of social insurance funds, the ultimate decision making power lies almost exclusively with the state. The management boards of social insurance funds consist of representatives of insured employees, employers and the state. Yet, these boards have very limited autonomy while the state exercises significant powers in key areas. For example, budgets proposed by the social insurance funds have to be approved by the relevant ministry and the government has the final say regarding the control and utilisation of assets.

Overall, areas of coverage include health insurance, unemployment insurance, main and auxiliary insurance (pensions and retirement lump sum benefits) and other forms of complementary social protection such as family, invalidity and maternity allowances. The majority of the funds fall under the competence of the Ministry for Health, Welfare and Social Security (MHWSS). Yet at least five other ministries are involved to various degrees in their administration (Petmesidou, 1996).

The following examples illustrate the fragmented nature and administrative complexity of the 'system'. The social insurance fund for those working in the merchant navy (NAT) falls under the competence of the Ministry of Maritime Affairs, while the

Ministry of Defence provides welfare benefits and health services for those employed in the armed forces. Further, although the responsibility for collecting contributions from private sector employees rests with the Institute for Social Security (IKA), it is the Organisation for the Employment of the Labour Force (OAED) that is responsible for the payment of unemployment benefits and family benefits to these employees. What is more, the IKA falls under the authority of the MHWSS, while the OAED falls under the competence of the Ministry of Labour.

Financing

The funding of social insurance schemes is equally diverse and fragmented. In principle, five sources of finance can be identified in Greek social security (Pieters, 1990, pp 147-8): contributions by employers; contributions by employees; 'social financing sources' (designated indirect taxes); income raised from the utilisation of funds' assets; and capital and state subsidies, that is financial support by the state granted on an ad hoc basis to social insurance funds in order to cover deficits. A sixth source, a fixed state contribution to social insurance funds, was established in 1992 – but this applies only to employees insured after December 1992 (see below). In 1993 employees' contributions comprised 27.7% of the total receipts for social protection expenditure, employers' actual contributions comprised 27.6%, state subsidies and contributions amounted to 17.6% and another 7.9% stemmed from other sources (Eurostat, 1995, p 5).

Table 4 provides contribution rates of each party, with regard to private sector employees, for the most important social insurance functions. However, there is a wide variation in respect of contribution rates, depending upon different arrangements for professional groups. For example, some self-employed groups pay a fixed rate of contributions while public sector employees pay no contributions at all. In the case of the IKA, the major source of finance are earnings related contributions by both employees and employers. However, in 1992 a tripartite financing system (employee, employer and the state) was established for persons insured after December 1992 for certain risks. A state contribution was added with regard to insurance to cover sickness, maternity, invalidity, old age and survivors (MISSOC, 1996, p 23). This arrangement formed part of new legislation (Law 2084/92) which was enacted primarily as a response to mounting financial problems of IKA as well as other funds. Yet, this legislation was also presented by the then conservative government as a move towards a 'rationalisation' of social security arrangements. As such, it has been at the centre of controversy both in terms of the consultation procedures that preceded its enactment and in terms of its capacity to respond to the seriousness of the funding problem (Robolis, 1993, p 59; Katrougalos, 1996, p 55).

Table 4: Earnings contributions for private sector employees insured after December 1992 (%)

	Sickness, maternity and employment injuries	Old age, invalidity and survivors' pensions	Un-employment	Family allowances
Employee	2.55	6.67	1.33	1.00
Employer	5.10	13.33	3.27	1.00
State	3.80	10.00		

Source: MISSOC (1996)

In comparative terms, state subsidies and contributions in Greece are the lowest in Europe. In 1993 they accounted for 17.6% of total social protection receipts while the average in the European Union was 29.9% (Eurostat, 1995, p 5). Moreover, they are not equitably distributed between social insurance funds. For example, the government contributed to IKA a sum that represented approximately 0.5% of total IKA revenue (Petmesidou, 1991). By contrast, the Common Fund of Engineers, Architects and Surveyors and the Lawyers' Fund received 55% and 54% of their revenue respectively. In the light of such inequalities, Petmesidou (1991, p 38) concluded that in Greece "the level of financial support by the state is primarily defined on the basis of access to the state machinery by socioprofessional groups and their unions rather than on the basis of the needs of these groups".

Expenditure

Social insurance expenditure represents approximately 83% of total spending on social protection. The level of social expenditure in Greece rose significantly during the 1980s, reaching 20.5% of GDP in 1990 (Figure 1). Still, this was among the lowest in the European Union (Eurostat, 1994). In fact, the combined effect of a series of cost containment measures seems to have halted the growth trend of the 1980s, and by 1995 social expenditure represented 18.75% of GDP.[1] Moreover, comparative data show that in 1993 expenditures as percentages of GDP were lower than EU averages for every area including pensions, sickness, etc (European Commission, 1995, p 67).

Pensions are by far the predominant area of Greek social expenditure. Figure 1 shows the almost parallel trajectories of social expenditure and expenditure on pensions. The growth of the latter sparked off a series of cost containment measures in the early 1990s which resulted in small decreases in expenditures from 1990 onwards.

Figure 1: Total social protection expenditure (SPE) and expenditure on pensions as % of GDP at market prices in Greece (1980-95)

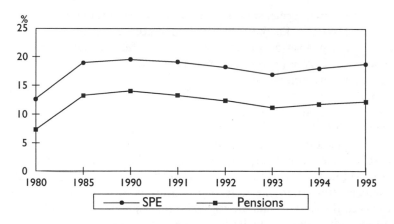

Calculated from Eurostat (1994) and European Commission (1995); figures for 1994 and 1995 estimated from data provided by the Ministry for Health, Welfare and Social Security

In terms of the other areas the picture is mixed, as Figure 2 shows. During the 1980s there was a significant growth in expenditure with regards to invalidity and occupational accidents' benefits which the adoption of stricter entitlement rules at the beginning of the 1990s seems to have contained. The very low level of expenditure on maternity benefits remained almost constant during the period 1980-95, partly because of low levels of benefits but also because of a falling birth rate. However, during the same period one can observe the continuous decline of expenditure on family allowances and housing, which resulted in very low levels of expenditure by the mid 1990s. Yet, one has to be cautious about the data on family benefits. Although it is true that in Greece expenditure is the lowest in Europe – in 1993 it was 0.1% of GDP compared with a European average of 1.8% (European Commission, 1995, p 67) – the effect of family tax allowances, which are not included in expenditure data, has to be taken into account. Nevertheless, the child support package for the average Greek family remains one of the lowest in Europe (T. Papadopoulos, 1996; Bradshaw et al, 1993a).

Figure 2: Social protection expenditure by function as % of GDP at market prices in Greece (1980-95)

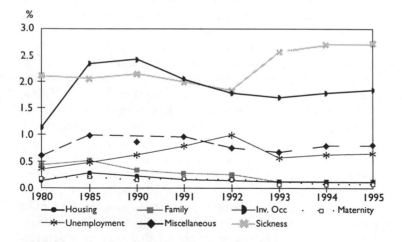

Calculated from Eurostat (1994) and European Commission (1995); figures for 1993 and 1995 estimated from data provided by the Ministry for Health, Welfare and Social Security. 'Inv.Occ.' refers to expenditure on invalidity and occupational accidents' benefits

Expenditure on healthcare increased significantly during the 1990s. During the period 1990-93 there was an average annual increase of 16.9% on health expenditure, compared with 0.8% per annum during the period 1985-90 (European Commission, 1995, p 64). Among the factors that have been suggested as the main causes of this development were the increase in the number of elderly and the overall increases in cost resulting from the advances in medical technologies (Petmesidou, 1996, p 20). Indeed, these increases have to be seen as additional challenges to the process of modernising the Greek national health system.

Finally, expenditure on unemployment benefits increased steadily in the first years of the 1980s following a rise in unemployment. However, while unemployment continued to increase during the 1990s, benefit expenditure actually decreased. A possible explanation for this is the rise of long-term unemployment and the absence of any social assistance scheme for the long-term unemployed in Greece. Hence, those who lose their entitlement to unemployment benefit after the maximum period of 12 months have to rely on the support provided by informal networks, and possibly on income from the informal economy.

The gap between revenue and expenditure is one of the key problems of the social insurance 'system'. However, no consensus exists among Greek analysts on what is to be considered as 'deficit'. As discussed earlier, government contributions to social insurance did not constitute an institutional feature of the 'system' until very recently. However, state subsidies became important in the 1980s in covering deficits in social insurance funds on an ad hoc basis. Furthermore, in the early 1990s a number of social insurance funds were in surplus although others were in deficit. Yet it does not necessarily follow that deficits of one fund will be covered by surpluses of another. Thus, the notion of a total deficit has to be treated with caution. Nevertheless, state subsidies have become one of the central issues in the current debate on welfare spending in Greece owing to their growth in relation to other types of revenue for social insurance. Figure 3 depicts total annual deficits calculated as the difference between total social protection expenditure and receipts, excluding state subsidies. The surplus at the beginning of the 1980s quickly turned into a deficit which rose dramatically towards the end of the decade. Government subsidies were fairly low during the first half of the 1980s but started to rise in 1986. Cost containment measures of the early 1990s brought the deficit down. However, the levels of deficit and government subsidies have become almost equal since 1990.

Figure 3: Total deficits in social spending and level of state subsidies to social insurance funds as % of GDP at market prices (1980-82)

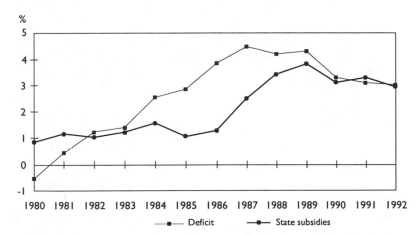

Calculated from Eurostat (1994); total deficits exclude state subsidies

Social insurance arrangements by function

Old age

Pensions constitute the largest sector of the Greek social insurance 'system' and in 1995 accounted for 71.5% of total social expenditure.[2]   Based on a pay-as-you-go principle, they are provided by a large number of social insurance funds, the most important of which are the Institute for Social Security (IKA) and the Agricultural Insurance Organisation (OGA).

An increase in the number of pensioners and the level of pensions during the 1990s were the most important factors behind the growth in pensions expenditure and the crisis in the pension sector (Figure 1). Moreover, demographic and economic projections conjure up an alarming picture about the future. As a result of the ageing of the population, pension expenditure is predicted to rise to an estimated 21% by the year 2030; and the ratio of the number of people aged 65 and over to the population aged 15-64 is expected to increase from 21% in 1990 to 32% in 2010 (IMF, 1992).   In an attempt to control mounting economic problems, new legislation was introduced in 1992 (Law 2084) which included an increase in the minimum pensionable age (set at 65 years of age for both men and women), an increase in contribution rates, disincentives for taking early retirement and a gradual reduction in pension levels in relation to previous earnings (by approximately 10 percentage points over 10 years).   The law also established a maximum income replacement rate of 80% of gross earnings during the last five years of earnings for those with 35 years of contributions.

The average level of pensions in Greece has remained comparatively low, and in 1993 pension expenditure per person constituted 47.6% of GDP per head, a figure well below the European average of 57.2% and among the three lowest in Europe (European Commission, 1995).   However, the fragmentation of provision and the diversity of insurance funds makes it extremely difficult to evaluate the overall standard of provision.   It is very difficult to calculate an average pension replacement rate, since pension levels and methods of calculation differ not only between different social insurance funds but within the same fund.   Indeed, the inequalities in the labour market and the privileges institutionalised within the social insurance 'system' are maintained in the pensions system.

An indicator of the extent of income differentials between Greek pensioners can be obtained if one examines the levels of maximum and minimum pensions as defined by Law 2084/92.   In 1992 these were 550,473Drs and 83,745Drs per month respectively – or roughly £1,673 and £254 (at an exchange rate of £1 to 329Drs in April 1992).   Hence, the maximum pension can be 6.6 times higher than the minimum pension.   What is more, the lower figure refers to those who have actually paid insurance contributions rather than to the national minimum pension. Aimed primarily at covering farmers, a non-contributory minimum is now available to all people of retirement age.   In 1994 its level was 22,500 Drs (£68) per month (Law 2163/93).   The maximum pension is almost 23 times higher than this minimum.

Medical care

Following the establishment of the national health system in 1983 (Law 1397), medical care is in principle free on demand in Greece. In practice, however, there is another 'system' in operation, favouring higher paid employees who are covered by occupational social insurance funds which entitles them to better hospital treatment.[3] There are thus obvious inequalities in the levels of provision between socioprofessional classes. In fact, although the above legislation required the sections of the funds that provide medical care to be integrated within the Greek NHS, this has not taken place yet and the two systems run in parallel. There are further inequalities with regard to preferential treatment arising from venality, disparities in healthcare infrastructure between urban and rural areas and the existence of a thriving private sector.

While medical care provided by the social insurance funds is financed by contributions from both employees and employers, the Greek NHS is tax-funded. In 1993 social expenditure on healthcare was very low, comprising only 14.8% of the total social expenditure (Eurostat, 1995, p 4). This was the lowest among the EU countries and far behind the European average of 24.3% for the same year. Nonetheless expenditure has increased remarkably during the 1990s and a debate was initiated in 1994 with the aim of creating a consensus with regard to structural reforms and cost containment measures (European Commission, 1995, p 111). By the middle of the 1990s a series of measures had been adopted, including patient charges of 25% towards the cost of medication and dental treatment. Finally, with regard to sickness benefits, these vary between the different social insurance funds. In 1995 the duration of sickness benefits provided by IKA was dependent upon the period of contributions, with an upper benefit ceiling (plus supplements for dependants) of 5,380Drs per day.

Unemployment benefits

In Greece, social expenditure on unemployment is remarkably low. In 1993 it comprised only 3.4% of total social expenditure, the lowest among the EU countries and less than half the EU average of 8.9% (Eurostat, 1995, p 4). Payment of unemployment benefits is the responsibility of the Organisation for the Employment of Labour Force (OAED), which falls under the competence of the Ministry of Labour. Unemployment benefits are strictly based on contributions, and the duration of benefit varies according to the period of previous employment, with a maximum benefit duration of 12 months for 250 days of employment and a minimum period of 5 months after 125 days of employment. For first-time claimants, the qualifying period is 80 days of work per year during the previous two years. There is no scheme of income maintenance for those unemployed whose entitlement has expired. However, there is a special first-time job seekers allowance of 25,000Drs per month for a maximum period of five months for those aged between 20 and 29 years who are searching for their first job. This comes into effect only after 12 months of job seeking; in other words, during the first year of unemployment first-time job seekers are not entitled to unemployment benefit (Maratou-Alipranti, 1995, p 145).

Various comparative studies of the adequacy of unemployment benefits have confirmed that the Greek income 'package' for the unemployed is among the lowest in the European Union (T. Papadopoulos, 1997; Fawcett and Papadopoulos, 1996; European Commission, 1995; Redmond, 1992). Table 5 provides replacement rates of unemployment insurance packages in relation to net incomes for different household types.[4] It was assumed that the head of household was the only income earner, was 35 years of age, had been unemployed for six months and was previously on average male earnings.

Table 5: Replacement rates of unemployment insurance income packages for different household types in Greece and the European Union (May 1992) (%)

Household types	Greece	EU average
Single person	35	57
Single parent with one child	40	64
Couple	34	58
Couple with two children	42	65
Couple with four children	56	72

Source: T. Papadopoulos (1997)

In all but one case, replacement rates are at least 20 percentage points below the European average. When one takes into account the fact that average wages in Greece are among the lowest in Europe and that there is no safety net after entitlement to insurance benefit has expired, the conditions for the Greek unemployed appear particularly depressing. In 1995 the long-term unemployed constituted more than half of the unemployed in Greece (European Commission, 1996, p 151). Hence, more than half of the unemployed did not enjoy insurance coverage and had to rely upon their families and other informal arrangements for protection. In this context, it is hardly surprising that dissatisfaction with social protection for the unemployed in Greece is extremely high. In a 1992 Eurobarometer survey, 85% of Greek respondents regarded state support for the unemployed as totally inadequate. Compared with a European average of 53%, this was the highest level of dissatisfaction in Europe (Ferrera, 1994).

Family allowances

Two categories of family benefits are provided in Greece: universal family benefits and income related family benefits. The first category includes schemes that, in theory, aim to increase the low birth rate by providing financial help to families with four or more children and incentives for parents to have a third child. Yet birth rates in recent years show that these benefits have been unsuccessful in their stated aims, and they cannot qualify as anti-poverty measures either, given their very low monetary value. The relatively high allowance of 34,000Drs per month given to mothers in respect of the third child lasts for only three years, and it can hardly be considered an incentive since research has shown that parents with one child in Greece either stop having children or postpone having further children (Dretakis, 1994).

The second category consists of insurance based family allowances for working and also unemployed parents. Different schemes exist for employees in the public and private sectors, with significant differences in terms of monetary value. The Organisation for the Employment of the Labour Force (OAED) is responsible for family benefits of those employed in the private sector and benefit levels vary according to the number of dependent children. However, benefit levels are lower for higher earners. For those working in the public sector the benefit is calculated as a percentage of a fictitious basic salary. This percentage increases with the number of children. Unemployed parents receive a 10% increase in their unemployment benefit for each dependent child (MISSOC, 1996, p 366).

As with unemployment, social expenditure on family allowances and maternity benefits as a percentage of total social expenditure is one of the lowest in Europe. In 1993 it comprised only 1.1%, almost six percentage points lower than the European average (Eurostat, 1995, p 4). Even after tax concessions are taken into account, the family allowance package for the average Greek family remains one of the lowest in Europe (see Bradshaw et al, 1993a). In the light of this finding it is hardly surprising that Greeks appear to be the most dissatisfied of Europeans with regard to the levels of child allowance (Eurobarometer, 1993, p 119). Indeed, this lack of support for the family results in the family itself, that is primarily women, undertaking almost solely the burden of care. As shown elsewhere (T. Papadopoulos, 1996), the type of family policy, as well as its passive nature, implicitly reproduces the socioeconomic role that families perform in Greece, with significant implications for the structuring of gender relations in Greek society.

Origins, foundation and development of the Greek social insurance 'system'

In recent years, a number of attempts have been made to formulate a chronology of the development of the Greek welfare state (Kremalis and Yfantopoulos, 1992; Katrougalos, 1996). This section is based on a critical synthesis of these chronologies. However, with any chronology, one has to approach the time periods with caution. Although the years adopted as 'boundaries' correspond to points in time of particular significance – either politically or in relation to the enactment of key social insurance legislation – the boundaries separating one period from another are blurred. These periods constitute historical phases of the same sociopolitical and economic continuum, within which a number of continuities – which are referred to as 'legacies' – and discontinuities – which are referred to as 'ruptures' – emerge, coexist and submerge in a continuous permeation of the 'boundaries'. The following chronology offers a brief introduction to these continuities and discontinuities in an attempt to establish the politico-economic determinants of social insurance development in Greece.

Origins: the legacy of patronage (1828-1909)

The end of the War of Independence in 1827 found the country in ruins. The newly established regime faced a large number of social problems with minimal resources. During the 1830s the first hospitals and orphanages were founded and attempts were made to meet the needs of the large numbers of refugees and victims of war. The role of the Greek Orthodox Church and the contributions of a large number of Diaspora Greeks were very significant during this early period. The second half of the 19th century saw the establishment of the first welfare schemes; for example, the fund for navy and army officers was founded in 1856, the funds for seamen and civil servants in 1861 and the fund for miners in 1882. The schemes provided insurance coverage, mainly against accidents and sickness, and were administratively independent (self-administered and self-financed).

The state provided only minimum universal welfare support which was not accidental. As a consequence of extensive borrowing during and after the War of Independence, the accumulated foreign debt imposed heavy restrictions on domestic economic policy. In turn, a relationship of dependency between the Greek state and the 'Great Protector Powers', that is, Great Britain, France and Russia, was established and this formed the backdrop of Greek foreign and domestic policy for many years to come. What is more, the efforts literally to impose a 'modern' centralised state (supported by the 'westernising' section of the newly formed politico-economic elite and the King) collided with the Ottoman traditions of patronage and localism, arrangements favoured by the 'traditionalist' section of the elite (Mouzelis, 1990, p 148). Despite the fact that universal suffrage for men was established in 1864, and although localism was gradually phased out towards the end of 19th century, the legacy of patronage proved to be very powerful. What was originally a system of mediation aiming to protect individuals from the arbitrariness of the Ottoman authorities became one of the key characteristics of the newly formed political system. Based on the principle of "having the right contacts who could mitigate the inertia and inefficiency of the bureaucracy", the maintenance of patron–client relationship entailed "the reciprocal dispensation of favours [as] the essential lubricant of a cumbersome and unresponsive state machine" (Clogg, 1992, p 63). Thus, during the 19th century state institutions became the arena for patronage.

Offering employment in the public sector was the key medium for 'compensating' voters for their political loyalty. According to Dertilis (1976), in the 1870s the number of public employees per 10,000 inhabitants in Greece was seven times that of the UK. In fact, since this type of employment was 'temporary' – ending with the change of government – a fragmented and dependent state bureaucracy was created, bearing no resemblance to western European bureaucracies of the same era (Mouzelis, 1990, p 150). Furthermore, given the predominance of pre-capitalistic structures in the Greek economy of this period, access to state power became the main vehicle for appropriating economic resources (Tsoukalas, 1987, p 67). Thus, the economic domain was 'subordinated' to the political qua state domain. In this context, the legacy of patronage in Greece is the establishment of a self-perpetuating spiral where the control of the state apparatus – a means for the sociopolitical elites to appropriate the economic surplus – was achieved via the maintenance of a web of clientilistic relationships with voters.

During the 1880s and 1890s a series of changes were initiated by the 'westernising' Trikoupis government with the aim of 'rationalising' administrative structures. Although limited, they were manifestations of power changes in the political domain. While the legacy of patronage remained almost intact, the phasing out of localism was accompanied by the emergence of new political elites during the late 19th and early 20th century. These new 'middle classes' consisted of sections of the military, public employees, teachers, lawyers, doctors, traders and few industrialists who eventually demanded their share of state power as well as the institutionalisation of their privileges (Mouzelis, 1990, pp 190-1).

First attempts: the legacy of institutional fragmentation (1909-33)

The military revolt of 1909 constituted a rupture with old political arrangements. The series of institutional reforms that its leaders demanded from the King was met with tremendous popular support. By 1910 a new government, headed by the charismatic young politician Venizelos, was in place. It signalled an era of economic and administrative reforms which took place amidst the turbulent years of the Balkan wars, the First World War and the war against Turkish nationalists.

The establishment of social insurance funds continued during the early years of this period and the fragmentation that characterised social insurance arrangements in the previous period was maintained. Thus, by 1925 the number of funds had increased to 21 and by 1933 to 77, more than double the number of the previous decade (Kremalis and Yfantopoulos, 1992, p 83). These funds provided insurance against unemployment, as well as pensions and medical protection, but only for a small proportion of the population. Yet there were voices arguing for a more comprehensive system. For instance, Amitsis (1992, p 12) points out that in the early 1920s there was a series of plans to establish a national system of social protection for all Greek citizens. Such ideas were never adopted, however. Instead, under pressure from predominant socioprofessional groups, the 'system' of social insurance was to be structured along categorical lines. Hence, institutional fragmentation became a key characteristic of the social insurance 'system' in Greece, which is by no means surprising, given the role of patronage. However, to interpret this development purely in terms of the interests of socioprofessional groups would be misleading because of two other important factors.

The first one was the political instability and, consequently, the insecurity that characterised this period, especially regarding the long series of changes of government and, above all, the tragic events in Asia Minor, particularly the massive wave of approximately 1.5 million refugees from Asia Minor in 1922, which followed the defeat of the Greek army by the Turkish nationalists, and which created a logistical nightmare for the Greek state. The newly founded Greek Ministry of Welfare in 1917 was faced with problems on an unprecedented scale, which called for immediate solutions rather than long-term planning and which made the discussion of a comprehensive welfare system almost irrelevant.

The second factor concerns the characteristics of the new pattern of social stratification. New class divisions did not express themselves at the ideological/political level in demands for reforms towards comprehensive corporatist arrangements. Rather, they were diluted within the vortex of the so-called 'National Schism', a massive cleavage in Greek society between the supporters of the King and the supporters of the liberal Prime Minister Venizelos.[5] Furthermore, although this period is considered to be the beginning of the expansion of Greek industry – aided by the influx of the cheap labour offered by the refugees and significant foreign investment – the state played a crucial role in providing support to industrial capital; the protective economic measures that the Venizelos government took after the economic crisis of the 1930s and the strict regulation of labour were at the basis of the industrial expansion. Thus, in the power dynamics between the state, industrial capital and labour, the state was the dominant force, with industrial capital being one of its (powerful) 'clients'. One has to realise that the size of both industrial capital and the working class in Greece were still very small, and although the strength of the latter was increasing it was very difficult for it to become a key player in the political domain.

In short, both the material and ideological prerequisites for creating a demand for corporatist arrangements, such as a comprehensive social insurance system, were absent in Greece during this period of instability and insecurity. Instead, new political elites and socioprofessional classes struggled to maintain and institutionalise their respective privileges via access to the state apparatus. In this context, the legacy of fragmentation in the domain of social security arrangements was consolidated.

Foundation: the legacy of authoritarian statism (1934-74)

For Kremalis and Yfantopoulos, the legislation that created the Institute for Social Security (IKA) in 1934 was "the founding stone of the Welfare State in Greece" (Kremalis and Yfantopoulos, 1992, p 84). According to Law 6298 of that year, IKA was to provide compulsory social insurance for the majority of employees in the private sector, that is, for approximately one third of the Greek population. In fact, this legislation has to be seen as a product of its time, constrained by the existing institutional arrangements and the socioeconomic developments of this period.

On the one hand, one has to take into account the consensus that emerged among the otherwise deeply divided political elites with regards to two key issues: the need for the state to play an interventionist role in economic affairs after the economic crisis of the 1930s, and the need for it to contain the increasing influence of the Communist Party. On the other hand, the strength of previous institutional arrangements has to be recognised. It is characteristic that the founding of IKA was not accompanied by any efforts to unify existing social insurance funds. Inequalities were thus to be maintained and the legacy of fragmentation was to continue.

In the political domain, the turbulence that characterised the first half of the 1930s reached its point of crisis in 1936 when, under the pretence of stopping a communist insurgence, a dictatorship was established by Metaxas, the leader of a small ultra-right-wing party, who had been appointed as a caretaker prime minister by the King. This signalled the beginning of a period of state authoritarianism which lasted until Greece entered the Second World War. However, after the occupation of Greece by the Axis forces, the outcome of the civil war provided the backdrop for postwar sociopolitical developments. Amidst the thousands of lost lives and unprecedented destruction, a deeply divided society emerged. The 'victory' of nationalists over the communists was to be consolidated through the authoritarian practices of a vindictive state. First, a series of post-civil war right-wing governments continued the legacy of patronage, now 'transformed' to serve as a means to exclude all those who could not provide credentials of their nationalistic purity and serve all those who were loyal to the regime. Second, the 'communist threat' was to be used as a pretext not only for the suppression of demands for economic and political reforms during the 1950s and 1960s, but also for the establishment of the colonels' dictatorship (1967-74).

The period under consideration is critical for an understanding of the underdevelopment of the Greek welfare state. Indeed, political repression made any debate on social/ citizenship rights or the welfare aspects of the state impossible. Thus, with the exceptions of the foundation of the Agricultural Insurance Association (OGA) in 1961, the introduction of child and marriage allowances in 1951 and the large families' allowance in 1972, no other major legislation concerning welfare issues was enacted during this period.

In the economic domain, however, the state was to play a key (albeit ambivalent) role which eventually led to the creation of new patterns of stratification and demands for political representation. First, a dramatic increase in emigration in the 1960s, actively promoted by the state, not only alleviated potential political pressures from unemployment but resulted in substantial economic benefits (Fotopoulos, 1985). The emigrants' remittances became (and remain) one of the most important invisible resources in Greek balance of payments accounts. Second, state support for an export led industrialisation and an open economy was combined with the active suppression of any demands for social rights made by the lower middle class, working class and the agrarian population. It was this mix of authoritarianism and statism[6] that produced the relatively high rates of economic growth during the 1960s of, on average, 8% per year. This allowed for rapid growth in total public expenditure but not in social expenditure which remained very modest (Petmesidou, 1991, p 36).

In sum, despite economic growth there was no attempt to establish a welfare state in Greece, contrary to expansionary trends in western Europe during this period. Institutional fragmentation continued while the system of patronage was transformed into a mechanism of exclusion and repression on purely political grounds. The state consolidated its role as the key modifier of power relations in Greek society, especially in relation to economic affairs.

Democratic consolidation through legitimisation: the legacy of liberal statism (1975-81)

After the rupture of seven years of dictatorial rule by the colonels and following the Turkish invasion of Cyprus, parliamentary democracy was re-established in Greece in 1974. One of the key characteristics of this period was the attempt by two consecutive conservative governments to consolidate a modern parliamentary democracy through a process of internal and external legitimisation. Internally, the legalisation of the Communist Party and the new Constitution of 1975, which offered a series of guarantees with respect to civil, political and social rights, were among the first steps in a process of transforming the authoritarian, vindictive state to a liberal one.[7] Externally, the revival of the procedures regarding Greece's participation in the European Community, which were interrupted during the dictatorship, resulted in Greece becoming the tenth member of the Community in January 1981.

However, the legacies of the past continued to set the boundaries within which the evolution of the social insurance 'system' was taking place. Statism remained the principal mode of power structuration within the Greek society, albeit adapted to the new reality of liberalism cum legitimisation. Although social expenditure increased slightly during this period, its levels remained very low. No major social security legislation was enacted, no genuine effort was made towards the creation of a more unified system and the privileges of various socioprofessional groups were maintained. Patronage and clientilistic networks (mostly controlled by the Right) continued to operate during this period. However, the balance of political power was changing as a result of the rise of the Panhellenic Socialist Movement (PASOK) in the rhetoric of which found expression the interests of those sections of the middle and lower middle classes politically excluded during the years of postwar authoritarian and dictatorial rule.

Last but by no means least, the ambivalent character of state intervention continued in the economic domain. Despite the ideological commitment to private enterprise and free market capitalism, the conservative governments of this period brought a number of financially problematic enterprises of key economic sectors, such as banking and transportation, under state control. The expansion of the public sector, serving mostly political rather than economic objectives, set the backdrop of developments in the years to come.

Expansion and crisis: the failed attempt to reach a social democratic consensus (1981-89)

In October 1981 PASOK won the election under the banner of *alagi* (change). In its first four years in office, the new centre–left government committed itself to a programme of income redistribution. Two important measures were the increase in average and minimum wages and pensions and the introduction of wage indexation in 1982. Their impact can be appreciated if one examines the levels of income inequality during the first years of the PASOK government: according to Tsakloglou (1988), approximately two thirds of the decline in inequality between 1974 and 1982 occurred between 1981 and 1982.

In the field of social security, the increase in the level of pensions was accompanied by the extension of social insurance coverage to include uninsured elderly farmers and repatriated Greek nationals (most of whom had fled to Eastern European countries and the ex-Soviet Union after the civil war).   The introduction of a minimum means tested pension for uninsured farmers was extended to cover all the uninsured elderly in Greece. Furthermore, the establishment of the national health service in 1983 (Law 1397) was seen as the first serious attempt to achieve equity and universality in healthcare provision.   Yet as Kremalis and Yfantopoulos point out, "despite the distributional and egalitarian objectives of Law 1397 very little reference was made to the efficiency and harmonisation aspects of the 365 existing insurance units" (1992, p 85). Even during its first period in office (1981-85), when PASOK enjoyed substantial popular support, the government did not attempt to alter the institutional features of the 'system'.   Indeed, the institutionalisation of the privileges of powerful socioprofessional groups, especially those who formed the electoral basis of PASOK, continued: the introduction of Law 1759/88 resulted in preferential insurance provisions for certain professional groups of the public sector (such as the Olympic Airways employees), while benefit rights of other less powerful social groups (such as various categories of the disabled) were restricted.

The creation of massive budget deficits constitutes the key characteristic of the social insurance 'system' during this period. This can be attributed mainly to three factors: the increase in the number of pensioners in relation to contributors, the general crisis affecting the Greek economy and the detrimental economic management of the insurance funds' financial reserves.

The increase in the number of pensioners resulted in the number of people employed per pensioner falling from 2.8 in 1979 to 2 in 1989 (OECD, 1990, p 48).   As a consequence, and given the increase in the levels of pensions, social expenditure increased dramatically (Figure 1).   Second, the combined effects of an increase in labour costs and the gradual lifting of measures protecting the Greek economy which followed Greece's entry in the European Community in 1981 resulted in massive deindustrialisation.   Unemployment reached approximately 8% in the late 1980s while economic growth plummeted from 3.1% per year in the 1975-80 period to 0.7% per year between 1980 and

1985, only to rise to 1.4% per year between 1985 and 1990 (Eardley et al, 1996, p 179). Furthermore, the chronic public debt problem worsened dramatically during the 1980s. From $7.9 billion in 1981, the total Greek external debt reached $21.3 billion in 1989, approximately 40% of GNP (Fotopoulos, 1993, p 41). Indeed, the achievements of the Stabilisation Programme initiated by the second PASOK government (1985-89) – a significant reduction in the budget and balance of payments deficits and a deceleration of inflation – were short-lived. Pre-election expansion in 1988-89 reversed these gains and resulted in a generalised economic crisis.

As far as the third factor is concerned, one can only question the motives behind the management of the social insurance funds' financial reserves during the 1980s. Funds were obliged by law to deposit their reserves into accounts in national banks bearing no interest. Thus, the dramatic decrease in the monetary value of the funds' reserves resulting from an average 18.2% annual rate of inflation (1981-89) and the increase in the number of pensioners resulted in social insurance funds accumulating enormous deficits. Furthermore, since the government did not take immediate measures, funds had to borrow at high interest rates from the national banks in order to cover their mounting deficits. Indeed, in the late 1980s, "out of the 860 billion drachmas accumulated deficit of IKA, 560 billion consisted of interest payments" (Robolis, 1993, p 59). As was shown in Figure 3, it was not until the late 1980s that heavy state subsidisation and a number of cost containment measures started to deal with this problem.

In ideological terms, PASOK continued the legacy of statism dressed up in radical social democratic rhetoric. Patronage and clientilism, modified to serve the new 'middle classes' that brought PASOK into power, thrived during this period. Public employment expanded dramatically in order to reward political loyalty and alleviate pressures from unemployment. The number of public employees, which increased from 344,000 in 1974 to 467,000 in 1981, reached 693,000 in 1989 (Fotopoulos, 1993, p 186). In fact, by 1989 one person in five of the economically active population was employed in the public sector, and spending on salaries reached 50% of the total general government costs (Karabelias, 1989, pp 249-50). Also, the ambivalent character of state intervention in the economy remained intact. The lack of a clear economic strategy necessary during a period of economic recession, deindustrialisation and increasing 'openness' of the economy to international market forces resulted in the loss of what was probably the best opportunity in the last 20 years to success-fully restructure the Greek economy. Statism under PASOK produced an overgrown public sector, created new state funded socioeconomic elites and placed the fragmented social security 'system' under a heavy burden of debt. Thus, the attempt to build a social democratic consensus was crashed under the combined weight of the legacies of the past decades and the accumulated economic problems of the 1980s. The end of PASOK in government took place amidst the economic crisis of Greek statism.

Readjustment: the emergence of a neo-liberal 'consensus'? (1989-present day)

After two inconclusive elections, the conservative party of Greece, New Democracy, formed a new government in April 1990. In the field of social security, priority was given to the reduction of insurance funds' deficits and the management of crisis in the pensions sector. Thus, Law 1902/1990 introduced, among other changes, stricter eligibility criteria for invalidity pensions, disincentives for taking early retirement, a gradual harmonisation with respect to IKA contributions, a uniform percentage of user charges in healthcare and measures aimed to raise revenues and deal with the administrative problems. Yet it was accepted that the provisions of Law 1902 did not address the seriousness of the problem in the pensions sector. In May 1991 an agreement between the conservative government and the trade unions resulted in the establishment of an independent scientific committee to study the structure of the social insurance 'system' and formulate proposals for reforms. In a manoeuvre typical of Greek politics, the government bypassed the independent committee and introduced Law 1976 in September 1991, thereby breaking the social dialogue with the social partners. In addition, the government invited the International Monetary Fund to investigate the problems of social insurance 'system'. In its report the IMF predicted a dramatic deterioration of the situation in the pensions sector and put forward proposals for cost containment (IMF, 1992). In September 1992, despite considerable protests by trade unions, the conservative government introduced Law 2084 for the 'Reform of the Social Insurance System'. It implemented a gradual increase in contribution rates, the establishment of a tripartite financing system (employee, employer and the state) for persons insured after December 1992, the age limit of 65 for retirement for both men and women and a decrease in the level of pensions for the newly insured.

These measures partially achieved the objective of cost containment. By 1993, social protection expenditure had fallen to 18.1% of GDP from 20.5% in 1990. However, they were also presented by the conservative government as an attempt to 'rationalise' social security arrangements. One can hardly find evidence for this argument. There were very few provisions for altering the institutional fragmentation of the 'system', addressing the seriousness of demographic developments or promoting the effective management of the funds' reserves. As Robolis pointed out, "while the deficits of the insurance system constitute a structural problem, [these] regulations are oriented mainly to immediate short term" (1993, p 59).

Public discontent with the neo-liberal economic measures of New Democracy brought PASOK to power in 1993. Although social protection expenditure increased slightly, reaching almost 19% of GDP in 1995, no major legislation was introduced in the field of social insurance. In addition, attempts to merge a number of small insurance funds with larger ones (MISSOC, 1996) were driven mostly by economic considerations concerning the funds' deficits rather than a commitment to create a uniform social insurance system. Indeed, the key characteristic of the policy measures adopted by both right and left-of-centre parties during the 1990s was their similarity. A neo-liberal 'consensus' (Fotopoulos, 1993) seems to have emerged in relation to economic and social policy. As Stathopoulos points out, given the current economic situation, "the major political parties [were] forced to pursue similar social polices. If the evidence from the 1980s suggested that party politics matter in welfare developments, the evidence from the recessionary 1990s suggests the opposite" (Stathopoulos, 1996, p 153). PASOK's continuation of the anti-inflationary strategy of New Democracy resulted in a series of austerity budgets which led to the dramatic decline in the real incomes of employees and pensioners. In the case of public employees this decline reached almost 40% (Stathopoulos, 1996, p

152).   Moreover, unemployment continued to increase and reached rates higher than 10% of the labour force in 1996.

After winning the 1996 elections, PASOK introduced even stricter economic policies which were met with a massive wave of strikes.   These policies embodied the main economic priority of contemporary government, that is to meet the criteria for participating in the European Monetary Union.   Although it is questionable if this aim is achievable, it nevertheless serves as the policy framework within which all other economic and social policies are formulated.   Thus, on February 1997 the government passed an amendment that obliged all social insurance funds to deposit their reserves with the Bank of Greece.   According to Robolis (1997), the most possible scenario is that the state will use the reserves, which comprise almost 8% of GDP, in order to reduce fiscal imbalances and contain the growth of indebtedness. In this context, the crisis of the Greek social insurance 'system' is far from over.

Conclusion

The end of the 1990s finds the Greek social insurance 'system' economically unstable, institutionally fragmented and under increasing pressure from high levels of unemployment and unfavourable demographic developments.   The emergence of a neo-liberal 'consensus' that followed the economic crisis of the late 1980s does not allow much room for optimism.   Indeed, it signifies a rupture with key aspects of the legacy of statism and will eventually modify the processes of power structuration in Greece and bring about a more polarised society.   In this respect, Greece is hardly a unique case.   As in other countries of the EU semi-periphery, the Greek welfare system is currently experiencing a structural crisis, the dimensions of which are qualitatively and quantitatively different from the crisis experienced by the welfare states of the 'core' countries (Ferrera, 1996; Petmesidou, 1996; Marinakou, 1996).   In the past the legitimisation of regimes in the semi-periphery was maintained primarily via the functioning of statism.   Access to political power and the state apparatus was the main objective of the middle classes because it provided access to revenue as well as security from the adversities of the market.   The 'opening up' of domestic financial and product markets to the forces of an internationalised market economy brought about the erosion of the state's economic sovereignty which, combined with domestic mismanagement, led to the economic crisis of statism. Since the latter is the major mode of power and class structuration, especially in Greece, one can imagine the consequences in terms of social fragmentation and polarisation.

Against this backdrop, social policy decision making in Greece faces two contradictory sets of priorities: the economic priority of competitiveness in the European and global markets, which calls for less welfare state presence, and the need to create a responsive welfare system since traditional forms of welfare provision such as family benefits are under tremendous pressure because of the impact of economic restructuring. With new patterns of labour market segmentation emerging and employment insecurity becoming the norm for large sections of the population, any attempt to 'roll back' the rudimentary welfare states of the semi-periphery will result in the deepening of social inequalities, a worsening of conditions contributory to social exclusion and increasing de-legitimisation. Thus, the challenge in the peripheral countries is to create an alternative to the neo-liberal consensus and to make the necessary institutional changes that will allow welfare state structures to respond before the crisis deepens. In the case of Greece, given the current consensus and the state of welfare institutions, such a development is rather unlikely.

Notes

[1] Estimates are based on the original method of calculating the Greek GDP. In 1994, a revision of national accounts raised the GDP estimates. As a result, levels of social expenditure in Greece appear even lower in recent Eurostat reports. For instance, the 1993 figure of total expenditure on social protection was estimated to be 16.3% of GDP (European Commission, 1995, p 61).

[2] Data from the social budget were provided by the Ministry for Health, Welfare and Social Security. The percentage includes old age, survivors' and invalidity pensions.

[3] This differential treatment concerns better hospital accommodation (rooms with fewer beds) and not the quality of medical treatment.

[4] For methods of calculation and assumptions see T. Papadopoulos (1997) and Fawcett and Papadopoulos (1996).

[5] The supporters of the King identified themselves with a traditional conservative autocratic regime and favoured a cautious approach with regard to wars over new territories. The supporters of Venizelos identified themselves with capitalist modernisation as well as the 'Great Idea', the "unification of all areas of Greek settlement in the Near East within the bounds of a single state with its capital in Constantinople" (Clogg, 1992, p 3).

[6] I adopt the term 'statism' as defined by Petmesidou (1991, p 46), namely "a type of state–society relationship in which the civil society is rather weak and market mechanisms, though extensively present in society, have a weak role in the process of distribution of revenue; instead access to political power and the state apparatus constitutes the primary means of appropriation of revenue and control of the state apparatus is the primary objective of social and political struggles."

[7] Other political and constitutional landmarks of this period were the referendum which abolished the monarchy and established the Greek Republic, and the trials of the protagonists of the dictatorial rule which resulted in their heavy sentencing.

ten

Social insurance in Hungary: the individualisation of the social?

Tony Maltby

Introduction

This chapter considers the present situation and future role of social insurance in Hungary. It will commence with a brief background description of the country, so as to place this analysis within a proper social, political and economic context. The chapter then considers the special meaning and ideological purpose that social insurance had during the state socialist[1] era and continues with a discussion of its present role and effectiveness in the period since 1989, when the process of 'transition' began.

What is clearly discernible is that the development of the 'new' system of social welfare (ie, since 1989), in which social insurance plays an important part, has been influenced largely by external 'actors', yet has built upon previous experience. Thus, what 'transitional' change there has been is of an incremental nature, organic rather than cataclysmic. The nature of this change is closely associated with the nature, role and purpose of economic and political decision making within Hungary. It has also led to a fragility in the political process at higher levels of government, particularly at cabinet level, where there have been a large number of resignations.

Thus, the present role of social insurance in Hungary has largely been determined by its sociopolitical and economic situation: by its (political) relations with its near neighbours in Central and Eastern Europe (CEE), that is, the former Yugoslavia,

Romania, the Czech Republic and Slovakia (in which a large
number of ethnic Hungarians reside); by its position as an
emerging economic force within a larger (capitalist) Europe; by its
relationships with the international financial and social institutions
(ie, OECD, EU, IMF and World Bank) (see Deacon and Hulse,
1997); and by the presence of the financial albatross of having the
highest per capita debt of the region and a growing level of
poverty since 1990.

   To underline these points, the chapter considers the case of
one of the major areas of social expenditure: pensions, and in
particular old age pensions.   Finally, and drawing upon the
foregoing analysis, a tentative assessment is made of the likely
future and role of social insurance in Hungary.

Background

Hungary is a landlocked country in the centre of Europe. In 1995
its population was 10.25 million, 19.4% of whom were over the
age of 60 (Statisztikai Ékönyv 1994, 1995). To the north of the
country lies Slovakia, to the west Austria, to the east Ukraine and
to the south Romania and the former Yugoslavia. Like the Czech
Republic (see Chapter eleven), Hungary is one of the European
countries usually considered by Western policy analysts to be 'in
transition' from state socialism to a particular form of capitalism.
For Hungary, most analysts suggest that this largely coincides in
type with the social market form pursued by Germany. However,
although in its past the country had a large number of similarities,
in terms of the role and structure of social insurance, to the other
Soviet satellites in Central Europe (viz Poland, the former GDR,
Czechoslovakia), Hungary must today be regarded as unique. This
is because it embarked upon the 'transition' towards capitalism
earlier than the other former state socialist countries of Central
Europe with major economic reforms dating from the mid-1960s
(ie, the New Economic Mechanism: see Swain, 1992), which made
the transition towards its particular brand of social market
economy in many respects easier to implement from 1989. More
contentiously, perhaps, Hungary could be considered to have
provided the stimulus (ie, by providing a glimpse of the
possibilities for change within the revolution of 1956) and the

catalyst (ie, through a relaxation of border controls to East Germans) to the breakdown of the old order in 1989.

However, the country's indebtedness has necessitated that it often has to abide by the advice of those organisations and governments underwriting its financial loans, in particular the IMF and the World Bank. This has constrained the country's room for manoeuvre, particularly in its social policy. It is these external agents, together with economic liberals within the country, that have argued that the level of social expenditure is too high, that the country 'consumes more than it can afford'. This, it is alleged, is one of the main contributing factors for Hungary's recent poor economic performance.

It is certainly true that social expenditures have been consistently high and have grown faster over the past decade (OECD, 1995). However, as Ferge (1995) and the OECD (1995) have argued, the country has faced particular difficulties as a result of the 'transition' process; for example, unemployment grew from 0.3% in 1990 to 15% in November 1996. In addition, 'old' needs, for example healthcare and pensions, still require solutions and expenditures which the state is obliged under law to provide. Moreover, Ferge (1995) suggests that, when expressed as expenditure per capita, Hungary spent a fraction of the amounts spent by most developed countries on pensions and healthcare. For example, after offering a cautionary note about the nature and difficulty of such comparisons, she cites published data demonstrating that per capita social expenditure in 1990-91 (in US$) for Germany was $23,650, for the UK, $16,550, for Mexico, $3,030, but for Hungary only $2,720.

During the state socialist period, social welfare costs were relatively high in proportion to the overall budget. Yet this was largely mediated by the country's political ideology of the time (ie, one with an objective of a 'societal' policy: see Ferge 1979, Maltby 1994). The centrality of the role of paid work and an unwritten contract with the country's intellectual elite (since 1956) were an important part of this strategy. Yet it should be remembered that the state had a unique position, being de facto the employer of all labour. This gave social insurance a unique role in its social contract with the people. Work (ie, paid employment) was "seen as the most important social activity for the survival and evolution of society as well as for the formation of the individual and of communities" (Ferge, 1979, p 89). A similar point is made by Sik and Svetlik (1988, p 276). They argue that it was employment (ie, involvement in paid work) and not citizenship that was the key criterion for participation in welfare schemes during the state socialist era. To underline this point, they note that one of the highest government medals in Hungary was Hero of Socialist Work.

Additionally, it should be underlined that the party,[2] the state and society must be considered, in any objective analysis of the state socialist period up to the mid 1980s, to be indistinguishable. 'Work' and politics affected the position in the social hierarchy not only of the economically active population, but also of the retired one. The 'old age' pension (*Öreségi nyugdíjak*) was (and largely remains) related directly to the work (employment) history. Society was founded upon and incorporated within a framework of political structures with an objective of a 'societal' policy (Ferge, 1979; Maltby, 1994).

With regard to the all embracing aspects of politics, the social milieu of the population was split between the public, where control was total, and the closed, private world within the home and 'family' (Ágh, 1989). Here there existed some degree of autonomy, of non-interference from the state. The controlling influences of the state/party resulted in the 'liquidation' of civil society (Ágh, 1989, p 11). Resistance to this overarching control of the state was expressed by the majority of the population by their involvement in the secondary economy (discussed later in the chapter). The secondary economy was not a unique feature of the Hungarian economy since it existed in all Soviet satellite countries in Central and Eastern Europe. As the state failed to exert a direct controlling influence over this widespread, often informal and unregulated aspect of economic activity (especially after 1956), its tactic was ultimately one of accommodation. Indeed, since the post-1989 transition, the existence of a secondary labour market has continued to flourish, particularly in north-eastern areas of the country where there are higher levels of unemployment than the norm. The continued existence of the secondary economy is also one of the many reasons for the crisis facing the social budgets (see below). Thus, the continued use of social insurance is largely a fine balancing act between the objective of poverty relief (not avoidance), the political economy of Hungary in relation to 'the West' (OECD, EU, IMF, World Bank), control of the secondary economy and control of the social budget expenditure.

The role of social insurance in Hungary

The contributory principle first established during the late 1920s survived the transition to state socialism in 1949 (Maltby, 1994). However, although the whole system was funded as part of the state budget, the contribution of employers (themselves part of the state) ranged from 12% of the total wages paid by the enterprise to its workers in 1946 to 17% in 1948, falling back to 12% only in 1958. In November 1948, contributions from wage earners were (re)introduced at 1% of earnings. Although this contribution was insignificant in amount, its introduction should be seen as a significant development, since it attempted, and certainly achieved, to underline to the worker that the resulting benefits had been 'earned' (Ferge, 1988).

This 1% contribution or 'payroll tax' was continued in 1951 and raised to 3% in 1954. In 1966, prior to the introduction of the New Economic Mechanism in 1968 (see Swain, 1992), the contribution was made progressive. Monthly earnings up to 1,800 Forints attracted a contribution of 3% of these earnings; 4% of earnings between 1,800 and 2,300 Forints; 5% of earnings up to 3,000 Forints and then rising by a single percentage point for each 1,000 Forints up to 7,000 Forints; earnings over this amount attracted a 10% contribution. This principle was extended by raising the contribution by a further percentage point for each 1,000 Forints over 7,000 Forints in 1982 to bring it in line with rising earnings, with an upper ceiling of 15% for all earnings over 14,000 Forints (Ferge, 1988). With the introduction of a personal income tax in 1988, the contribution reverted to a uniform rate of 10%. In 1989 this resulted in the social security budget not only being self financing (creating a surplus equivalent to 1% of GDP) for the first time since 1948, but contributing to the overall national budget.

Employers' contributions have increased since 1967 and are levied at differing rates according to sector. The state enterprises paid a constant 10% of their wage fund from 1967. For other sectors and enterprises the rate varied, from 17% in 1967 to 24% in 1979 and 40% in 1984. For agricultural and other coopera- tives contributions have similarly varied from 8% to 17% and 33% respectively. However, it should be emphasised that these contributions served a different purpose within a state socialist society. Rather than acting as a redistributive mechanism, they were used to impose, in theory at least, some efficiency in the use of labour, for example to avoid overstaffing.

The administration of the social insurance scheme was delegated to the Central Council of Trade Unions (SZOT) in 1950. The SZOT was, in effect, an arm of the party and allowed for a controlling influence to be extended down to individual workplaces. It did not have any formal authority and simply acted as a part of the bureaucratic mechanism to transfer social welfare payments from the state to individuals. Further, the SZOT did not have any influence or control over decisions affecting the balancing of the social insurance budget. Indeed, up until quite recently, one of the ministers on the Council of Ministers (usually the finance minister) "exercised supreme supervision over the social insurance activity of the trade unions" (Ministry of Finance, 1982, p 12). Thus, the insurance payments made by both employee and employer became part of the overall state budget and were not accounted separately.

In 1984, however, the control and everyday running of the social insurance system was taken away from the National Council of Trade Unions and given to the National Administration (or Directorate) of Social Insurance (*Országos Társadalombiztosítási Föigazgatóság*, OTF). This is a government agency and operates a similar network of offices to that adopted prior to 1984. In 1988 a decision was made to separate the social security budget from the central budget. Even so, under this new regime OTF was still unable to make unilateral decisions regarding expenditure and income (Adamik, 1990).

Social insurance since 1989

Social insurance as a system of funding social expenditure has survived the transition, but with a number of significant reforms. The requirement that employers and employees contribute to the Social Insurance Fund continued, but separate payments have also to be made to the Solidarity Fund. This was created to provide unemployment benefits and other compensatory payments for those out of employment, as well as for the pre-pension payments, similar in nature to redundancy payments. However, as already indicated, in early 1989 the Social Insurance Fund became separate from general government expenditures and budgetary forecasts. This was largely in an effort to promote accountability in the financial arrangements of the funds.

Early in 1992, this process of giving the system greater 'democratic transparency' continued when the Social Insurance Fund was further divided into two separate parts, the Health Fund and the Pension Fund. Separate contributions are now paid into each fund by employers and employees. Although the two funds must be regarded as separate entities, having separate budgets and management structures, internal transfers between the two still occur; for example, the healthcare costs of pensioners are paid from the Health Fund and, conversely, pensions of health staff are paid from the Pension Fund. In order to enhance further the accountability of the system of administration, elections were held in 1993 to elect the 60 members each of the governing bodies of the Health Insurance Bank and the Board of the Pension Funds. This push for an increasing openness in the governance of the system did not however match the public mood, and only 35% of the electorate voted.

Employers pay 44% of their total payroll in contributions towards the Health and Pension Funds. In addition they were required to pay 7% to the Solidarity Fund, but since 1994 this has been reduced and at the time of writing stands at 5%. Employees are required to pay 6% of their gross income to the Pension Fund, 4% to the Health Fund and 2% to the Solidarity Fund. From 1994 these contributions became exempt of income tax largely to reduce non-payment, which remains a major problem owing to the continued existence of the secondary economy.

Present social security law requires employers to register the total value of earnings paid to employees. If the contribution is not paid, the employer becomes liable to a penalty payment of 48% of the total contribution due. For the small scale entrepreneur, the threat of this penalty is hence considerable. Because of this and the considerable 'knock on' effects on the whole economy, the government has allowed payment of such fines in instalments. However, should a firm be forced into liquidation, the State Treasury has first call on any assets, with the social insurance administration having second call and becoming responsible for all collection and administration.

The pension system in Hungary to 1990

Having outlined the social insurance system in general, I now turn to the analysis of the structure and function of the Hungarian pension system. Like Britain and indeed most of the countries in this volume, the current practice in Hungary reflects that of the past. Indeed, the framework adopted since 1949 reflected and built on the existing structure, modifying it to account for changes in the political economy.

The introduction of a national scheme of social insurance in Hungary in 1891 predates British moves in this direction. In fact, Hungary ranks third after Germany and Austria of the European countries to commence such a system. In 1907, Act XIX unified benefit provision and made accident insurance compulsory. However, it was not until the late 1920s, during the Horthy regime, that the social insurance scheme was consolidated. Compulsory pension provision was not introduced into Hungary until 1928 (Tomes, 1968, p 413). In that year, through the passage of Act XL, the provision of insurance for workers and employees against invalidity, old age and death was made compulsory.

In spite of this requirement for compulsory provision, however, the administration of that provision was not universal in scope, being linked to a framework of what could loosely be called occupational welfare. Indeed, coverage before 1939 was confined to 30% of the population, mainly urban workers; the whole of the rural landless and peasant workforce was omitted from the scheme's coverage (Ferge, 1986). Indeed, the 1939 modification to the pensions system specifically excluded female agricultural workers (SZOT, 1975, p 10). Many of the larger private and public sector companies (eg, Hungarian State Railways [MÁV], the Hungarian Shipping Company and the Royal Hungarian Mail) administered their own schemes. Altogether in 1935 there were 83 approved funds of undertakings, mostly private insurers, who paid out a total of 3303,780 Pengö (the unit of currency of the time) (NISI, 1935). Such schemes provided not only a pension but also sickness insurance, with many having sanatoria for their employees in the countryside areas of Hungary, especially Lake Balaton (NISI, 1935), a popular tourist resort.

Those organisations that could not afford to administer their own schemes devolved the administration to the National Institute for Social Insurance. The number of persons insured in this way was 373,000 in 1933 (NISI, 1935, p 7). It should be noted that agriculture, based on a feudal form of land distribution, was the predominating form of employment in Hungary before 1945 (Répássy, 1991, p 23). The migration to the urban environment since 1949 was a direct result of the industrialisation policies during the Rákosi period, which, owing to the particular reliance upon heavy industry, offered the men better paid yet demanding work. As a result, the predominantly rural population (63.2%) in 1948 been transformed into an urban one (59.4%) some 40 years later (Maltby, 1994).

However, what is important in terms of pension provision is that, as Ferge (1988, p 147) notes, social benefits were targeted at the urban industrial worker, leaving the majority of (female) rural peasants excluded and living in extreme poverty. This particular outcome underlines the importance of the ideological underpin-nings of the social policy of the period. It should be emphasised that the marked change of socioeconomic and political regimes after the Second World War, following the imposition of 'socialism' from above, led to a different theoretical emphasis in the implementation of social policy. Social policy had not only a redistributive role but also an ideological function, which was particularly the case after 1956 (see Ferge, 1979). In brief, it became a constitutive element of the 'societal policy', occupying a preventative and formative role and was proclaimed as the basis on which the population would have "not only a right to live, but indeed the right to live equally well" (Ferge, 1979, p 2).

The modern Hungarian pension scheme, however, dates from 1952, some seven years after the foundation of the state, when the right to a pension was extended to all in employment. Retirement ages were fixed at 55 for women and 60 for men, and the minimum length of service was set at 10 years. The pension, which was set at 15% of wages or earnings, did not cover workers in the agricultural sector, however, and was part of the policy of industrialisation mentioned earlier. As has been emphasised, the definition of employment, and hence entry into the social welfare system, was determined by the state (and hence the party).

The most significant departure in terms of pensions was the link between (paid) work and the payment of a pension. The separate privately funded schemes that existed before the Second World War were all unified under the National Directorate of

Social Insurance. However, not all workers in the economy were covered. As Ferge (1988) has noted, members of cooperatives were included from 1957 (with a retirement age of 65 for men and 60 for women), self employed crafts*men* (sic) from 1960 and 'shopkeepers' from 1969. It is important to underline that the nature of this coverage was not uniform; for example, members of the agricultural cooperatives had higher retirement ages than industrial workers until as late as 1975. There thus existed a dichotomous approach to social policy on old age pensions: dichotomous not only in its division between the urban and rural worker, but also, as a result of this, a division between men and women, since most agricultural workers were women (Maltby, 1994).

In October 1954, 50% of average earnings since 1945 were counted towards the pension. In 1959 this was extended to include earnings from 1929 onwards when the pensions system in Hungary was implemented. These earnings had to be proved with documentary evidence. This was, and continues to be, difficult because of the massive destruction caused during the Second World War and the loss of many official documents during the 1956 revolution.

The 1952 system for the calculation of pensions continued until 1970 when, as a result of the expansion of the private sector resulting from the 1968 economic reforms under the New Economic Mechanism, that sector was included in the state scheme. In 1972 an annual increase of 2% or 50 Forints[3] was added to the pension to allow for the effects of inflation. Although there was no official recognition of inflation, Széman (1989) estimated that during this period the rate was as high as, and sometimes over, 20%, and so these additions must be considered to have been superficial in effect.

Indeed, the poverty experienced by increasing numbers of pensioners as a result of high rates of inflation was one of the factors accounting for the growth of a specific labour market for pensioners (disability and old age) from the 1970s and 1980s. During this period a demand for labour was created as a result of two main factors: a reduction in the numbers of first time job seekers, and the disappearance of women from the labour force to undertake childcare following the introduction of childcare assistance payments in 1967 (GYES) and their subsequent expansion in 1985 (GYED). Thus, pensioners became one of the principle sources of labour, and as a result, changes in the regulations governing the employment of pensioners were relaxed; that is, the maximum hours that could be spent in paid work without forfeit were extended (Széman, 1989).

Pensions policy from 1975

From July 1975 pension provision, including the age of retirement, was made uniform throughout "for all strata and in all respects" (Ministry of Finance, 1982). The reduction of pension ages in the agricultural sector to that of 55 for women and 60 for men was phased in over a five year period. Workers who have worked in environments hazardous to their health (eg, mining, chemical industries, some heavy manufacturing) are entitled to retire earlier. To obtain this concession, women have to have worked for eight years (men for ten) in such hazardous conditions, for which they 'earn' an extra two years earlier retirement; this can be extended by one year for every additional four years (five for men) worked. Obviously, workers in such life threatening environments may not be able to enjoy the full benefits that could ensue from such a policy, owing to the risk of premature death or ill health in retirement (see Carlson, 1979; Forster and Józan, 1990; Meslé, 1991).

In addition to these changes, the minimum period of service for entitlement to a pension, established at 10 years in 1981, was extended to 20 years in 1991. This service period is calculated from 1929 (if proved with documentary evidence) and interruptions of up to five years do not at present result in a loss of rights. Thus, the size of the pension is presently calculated on the basis of two factors: the number of years in work, and the size of earnings. According to these guidelines, older people are entitled to a pension of 33% of 'average monthly earnings' (see below) for a service period of the basic 10 years, 43% for 15 years and 53% for 20 years; for each additional year worked up to 25 years, the pension is increased by 2%, then by 1% up to 33 years' service and by 0.5% for each subsequent year worked over 33 years.

'Average monthly earnings' are calculated by determining the most favourable gross earnings of three years within the five year period prior to retirement. Before 1982 the maximum average earnings figure that could be applied was 10,000 Forints, but from January 1982 average earnings above this figure can be taken into account with replacement factors applied to such earnings. Since

1994 these have been calculated in nine percentage bands of 10% each, starting at 100% of earnings up to 16,000 Forints then progressively to 50% of earnings between 50,001 to 60,000 Forints, reaching 10% of earnings for 80,001 Forints and over.

In order to claim a partial pension, 15 years' pensionable service has been required since 1993. Widows' pensions are paid to 'a wife, a divorced wife, a common law wife and a husband' (Ministry of Finance, 1982, p 25). This is a temporary pension, payable for one year, if the minimum service period has been accumulated or if the spouse died as a pensioner; a permanent pension is paid to women who have reached pension age, are incapable of working through disability or who have to support at least two children. The amount of the pension was 50% of the deceased person's pension but this was increased, from January 1989, to 60%. The temporary pension of divorced or separated women cannot exceed the total amount of maintenance they were receiving.   All pensioners are now entitled to a 'minimum pension', which in 1990 was 3,968 Forints per month and in 1994, 7,480 Forints.   These minima do not allow pensioners to receive more than their previous monthly earnings.

The payment of various forms of 'retiring allowance', as they are known (ie, all types of pension including orphan's allowances, disability and widows pensions), consumes a large proportion of the total welfare expenditure.   For example, in 1994 the total expenditure on all forms of 'retiring allowances' was 384,436 million Forints with an average (mean) payment 13,977 Forints, paid to 28.6% of the population (Statisztikai Ékönyv, 1994; 1995). The total revenue received by the Pensions Insurance Fund was 385,971 million Forints and total expenditure 408,749 million Forints; thus it was in deficit, a common trend today. Similarly, the Health Insurance Fund in 1994 had a total revenue from contributions of 341,953 million Forints and a total expenditure of 360,771 million Forints (Statisztikai Ékönyv, 1994; 1995).

Recent trends

The rising levels of expenditure can be seen to be due to a particular phenomenon associated with the 'shake out' of older industries, which have accommodated the 'transition' to capitalism by reducing their workforce through a variety of measures. Széman (1993) has demonstrated that whereas, before 1990 retirement pensioners had remained in the labour force because of the low value of their non-indexed pension, this has now been ruled out. Indeed, one commentator suggested that such employees often earned more money working full time in the secondary economy than in the first or principal one (Szalai, 1990; 1991).

Following the privatisation process in Hungary since 1990 (or what is more often known as the 'marketisation' process in CEE countries, since market principles are being applied), employers use a variety of mechanisms to remove older workers from their enterprises (eg, phasing out the use of working pensioners; offering pre-retirement packages, making use of disability pension payments which have increased rapidly). As a consequence, statistical surveys demonstrate a pronounced trend towards lower retirement ages for men. Associated with this growth of 'discouraged' workers, there has been a shift towards the employment of younger workers (ie, those under 40) mainly by Western European and US based companies (Széman, 1993).

There are two main programmes that cater for early retirement, the Pre-pension and Early Retirement schemes. The Pre-pension scheme is intended for older 'discouraged' workers who are within three years of retirement, who earn less than the minimum wage and who have been unemployed for at least the previous six months. Funding for the scheme is borne from the Solidarity Fund (OECD, 1995). The Early Retirement scheme is intended to assist workers at risk of layoff in firms that are in financial difficulty and provides them with a pension five years earlier than the usual retirement age; it is limited to those workers who have long service records (30 years for men, 25 for women) (OECD, 1995). However, it should be noted that the disability pension route is used more often than either of these by employers (Széman, 1993). Indeed, between 1990 and 1993 those entering retirement in this manner, often involuntarily, accounted for a third of all retirees and double the number of those entering early retirement by other methods. There are many parallels here with the other European countries where similar trends are noted (see Walker and Maltby, 1997).

The second(ary) economy

Since the secondary economy has had considerable negative effects on social insurance revenue, yet is often crucial to the maintenance of family incomes in Hungary, attention will now turn to this important and in many respects unique socioeconomic phenomenon.

Involvement in the secondary economy is considered normal practice for many Hungarians. This is largely because it continues practices of the state socialist period when (official) wages were low and one routinely took a second job to boost income. Indeed, most commentators have noted that in the socialist era involvement in this (usually) cash based economy was often a necessity for daily survival (Galasi, 1985). Since 1990 it has adopted more overtly political overtones, for example the embodiment of political freedom (thought, movement, actions) under a capitalist economy.

Although there is an extensive literature on the second economy in Hungary,[4] as Gábor and Galasi (1985) indicate, there is no accepted and agreed academic interpretation as to what constituted it in the Hungarian context up to 1990. However, Gábor and Galasi (1985, p 123) suggest that the term included "all income-producing economic activities which are carried out by households or individuals not as employees in the organisations of the socialist sector". The authors exclude mutual networks based around neighbourhood and kinship ties, the subsistence economy (household production for its own consumption) and illegal activities within socialist enterprises. Unlike the first economy, the second economy was regulated, not directed, by the state. Thus, to cite Gábor and Galasi (1985, p 125) again, "the socialist economy is dual, that is, it consists of two economies with differing rules of operation. At the same time, however, the two economies are in symbiosis, as they are connected to one another through markets."

However, data concerning the second economy were not officially collated, since (officially) this economy did not exist.[5] It has been estimated (Gábor and Galasi, 1985, p 130) that the 'total time input' represented approximately a quarter of the total work time in the first economy and generated about one fifth of the annual GNP. This compares well with another estimate of Szélenyi (cited in Hann, 1990, p 22) that by the mid-1980s 70%

of households in Hungary had incomes derived from the second economy and that about a fifth of income earners received between a third and a half of their incomes from this source. Not only does the second economy occupy a central role in contributing to the total income of households, but it has had an important bearing upon the growth and formation of a civil society. This particular thesis is offered by Szelényi (1989), who sees the rise of the second economy in Hungary as a particular aspect of an embourgeoisement process resulting from the compromises made by the Kádár regime, that is, post-1956.

Coping with change: social insurance in the present and future

It is clear from all the objective evidence from a number of surveys since 1989 that poverty has increased and is increasing in Hungary (Ferge, 1996). This poses a considerable challenge to future social policy in the country. Whether the social insurance model is the way forward, and whether it has succeeded in the past, can be debated at length. However, what is clear is that since 1990 governments of both the centre–right and more recently the centre–left have adopted a less interventionist, more market driven, policy towards welfare, with means testing rather than social insurance being the dominant form of distributive mechanism.

In any analysis, it should be clearly stated that Hungarian social policy is hostage to the loans provided by such organisations as the World Bank and the IMF, without which it cannot survive. It is also hostage to the past, a past that can be seen to undermine the principle of social insurance today. During the state socialist period up to October 1989, evasion of payment of taxes and contributions was seen as a legitimate form of political subversion. This view persists today particularly among the entrepreneurial classes (Árvay and Vértes, 1993; cited in OECD, 1995) and is a major problem for the legitimacy of the continuance of the social insurance system itself. Indeed, the government as recently as November 1996 introduced a reduction in income tax and other forms of direct taxation (but not social insurance contributions) in a desperate effort to encourage the collection of these particular types of revenue.

Clearly, the present Horn government has a fine balancing act to perform. On the one hand, it wishes to convey to the rather disillusioned electorate that it is not still wearing its old communist party clothes and that it belongs to the social democratic tradition of socialism. It has also expressed a desire for the introduction of measures (in which social insurance has a vital role) to combat the increasingly widespread levels of social deprivation and poverty. Yet on the other hand, the government has to appeal to the international financial institutions for credits, and these often apply criteria such as a drastic and wholesale reduction of social expenditures and/or an extension of means testing.

The recent 'austerity measures' are a clear example of this dilemma (see Economist Intelligence Unit, 1995). These placed reductions on all forms of social expenditure ranging from child welfare payments to the funding of higher education. Additionally, in January 1996 the Hungarian Finance Minister Lajos Bakros announced additional austerity measures. These, he suggested, would further 'streamline' public welfare. However, the cuts were largely a reaction to the news that the Health Insurance Fund had a deficit of 20 billion Forints in 1995; they also helped to secure a vital financial credit (a standby loan) from the IMF of $387 million, which led to the entry of Hungary into the OECD in March 1996, thus improving its creditworthiness.

Yet such 'austerity measures' created not only widespread unease (and in some cases antagonism) within the general population, but ultimately many cases of severe hardship. In February 1996 the World Bank itself reported that poverty in Hungary had increased fivefold since 1989: at that time 1.6% of the Hungarian population were relying on incomes below the minimum pension level, which even then was comparatively low; by 1993 this rate had increased to 8.6%. Yet to counter such rising levels of poverty and deprivation, the World Bank proposed changes to the social safety net which involved not social insurance, but an expansion and broadening the role of means testing.

A more radical and imaginative solution than this is required. The 'social' benefits of social insurance (greater social cohesiveness, greater possibility for redistribution across the life cycle, etc) should be seen as a way forward. Social insurance should be regarded not simply as a financial instrument but as a reinvigoration of the 'social' (Ferge, 1996; Guillemard, 1986;

Rosanvallon, 1995). The present policy, focusing simply on means testing, acts to individualise it (Ferge, 1996). In short, and as Ferge (1996, p 4) suggests, "the new project is about the retraction of social commitments, the refusal of the importance of an integrated society or even of society, *the individualisation of the social*" (original emphasis).

For example, one of the strategies employed has been to raise the statutory retirement age. There is nothing unique or original in this. A similar tactic has been used by a large number of governments worldwide, the UK among them, as a response to their often pessimistic projections and expectations of the so-called 'demographic time bomb'. In Hungary the changes are to be to implemented from 1997 and will increase the retirement age to 62 (from 55 for women and 60 for men) by 2005. Yet as has been noted (Walker and Maltby, 1997), in the European Union and in many other industrialised countries the actual age of retirement is falling *below* the pension age, and the pathways into retirement are more varied, not simply through receipt of a retirement pension.

On 12 March 1996, just before Hungary's entry to the OECD (on 29 March), the social security budget for 1996 was approved. It aimed to cut the accumulated social security deficit for 1996 to 17.8 billion Forints from 47.2 billion Forints in 1995, which would comply in full with conditions set by the IMF that the overall budget deficit should fall to below 4% of GDP. To achieve this monetary target, a concerted effort to collect unpaid social insurance contributions was planned, even though this strategy had been attempted none too successfully in the past. In May 1996 the Finance Ministry announced that the accumulated social security budget deficit would be 41.3 billion Forints by the end of 1996, allowing for a stand-by credit of $300 million from IMF. This meant that the budget deficit would be 3.9% of GDP in 1996 and thus would meet the targets. However, in July 1996 it was predicted by the government that the Pension and Health Insurance Funds would run up a total deficit of 68 billion Forints by the end of 1996. This is four times higher than that stipulated by IMF (17.8 billion Forints) as a condition for a future stand-by loan of $387 million. Again, this deficit was simply blamed on low collection rates of contributions.

More recently, in early December 1996, a revised draft budget for the Pension and Health Insurance Funds showed that the debt for 1997 would be 13 billion Forints. Previously it was estimated that it would break even. The increase is largely attributed to a 'modest success' in the collection of outstanding debts on social insurance payments. Thus, the emphasis of many policy documents is that social insurance has failed (and is seen to be failing) and that, as a mechanism for raising finance for social welfare, it should therefore be abandoned.

In fairness, the Hungarian government can be said to be caught between the 'devil and the deep blue sea' in seeking a pragmatic solution. Their financial backers are insistent upon a reduction in welfare expenditure, even though such reductions and the greater reliance on means testing has resulted in increasing levels of poverty and greater social conflict. It has been suggested that social insurance, as a mechanism, has the potential for uniting what is increasingly becoming a polarised and individualistic society (Ferge, 1996).

In conclusion, although it would appear in any objective analysis that social insurance has failed in Hungary, the solution remains complex, since it involves not only the Hungarians themselves.

Notes

[1] This term is employed for the sake of brevity and because of its popular usage. It is not used in a descriptive capacity. Other phrases, eg, 'really existing socialism' or 'bureaucratic state collectivism', could equally be employed, but they are a bit longwinded and open to similar criticisms.

[2] That is, the MSzMP, the Hungarian Socialist Workers Party.

[3] In May/June 1990, 100 Forints were worth approximately £1. In October 1992 the exchange rate was approximately £1 to 146 Forints, and more recently (November 1996) it was £1 to 265 Forints.

[4] An extensive survey of the second economy is provided in Swain (1992), Galasai and Sziráczki (1985) and Gábor (1979), from which much of this analysis derives.

[5] In much the same manner as 'moonlighting' activities are not officially recorded in Britain. However, it should be stressed that such a term does not equate with the Hungarian secondary economy.

eleven

Social security and social insurance in the Czech Republic

Mita Castle-Kanerova

Introduction

After six years of reforms repudiating the logic and legislation of previous paternalistic state provision, a fully comprehensive social security system came into effect in the Czech Republic in January 1996. In some sense it provides a bridge from one social system to another, linking the past with an uncertain future. Yet its stated aim is to break away from the ubiquitous system of social protection under communism which was in operation until 1989, and replace it with a transparent, decentralised system of income transfers which is able to cope with the exigencies of a market economy.

Since 1990 reforms have aimed at constructing a social policy system based on three components: social insurance, state social support and social assistance. These were conceived as three Roman pillars, as separate but part of the same integrated whole, reinforcing each other to offer incentives, social protection and a guaranteed safety net. However, in the late 1990s the Czech Republic finds itself in the midst of rapidly deregulating world markets, and its social security system is accordingly giving way to a much slimmed down version of social policy resulting from the cost cutting exercises which began under the Czech government of the Civic Democratic Party of 1992 and continued under the present coalition government (Civic Democratic Party – Social Democratic Party) which was elected in 1996.

Many European models of social insurance have come about within a long history of market led concerns, and economic parameters are visibly influencing current welfare strategies and reforms in many countries.   The latter applies to the Czech Republic as well.   However, as a society in transition, questions of social insurance arise from a different vantage point, and it remains to be seen how far current economic criteria can be reconciled with meeting social needs.

One of the concerns of Czech policy planners is how far their social security system is compatible with the rest of Europe for reasons of accession to the EU.   However, of equal importance is the question to what extent it can meet early promises of creating a system based on principles of fairness, justice and equity.   It is not a small task to be 'European', to face new pressures of cost effectiveness and at the same time to turn around a history of forty years of communism which has produced a welfare system based on false egalitarianism.

This chapter will begin with a brief discussion of the context of social reform in the 1990s, followed by a description of the current social insurance system and the ways in which it relates to the other two aspects of social security in the Czech Republic, ie, state social support and social assistance.   Finally, an assessment is made of the possible direction of social insurance in the light of relatively fragile economic and social structures brought about by the introduction of a Western style market economy.

Social security since 1990

Social security reforms which came into effect in January 1996 have to be considered against the backdrop of the political climate in what was then Czechoslovakia after the demise of the communist-led government at the end of 1989.   Initially, social policy legislation was conceptualised with an explicit reference to the social democratic past of the 1920s, characterised by progressive social insurance legislation under the first independent Czechoslovak government of T.G. Masaryk.   Thus, reforms of the early 1990s emphasised principles of social justice, social solidarity and the guarantee of a minimum wage.   As an accompaniment to economic reform, they were regarded as a means to smooth the transition towards a fully fledged market economy (Zizkova,

1996). Hence, new social policies came about as part of a set of socioeconomic reforms which consciously addressed labour market issues such as unemployment, social differentiation and other macro social issues.

Early schemes were comparatively generous, such as unemployment benefit, which was payable for a period of 12 months (but was later reduced to 6 – see below). Gradually however, a more cautious and cost conscious approach gained ground and became dominant after the election in 1992, which was won by the conservative Social Democratic Party, led by Vaclav Klaus who had been Minister of Finance within the ruling Civic Forum. Benefit levels were reduced and some of the allowances under the state social support scheme became means tested in 1996 (see below). However, even at the height of Klaus's drive for what was referred to as 'demonopolising' welfare, ie, taking social policy programmes out of state control and cutting down social expenditure, no measures were taken that left any social group entirely without social security entitlement. Indeed, the neoliberal rhetoric regarding economic policy has never been matched by overt neoliberal policy making in social policy (Castle-Kanerova, 1996a). For example, during the period of price liberalisation between 1992 and 1994, a special top-up benefit was introduced to compensate pensioners and families with children for price rises (Zizkova, 1994).

The current social security system is based on a clearly defined 'social minimum' as the safety net or guarantee, which is legally codified and embodied in the 1991 Minimum Subsistence Amount Act, since amended. It stipulates the calculation of benefit levels within the state social support system based on a basket of goods necessary for subsistence (see below).

The introduction of a right to a social minimum firmly established an official poverty line below which no one should fall. It also provided a unique opportunity to introduce a package of reforms as part of a dramatic shift from one socioeconomic system to another. Since poverty had not been regarded as a social problem or concern prior to 1989, social policy planners in the early 1990s did not see themselves as having to devise programmes to deal with poverty in a direct way. Instead, their main concern was to design a system that could prevent the emergence of poverty on a large scale. This policy context is important to note, particularly with regard to the intermeshing of the three pillars of social security in the Czech Republic system and the somewhat ideological connotations of pledges of social justice and social solidarity.

In order to comprehend fully the role of any one of its components, such as social insurance, it is important to consider the three elements of the social security system as a whole. Social insurance was to be run as a separate system of protection for those who are able to contribute based on employment. However, as will be demonstrated below, the state still plays a large role in the system as far as control over finance, coverage and legislation is concerned. This has been criticised by some Czech commentators. They consider social insurance to be more akin to aspects of Czech-style state social security of the past, rather than a system governed and characterised by social insurance principles common in many countries (eg, separate contribution funding, management by social partners and only limited political influence by the state).

Social protection in the Czech Republic

In 1994, social spending as a whole was equivalent to 21.5% of GDP (Friedrich et al, 1996, p 26). The largest proportion went on pensions (8.5%) followed by healthcare (7.8%); social assistance absorbed only 1.1% and employment policy (including unemployment benefits) 0.2%. According to trade union sources, the overall level of expenditure dropped to 21.1% of GDP in 1996 (Fassmann, 1996, p 5). This relatively low level of expenditure has to be considered within the context of low unemployment. In 1996 the registered unemployment rate was 3.2% (Socialni Politika, 1996, p 17). However, it should be noted that there is a public debate about the validity of some official statistics.

The overhaul of the social security system, finalised in the reform package of January 1996, rests on the complementarity of its three components: social insurance, state social support and social assistance. At least on paper, there was to be a clear demarcation between these three in terms of finance and adminis-tration. According to government sources, insurance represents a delayed consumption needed for future eventualities (Vodicka, 1996). Covering pensions, sickness and unemployment, social insurance was to be a system based on earmarked social insurance contributions, to be paid into a fund separate from state finances and control. By contrast, state social support was to provide a tax-funded guaranteed social minimum for all citizens based on a variety of universal and means tested benefits. Both social insurance and state social support were to be governed by the principle of solidarity, which was portrayed as an integral part of the then Czechoslovak way towards democracy, as expressed in the first set of social legislation in 1990 (Zeniskova, 1995).

The social assistance component was, and still is, the least developed of the three pillars. It was designed for those who are not, or not adequately, catered for by social insurance and state social support. Within the context of preventing poverty, it deals with residual welfare at a local level and includes cash benefits, social services and counselling. In principle, there is a clear division of roles between the central and local administration. While the state confers social rights to certain minimum standards on all citizens, local authorities are legally obliged to actually provide those minima regarding income, shelter, food and basic clothing for those in need.

In practice, the division of responsibilities is less clear, and the separation between insurance, support and local assistance is often blurred. For example, until 1996 pension funds had been incorporated directly into the state budget. A separate account has since been established (Czech Social Security, 1995, p 27). However, it can be argued that social insurance funds are still firmly controlled by the state, a fact that has been widely criticised. What is more, the existence of fairly low benefit ceilings in both sickness and pension insurance led to the accusation of a 'levelling tendency' which, while favouring lower earners, has created resentment on the part of higher income groups.

Social insurance

What follows is a brief description of the three social insurance branches: pensions, sickness and employment insurance. Contributions to all three of these schemes are mandatory for those in work, with the exception of sickness insurance which is optional for the self-employed. Contribution rates by employers, employees and the level of tax subsidies are laid down by law (Zeniskova, 1995). The Czech Office for Social Security with its

85 regional centres is responsible for the administration of pensions and sickness benefits. The Office is subordinated to the Ministry of Labour and Social Affairs.

Pension insurance

The 1995 Pension Insurance Act, which became effective in January 1996, is the legal framework for mandatory pension insurance covering old age pensions, full and partial disability pensions, widows' and widowers' pensions and orphans' pensions (Czech Social Security, 1995, p 12). The pensionable age is currently being raised: by two months per year for men until it reaches 62 by the year 2006, and by four months per year for women until it reaches 61 in the same year; however, depending on the number of children raised, the pensionable age can be as low as 57 (Czech Social Security, 1995).

The combined contribution rate to pension insurance was 26% of employees' wages in 1996, with 19.5% paid by the employer and 6.5% by the employee. Entitlement to an old age pension is conditional on a minimum of 25 insured years at retirement age, or 15 years for those who have reached the age of 65 (Czech Social Security, 1995, p 13). The level of individual pensions is based on two elements: a basic assessment element (fixed amount) and a personal assessment element. The basic assessment of all types of pension was 920 Czech crowns per month in 1996. By comparison, the average monthly wage in 1996 was about 8,000 Czech crowns, which, based on currency exchange rates, was equivalent to about £200. The personal assessment element is equivalent to 1.5% of annual earnings during insured employment, with a maximum benefit ceiling of 5,000 Czech crowns per month.

The new pension system has replaced the previous state old age pension system which included a guaranteed minimum 'social pension'. However, as mentioned above, a pension is still payable for those with at least 15 years' insured employment by the time they reach the age of 65, and there are other exceptional qualifying criteria for those who fail to meet this condition (see Czech Social Security, 1995, p 122). Only those without any entitlement to an insurance pension will have to resort to social assistance. However, the Ministry of Labour and Social Affairs denies that destitution among old age pensioners is a problem because of the indexing of pension levels. Each time the cost of living rises by 10% (5% since April 1996), the value of pensions is adjusted accordingly. In the words of a government minister, "even a low pension which is the only source of income is higher today than the social minimum" (Vodicka, 1996, p 2).

However, the value of average pensions declined from 64.9% of net income in 1990 to 56.2% in 1996. While this level is generally expected to decrease further, the government has recently promised that it will not decline below 45% (Friedrich et al, 1996, p 15). Trade unions have pointed out that, as a share of gross income, average pensions already stood at 43.8% in 1996 and can be expected to decline to 35% by the year 2005.

Other types of pension are covered by the pension insurance scheme, such as invalidity pensions, widows' (and widowers') pensions and orphans' pension (for details, see Friedrich et al, 1996). A full invalidity pension can be claimed if a person's work capacity has been reduced by at least 66%, or if a person is capable of performing gainful activity only under special conditions. It is the employer's responsibility to insure employees against occupational injuries with one of currently three private commercial insurance companies (Friedrich et al, 1996, p 8).

Recently there has been a tendency to encourage people to take up supplementary private pensions. Such an option has existed since February 1994, and at present there are 44 private supplementary pension funds which cover 10% of the population (Friedrich et al, 1996, p 12). These are joint stock companies which have been granted a licence by the Ministry of Labour and Social Affairs.

Unlike in many industrialised countries, the 'ageing' of Czech society is not regarded as a major problem in the medium term. In fact, the share of the so-called 'post-productive' population (those over and above retirement age) in relation to the 'productive' population actually declined from 36.2% in 1995 to 32.7% in 1996, and a return to 1995 figures will not be reached until the year 2012 (Fassmann, 1996, p 6). This is partly explicable by the change in the pensionable age.

Instead of demographic change, the most debated issue regarding pensions is the effect of the so-called 'solidaristic principle' within the mandatory pension insurance scheme, which has been widely criticised as a remnant of the previous communist era of imposed egalitarianism. Because of a benefit ceiling, the replacement rate of old age pensions for lower and average earners is currently about 50% of previous income. However, for higher earners this rate is much lower, falling to 22% for those with 2.8 times average earnings (Ministry of Labour and Social Affairs, 1996). A similar so-called 'levelling down effect' is visible for sickness benefits (see below). What is more, pensions that are at least 2.5 times higher than average are liable to taxation.

Sickness insurance

The mandatory sickness insurance scheme is funded by contributions from employers (3.3% of employees' earnings) and employees (1.1%). It covers sickness benefit, short-term benefit for those who care for a family member, income support during pregnancy and maternity, and maternity benefit. Current legislation is still based on the amended 1956 Employees' Sickness Insurance Act (Czech Social Security, 1995, p 10). Sickness benefit is payable for a maximum period of one year. Up to a certain ceiling, benefit levels are related to earnings, representing 50% of average income for the first three days and 69% thereafter. However, because of the benefit ceiling of 270 Czech crowns per day, actual replacement rates are lower for many claimants. Thus, as with old age pensions, the existence of a benefit ceiling produces the so-called 'levelling tendency' between higher and lower earners. While the replacement rate for employees on average earnings can reach 78% of gross monthly wages, it declines to 32% for an income that is 2.8 times higher than the national average (Ministry of Labour and Social Affairs, 1996).

Sickness insurance also entitles employees to short-term benefits in order to care for a sick family member living in the same household. This covers not only spouses, including common law spouses, and dependent children, but also others whose subsistence might be dependent on the insured employee, such as school-aged grandchildren, siblings, parents, grandparents and parents-in-law and other groups (Czech Social Security, 1995, pp 86-7). Benefits are available for nine calendar days only, and 16 days for employees who are single (Czech Social Security, 1995, p 11). Maternity benefits entitle female employees to a paid maternity leave of 28 weeks at 69% of the daily wage (up to a ceiling), and 37 weeks for single mothers and in the case of multiple births (Czech Social Security, 1995, p 11; Friedrich et al, 1996, p 18). There are additional types of benefit in relation to raising and caring for children within the context of state social support (see below).

In January 1994, sickness insurance became optional for the self-employed, who, for purposes of social insurance membership, must define their income which has to be equivalent at least to 35% of the difference between profits and costs (Zeniskova, 1995).

Employment insurance

Employers pay 3.6%, and employees 0.4%, of their wages into a mandatory employment insurance scheme which provides unemployment benefits and also functions as a funding mechanism for active employment policy and for meeting the cost of maintaining labour exchanges (Zeniskova, 1995).

There are about five million employees contributing towards employment insurance, which means that, according to trade union sources, the present level of contributions would be sufficient to meet the costs of unemployment of up to 7% of the labour force (Fassmann, 1996, p 5). The level of unemployment benefit is equivalent to 60% of average monthly wages for the first three months, and 50% for another three months, after which entitlement ends (Friedrich et al, 1996, p 20). Also, there is a maximum benefit ceiling of 3,990 Czech crowns, equivalent to 1.5 times the social minimum, rising to 1.7 times for those taking part in a retraining course (Friedrich et al, 1996, p 20). Benefit entitlement is conditional upon 12 months' employment within the previous three years prior to becoming unemployed.

Although the unemployment rate of 3.2% in 1996 was one of the lowest in Europe, there are indications that both long-term unemployment and youth unemployment are becoming more prevalent. Available data suggest that the share of long-term unemployment has risen from 14.8% in 1993 to 23.7% at the end of 1994. Youth unemployment in 1994 stood at about 30% of total unemployment (Friedrich et al, 1996, p 19). Also, regional variations of official unemployment rates ranged from below 0.5% in Prague to 7.6% in industrial towns of the north-west (Friedrich et al, 1996, p 19). Inevitably, this has a bearing on local authorities' finances, since social assistance, payable once unemployment insurance benefits have been exhausted, are funded at the local level. What is more, there is a low level of assistance benefit take-up (estimated to be 50% in 1993) by those who have run out of insurance cover. This is partly due to the role of the informal economy and the reluctance to register with labour exchanges and seek means tested assistance, which requires a declaration of all personal earnings and assets.

Health insurance

The health reform which came into effect in 1991 was one of the most radical changes in social welfare. It implemented a general health insurance system which differs from the social insurance schemes discussed above in the sense that it is clearly separate from and independent of the state budget. It is administered by, in total, 16 health insurance companies (Friedrich et al, 1996, p 23). The provision of healthcare services, including pharmacies, has been virtually privatised, except for large teaching hospitals. However, health insurance is mandatory and insurance companies are answerable to the Ministry of Health. What is more, the government sets contribution rates while insurance companies administer and manage funds.

Doctors are paid by insurance companies according to a system of performance categories and indicators. The replacement of the Minister of Health in 1995 and strikes by doctors in the same year indicated problems within the system, which was criticised as too expensive and inefficient owing to the lack of competition. One single insurance company, the General Health Insurance, covers about 75% of the population (Friedrich et al, 1996, p 35).

There is a current debate in parliament as to whether a more universal system of health insurance for all primary healthcare needs should be introduced alongside a second tier for non-primary healthcare needs, following the so-called Singapore model (Friedrich et al, 1996, p 35). Health insurance has been mandatory since 1993 for everyone with permanent residence in the country. Contribution rates in 1996 were 9% for employers and 4.5% for employees (Czech Social Security, 1995, p 25).

All insured persons have a right to choose their health insurance company, and the right to choose their doctor, or any other healthcare specialist or healthcare facility. Insurance covers all diagnostic inpatient and outpatient care, including rehabilitation and care for the chronically ill, transportation costs and reimbursement of travel expenses to the nearest healthcare centre, as well as special therapeutic care deemed necessary as part of a cure (Czech

Social Security, 1995, p 270). Legislation stipulates that the state pays premiums on behalf of a number of social groups, such as dependent children, pensioners who retired before January 1993, recipients of parental allowances, women on maternity leave, the unemployed, those on short-term contracts, recipients of social assistance, some categories of carers and some other groups (see Czech Social Security, 1995, pp 276-7).

Overall, this implies that for about half of the population it is the state that actually meets the cost of healthcare (Friedrich et al, 1996, p 24). There is also another type of interpersonal redistribution. In order to compensate for the costs of catering for people with different needs, insurance companies are obliged to pool 60% of their revenue from premiums into a common fund which compensates those funds that, for example, have a high proportion of older members. Health care costs for those over the age of 60 have been estimated to be about three times as high as average costs.

State social support

State social support is entirely tax financed. An agreement on the scheme was finally reached in 1995 which allowed parliament to pass the State Social Support Act, after a compromise had been found between parties which introduced means testing for four out of the nine types of benefit available under the scheme. Targeted mainly at families, the main aim of state social support is to top up insufficient income. Benefits are administered by 460 regional contact offices, which represent a newly established tier of the state administration at local level (Friedrich et al, 1996, p 7).

The four means tested benefits are child allowance, social allowance, housing allowance and transportation allowance. There are three rates for child allowances. Families with an income below 110% of the official social minimum are entitled to an increased allowance. The basic rate goes to families with an income below 180% of the social minimum and the reduced rate to families with an income not exceeding three times the minimum income.

A person caring for at least one dependent child is entitled to a social allowance provided the family income does not exceed 160% of the social minimum (Czech Social Security, 1995).

Housing allowance is payable to families with permanent residence whose total income is below 140% of the social minimum, and transportation allowance covers part of the expenses for travelling to a school outside a child's town of permanent residence (Czech Social Security, 1995, pp 20-1).

The non-means tested benefits within the scheme are parental allowance, maintenance allowance, foster care allowance, maternity grant and funeral grant (Czech Social Security, 1995, pp 206-7). In principle, there is a provision that allows either parent to receive a parental allowance for staying at home and taking care of a child under the age of four (Friedrich et al, 1996, p 18). In all types of legislative documentation however, this provision is referred to in relation to mothers only, and there is little evidence of any actual take-up by fathers. If a child suffers a long-term illness, entitlement can be extended up to seven years on condition that the parent does not claim sickness benefit and is not working for more than two hours a day (Friedrich et al, 1996, p 22). This provision dates back to the original social security reforms of 1990, when it was conceptualised as one way of preventing, or at least delaying, a rise in official unemployment. However, there is some uncertainty as to the interpretation of this provision. While claimants might receive the allowance normally for up to four years, employers are obliged to keep jobs open only for three years under the current Labour Law.

A care allowance and a lump sum are granted to foster parents who care for a child. Foster parents with at least four children in their care are also paid a grant of up to 70% of the purchase of a car (with a ceiling of 100,000 Czech crowns). Maternity grants are paid as a lump sum, calculated according to the number of children born. Funeral grants are another flat-rate universal benefit (Czech Social Security, 1995, pp 21-2).

Social assistance

While social insurance is geared primarily towards those in employment, state social support provides supplementary protection targeted mainly at families. However, there are groups of people, and particular needs, that are not catered for in either scheme. For those there is social assistance, which is very much a residual scheme, or last safety net. In principle and in law, the scheme deals with problems of poverty and destitution. It is financed through government grants to local authorities who are responsible for the assessment of need, the payment of assistance benefits, the provision of existential minima (such as shelter, food and clothing) and the provision of statutory social services. On a discretionary basis, and funded out of local budgets, local authorities can provide additional services which are deemed to be in demand in a particular locality (Castle-Kanerova, 1996a).

In principle, then, social assistance is supposed to prevent destitution through the payment of benefits in cash or in kind for all residents in a locality. However, in practice there are difficulties. On the one hand, the financial as well as administrative separation between central and local government is not yet fully complete and some claim that their respective roles have so far remained indistinguishable (Friedrich et al, 1996, p 36). Second, professional social workers who are in principle responsible for the assessment of needs at local level have not yet been fully prepared for this function.

Currently, about 5.5% of the population qualify for social assistance, but an estimated 15%-16% live just above the poverty threshold (Ministry of Labour and Social Affairs, 1996). However, local authorities are neither prepared nor sufficiently organised to cope with the potential demand, and there is no legislation that could ensure uniform standards across regions. Compounding the problem is the lack of legislation dealing with the non-payment of local taxation or rent for what is still largely local authority housing, depriving local authorities from revenue or tempting them to adopt measures that are not sanctioned by law (Castle-Kanerova, 1996a). In this situation, it is the voluntary sector and charities that are heavily relied upon for local support and services, while the debate about the meaning of citizenship, social rights and equity continues without a resolution of the problem of poverty, which has been 'dumped at local authorities' doorsteps'.

What future for social insurance?

Seven years after the political and economic changes towards a full-scale marketisation, there are no visible signs of public disillusionment with the political system in the Czech Republic, no large scale poverty or problems of foreign debt. In that sense, the transition of Czech society has to be regarded as successful. However, within a context of a prospering economy, it has to be remembered that social protection schemes have not yet been properly tested. Pockets of high unemployment, low average wages and other signs of social and economic differentiation have so far been dwarfed by macro indicators such as high annual economic growth rates and low levels of official unemployment. The social security system has not had to cater for large numbers of homeless or long-term unemployed people, and there is little pressure for change since costs have remained relatively modest owing to low unemployment, and also because of imposed wage controls which were in place until 1995. As a consequence, for the moment at least, social security can be characterised as a fairly stable, centrally managed system. The question is how long this stability will last.

Opposition parties and trade unions are warning of a possible collapse of the 'economic miracle', and of a steep rise in unemployment once the privatisation of all old industries has been completed (Hirsl et al, 1995). The likelihood of such a scenario is hard to predict. However, an assessment of the social security system has to question how far the three pillars of social security will be able to legitimise economic and social change.

Concepts such as social exclusion and marginalisation have not entered the social policy vocabulary, or even been sufficiently conceptualised within the Czech context. That does not mean that processes of social marginalisation do not exist; it merely illustrates the current social security system as concentrating on a neat, 'pre-packaged' set of needs which does not reflect the increasing pluralisation of society. While the social protection of some groups, such as pensioners, the unemployed and families, has been relatively successful, the needs of others who might fall through the net of social insurance and state social support have been neglected. The discrimination against the Romany population, who do not qualify for social security benefits because of unresolved issues of citizenship and nationality, is one such example of social marginalisation which has yet to be addressed by social policy. Another, more indirect, example is the nuclear family, with the husband as the chief earner, as the dominant normative orientation in social policy formulation.

If meeting needs and expectations is a key to the legitimacy and stability of a social security system, then the introduction of the social insurance scheme in 1996 has to be questioned with regard to the impact of the benefit ceiling, promoting the so-called 'solidaristic principle' in pensions and sickness insurance at the expense of a higher degree of life cycle redistribution according to the principle of status maintenance. In other words, higher income groups have been asked to subsidise a system with an inbuilt 'levelling tendency', as was discussed earlier. This has led to resentment among the aspiring middle classes and has also triggered criticism of neopaternalism and accusations of embezzlement of pension funds by the state (Konopasek, 1995).

The conflict between the 'solidaristic principle' and the principle of status maintenance, which is common in social insurance schemes of other countries such as Germany or France, exemplifies a crucial problem within Czech social insurance and social security as a whole. As a consequence of economic liberalisation, the country has opened up to new forms of social differentiation. However, the social security system appears to be operating on the premise of a homogenised society rather than embracing social differentiation and providing incentives, and thus positively including the new middle classes and high earners, which are found mainly in the private formal and also the informal economies. This issue has not yet become a central concern, but it highlights a crucial question regarding the future of a society that has so far remained relatively homogeneous as far as living standards are concerned, characterised by a relatively small proportion of the population with incomes below the official poverty line, a relatively large proportion (about 60%) with incomes below the national average, and a relatively small proportion of rich people (Fassmann, 1994, p 9).

There is also the wider question of the relationship between social security and citizenship. Some of the governmental documentation implies that, among other things, the social security system aims at promoting the notion of citizenship by, for example, appealing to people not to claim benefits when it is not warranted by their financial situation (Castle-Kanerova, 1996a). On the other hand, citizenship in the new democracies of Eastern Europe has been associated with a process of individualisation and the breaking of old ties of imposed communitarianism. Although public debates on such topics have so far been rare, these and other apparent contradictions will take a long time to resolve.

Overall, the current Czech situation has been likened to what Pick (1996) calls an 'Asiatic model' of fast economic growth based on domestic demand and short-term consumerist trends, rather than long-term economic investment (Pick, 1996, p 11; Hirsl et al, 1995, p 11).   Economic concerns are dominant and the new socioeconomic balance between productivity, profitability and social cohesion is still very vulnerable.   However, some form of desegregation between social policy and economic policy has occurred since 1994, with social policy issues gaining greater prominence.

Several anomalies within the present system of social security have been noted and are widely criticised.   For example, the introduction of a means test for the receipt of child allowances has hardly altered the pattern of overall takeup.   Only 5% of families do not qualify for the allowance because of their income (Friedrich et al, 1996, p 22), putting into question both the purpose and the cost of means testing child allowances.   Another anomaly regarding the explicitly strong pro-family orientation in social policy has been underlined by evidence that families with children are becoming worse off compared with childless families (Hirsl, 1994, p 7).   What is more, a study conducted in the region of Olomouc (north-east Bohemia) demonstrated that the introduction of means testing for family benefits pushed people further into, rather than away from, participation in the informal economy (Janyska, 1996, p 8).

Further criticism can be made regarding the adherence to the traditional view of the family as the normative orientation for social policy.   Unlike in other post-communist societies such as in the former GDR, female labour force participation has remained very high in the Czech Republic and about 45% of all jobs are taken up by women.   However, one characteristic of the social and economic transition of the Czech Republic is the lack of debate on gender issues which have clearly not been included in the new social reforms; for example, there is no regulation that would prevent companies from advertising new, especially managerial and high paid, jobs for male applicants only (Castle-Kanerova, 1996b).

In conclusion, the previous 'socialist' Labour Law model which guaranteed work, income and social protection for everyone is now seen as outdated, and further labour market deregulations are under review. Meanwhile, the Czech social security system in general, and its social insurance scheme in particular, have not yet been fully tested. Reforms have evolved within the context of deinstitutionalising the former state social protection. As such, social insurance has achieved limited success but, as discussed, reforms have also led to criticism, not least regarding the so-called 'levelling tendency' within pension and sickness insurance. New issues and problems will undoubtedly arise within the move towards a fully developed market economy. The question of the future role for social insurance has not come up for discussion yet but will need to be addressed within a country striving to strike a balance between democracy and the market.

twelve

Social insurance in Europe – adapting to change?

Angus Erskine and Jochen Clasen

Introduction

The chapters in this book have demonstrated the, at times confusing, complexity and diversity of national social insurance arrangements and their interface with universal benefits, social assistance as well as voluntary private insurance schemes. Some schemes provide benefits in kind (eg, healthcare, long-term care) but the bulk of social insurance programmes is geared towards providing an income for people out of work.

However, social insurance is not a simple discrete part of the income package of those who do not have an income from paid employment. It is one of the ways in which income is replaced when risks such as unemployment, old age, sickness or disability reduce earnings from paid employment. Reading about the specificity of social insurance schemes in different countries may lead the reader to ask, what do they have in common? In Germany we see a fairly resilient social insurance system; in Portugal, Hungary, Greece and the Czech Republic we see new social insurance schemes; in Britain, insurance is being subsumed into general social protection; in Sweden and Denmark insurance against unemployment is voluntary; in France cost cutting measures have resulted in more state involvement; while in Switzerland the institutional structure of the political system has influenced the contraction of some elements of social insurance and the expansion of others. In each country, social insurance schemes are organised under different administrative, fiscal and legal arrangements which have their roots in historical developments. In some countries, (eg, Greece and France) social insurance is highly fragmented, with a large number of insurance organisations covering different sectors of the workforce. In others, such as Britain, there is one system of social insurance run by the national government. These variations result in a wide diversity in coverage and organisation of social insurance.

However, the chapters in this volume illustrate that there are five common characteristics shared across countries which distinguish social insurance from other forms of social protection.

First, unlike private insurance, one of the fundamental characteristics of social insurance is a pooling of risks without differentiating contributions according to exposure to risk (despite rare exceptions such as Swiss health insurance premiums, which, until 1994, varied according to age and gender). Generally, social insurance contributions do not distinguish between those who might be more exposed to a particular type of risk and those who are less exposed. Therefore someone in an insecure job will be covered through social insurance with contributions calculated on the same basis as someone in secure employment; a person with a chronic health condition will be covered on the same terms as a healthy person. Of course, the pooling of risk in social insurance schemes is more pronounced where there is less fragmentation within the system. In general, however, social insurance promotes solidarity between poor risks and good risks.

The second common feature is the involvement of the state in social insurance arrangements, the form of which varies and the extent of which differs from country to country. In all cases however the state is involved in establishing minimum standards for contributions and benefits and in the regulation of social insurance schemes.

Third, social insurance schemes are distinct from other income maintenance arrangements in that they are conditional upon contributions. Social insurance may contain categorical conditions (eg, that to benefit a contributor must be in a particular category), but membership is defined by contribution, although in many schemes these contributions may be notional, as in the case of credited contributions for carers or students.

Fourth, notwithstanding rare exceptions such as unemployment insurance in Denmark and Sweden, social insurance schemes are generally of a compulsory nature for the majority of wage earners, which enhances their redistributive impact.

Finally, the risks or contingencies which social insurance typically covers, such as old age, ill health, occupational injuries and unemployment, are generally those associated with wage labour. Many countries require their inhabitants to hold insurance against other risks (eg, motor car insurance) but these forms of insurance are not part of any social insurance scheme.

In addition to these core characteristics (the pooling of risks without differentiating between contribution rates; state involvement; contribution conditions; compulsory nature and the coverage of labour market risks), social insurance schemes tend to have two other common features. First, contributions for statutory minimum coverage tend not to be determined by the extent of coverage provided, but are either flat-rate (the same for all contributors) or related to the income of contributors up to a ceiling. In most countries some benefits, such as pensions, may have a second complementary contribution which enhances the basic minimum provision. However, the extent of coverage is usually not determined by contributors choosing to make enhanced contributions to increase their benefits, but is based upon statutory requirements. Second, social insurance schemes contain a tension between what might be called the 'solidarity principle' on the one hand, which is enforced through the pooling of risks, as well as undifferentiated and credited contributions, and the principle of status maintenance on the other, through providing higher benefits to those who have contributed more and have thus protected their relative living standards when exposed to risk. This tension, which will be returned to below, appears to be at the heart of the question as to whether social insurance will survive as a major form of social protection in Europe.

Social insurance: historical function and current challenges

While social insurance arrangements in European states and the administrative structure of schemes vary, cross-national similarities have to be viewed against the backdrop of a common historical legacy which has led governments to provide some form of social insurance for wage earners and their dependants. Schemes to cover the risk of income loss associated with ill health, industrial disability, retirement or unemployment have arisen across Western Europe over the past one hundred years. While the rate of development and the nature of the intervention were not synchronous between countries, and the immediate political forces that led to the introduction of social insurance arrangements differed, the underlying common factor seems to have been the need to develop forms of protection against the risk of loss of income associated with industrial wage labour in market economies.

The roots of social insurance in a particular standard industrial employment relationship can be illustrated with reference to historical developments. When social insurance was introduced in Britain in 1913, for example, unemployment insurance cover was limited to certain industrial sectors – those most likely to experience fluctuations in trade within the context of overall consistent patterns of employment (Gilbert, 1966). Other groups, such as domestic servants, were excluded. In other countries, it was not until after social insurance schemes had been established for industrial workers that agricultural workers, especially in those countries where agricultural production was organised on the basis of small farms, were included within compulsory social insurance. The chapters on Hungary, Portugal and Greece in this volume confirm the 'path dependency' of this development.

However, more than a hundred years after the implementation of early programmes, changes in the socioeconomic context within which social insurance schemes operate have led to questions as to the appropriateness of the model of social insurance as an effective type of social protection. While some of these changes have already been identified in the introductory chapter, three aspects seem to be most important in this respect: labour market changes, changes in family formation and social relations, and the salience of new types of risk.

Wage labour in market economies creates a dependence on the part of the employee upon a sole income type. This must maintain living standards, or at least the minimum standard necessary to ensure that the basic needs of workers, and also their dependants, are met. While the risk of loss of income itself is the product of social and economic arrangements, because of the way the burden falls, it is possible to provide insurance for individuals and their families financed in part by their own contributions and partly by contributions from employers and, in certain instances, the state.

Under Fordist methods of production, with fairly standardised employment arrangements across the workforce and where, with relatively full, male employment for industrial workers, interruptions in earnings are either predictable (as in retirement) or short term (as with periods of unemployment) or where the risks are haphazard, albeit concentrated upon certain groups of workers (as in the case of industrial injury), social insurance against these risks contributes to solidarity among employees and to a redistribution of income over the life cycle of any individual worker.

However, current trends in European labour markets may indicate that the form of employment for which social insurance was designed will decrease in importance in the future. Levels of employment are falling and unemployment is high. At the same time, the new jobs that are being created are increasingly part-time and temporary. In addition, employment is shifting away from agriculture and industry towards the service sector (European Commission, 1996). The significance for social insurance of these trends lies in the way in which the risks of loss of income from employment is being redistributed among the working population and the consequent patterns of income loss among those who are concentrated in part-time or low paid employment. Those in more marginal labour market positions are more vulnerable to unemployment and, when unemployed, to long-term unemployment. Low levels of income in work result in low returns on earnings related pension provision.

Changes in the structure and nature of family relationships also call into question traditional social insurance responses to income loss (Lister, 1994; Webb, 1995). The increasing participation of women in the labour market and the consequent growth of two-earner households provides an alternative form of protection against the risk of the loss of one income leading to the household's inability to meet basic needs or protect itself against income loss through intra-household transfers. Whether the male breadwinner model (Lewis, 1992; Land, 1994) of social insurance was ever an appropriate model to ensure the protection of the dependants of insured men, particularly against the risk of separation from, or death of, their partner is questionable. With changing family structures, married women's participation in the labour market and emerging new family forms, the traditional model of insurance has to, at the least, adapt. On the separation of a couple, dividing pension rights in particular is problematic where entitlement is based upon the contributions of a single wage earner. Similarly, the allocation of family benefits where care may be a joint responsibility between two families is difficult if benefits are derived from entitlement based upon the contributions of one wage earner.

If social insurance is to adapt to these social changes, there must be an introduction of elements which extend entitlement to benefits to individuals neither on the basis of their contribution record nor on that of their direct dependence upon a contributor. As referred to earlier, this is an issue that is crucial to the continuance of social insurance as a major form of social protection but also an area of increasing tension, leading to possible growing resentment on the part of traditional contributors to social insurance (see below).

In addition to changes in labour markets and family structures, the prominence of types of risk other than those associated with wage labour call into question social insurance as a form of social protection. These more general risks include crime, environmental pollution, terrorism, food scares and death from AIDS. Generating social insecurity, they may have replaced, in the minds of some social groups, the central place that was previously occupied by interruption in earnings. Amongst better paid employees, private insurance and savings plans present the possibility of a private and personal response to loss of income, whereas the new forms of social insecurity grow in prominence and generate demands for action to produce social protection and prevention measures. These new risks are ones that fall across society and against which social insurance providing for the replacement of lost income cannot protect (Beck, 1992). The development of policies to prevent, and provide protection against, some of these new global forms of risk has become the central concern of the radical politics of ecological movements. These movements also argue for new forms of provision for income security through a basic income (see Chapters four and seven, for example). On the right, a concern about some of these new risks (eg, crime and terrorism) has become a central part of their political platform along with arguments for individual market responses to income insecurity through savings and private insurance.

Challenges and policy responses in social insurance

Changes in family structures and in European labour markets are taking place at a time when, in many countries, the role of the state in the provision of welfare services is being called into question both economically and politically. Thus, contributions to this book demonstrate that, rather than attempts to incorporate new types of risk, or to adapt social insurance programmes so that changing family formations and the growth of non-standard types of employment can be accommodated, governments are primarily concerned with other issues – foremost with the level of expenditure on social insurance.

Deteriorating economic conditions and high unemployment are undermining the funding of social insurance schemes based on pay-as-you-go principles and have led many countries to introduce cost cutting measures in order to minimise or remove deficits (as in Greece or France) or to relieve pressures for raising social insurance contributions, perceived as imposing high additional costs to the wages bill. While the severity of demographic pressures differs between countries, a common policy pattern has been the reduction of public expenditure in the area of pension insurance through the increase of statutory retirement ages and the introduction of stricter qualifying criteria for early retirement. Pressure on healthcare costs resulting from rising demand at a time of increasingly expensive treatment and an ageing population is another area that has led many countries (eg, France, Switzerland, Germany) to introduce similar changes. These have included increasing competition between health insurance funds, widening the scope for private provision and raising charges and fees for medical care and provision in order to contain costs.

In addition to the restricted scope for expanding or strengthening of social insurance schemes owing to economic and labour market pressures, different governments are confronted with two types of real, or self-imposed, external constraints arising from European social and economic integration. Coordinating social security provision and harmonising social protection, provided for within the Treaty of Rome, has not been a priority for European Community policy making (Hantrais, 1995; Spicker, 1993). The limited nature of intercountry labour mobility within Europe up to now and the predominant pattern of migration – from areas of poor social protection to areas with better social protection – has meant that the lack of harmonised systems has not been a significant brake on economic integration. However, the more recent emphasis on social cohesion, which has developed over the past decade within the European Union, may result in a new focus on issues of harmonisation and on questions about the appropriateness of current social insurance schemes in the member states of the EU.

There are two areas in which a European consideration of social insurance may become both necessary and significant. Pensions and other long-term insurance cash benefits may be relatively portable and so may not create any significant problem either for migrants moving from northern Europe to southern Europe or for the countries to which they move (Leibfried and Pierson, 1995). However, this pattern of migration may create problems in relation to the provision and funding of benefits in kind such as healthcare. Credited contributions to social insurance for periods of childcare or education may also lead to future inconsistencies in the treatment of migrants and their families. The issue is how far these credited contributions give rise to transportable benefits if those eligible for them subsequently migrate.

The second area in which the development of increasing European integration may impact upon social insurance arrangements is the move towards economic and monetary union. The freedom of financial services to trade across Europe may affect the future of social insurance schemes by imposing similar financial regulations and conditions particularly upon complementary insurance arrangements. Given the diversity of pension arrangements, movements in this direction would require European regulation of social as well as private provision. Whatever the course that European legislation takes, the globalisation of financial markets will have a common influence on long-term social insurance schemes. The role of the IMF in Hungary, the deregulation of markets in the Czech Republic and the overriding aim of meeting the convergence criteria for European Monetary Union, which looms large in most EU countries, all illustrate these pressures.

While the chapters in this volume demonstrate that there is a widespread perception that social insurance expenditure needs to be constrained and some of the policy measures bear broad similarities across countries, the actual course taken in many other areas depends upon particular national circumstances as well as institutional and political arrangements within which social insurance is embedded. In Hungary, for example, the difficulty of collecting social insurance contributions has to be understood in historical context. The persistence of occupational privileges inherent in the fragmented social insurance systems in Greece and Portugal is responsible for some mismatch between legislation and implementation and the failure to introduce more uniform social insurance principles and arrangements. What is more, the lack of self-control for social insurance funds in Greece has seriously undermined financial scope for manoeuvre. Blurred boundaries between state budgets and social insurance funds, or between supposedly contribution-funded and tax-funded social protection schemes, hinders a more stable and transparent development of social insurance in the Czech Republic and other countries.

At the time of writing, a move to a more pronounced and more clearly distinguished social insurance framework does not seem to be high on the policy agenda in any of the countries discussed in this book. On the contrary, even in countries with a more established tradition of social insurance such as France, the role of social insurance seems to be declining. Indeed, rather than expanding arrangements, social insurance across Europe seems to be in a process of contraction, or at least under strong pressure to contract. The introduction of the long-term care insurance scheme in Germany might suggest otherwise (see Götting et al, 1994) but it has to be remembered both that this is a country with a very strong history of a particular social insurance tradition, and that its implementation was decided upon before the latest economic recession which led to record unemployment levels.

On the other hand, the chapters in this volume suggest that there is no sign of an immediate abolition of social insurance programmes or serious threat to the continuation of social insurance principles. The exception is perhaps Britain, where a process of gradual erosion of the National Insurance scheme has received further impetus owing to recent policy changes, and where the general uncertainty and ambiguity about its role persists. Yet even here contributory benefits represent a significant part of social security spending. What is more, given the general assumption of a greater public acquiescence to raising insurance contributions rather than increasing direct taxation, the abolition of the National Insurance scheme might be considered as counterproductive in the light of its role as a device for revenue raising.

Unlike in Britain, social insurance programmes in most European countries are geared towards reproducing inequalities in the labour market through mechanisms that ensure horizontal rather than vertical income redistribution, or, in other words, promote 'status maintenance' rather than solidarity. The exact balance between these two principles depends on institutional arrangements including benefit formulae, contribution and benefit ceilings and the degree of contribution crediting. However, there is a tension between the conflicting objectives of status mainten-ance and solidarity. While the funding of 'insurance alien' elements within schemes and the crediting of contributions for non-workers may mitigate some of the exclusionary effects of social insurance based solely upon contributions from waged workers, the changes in the labour market that we have drawn attention to above have the potential to increase the exclusionary effects of social insurance unless strict contribution conditions are relaxed. Yet, the relaxing of contribution conditions can lead to a loss of political support for social insurance from those who are funding it through their actual contributions. The increasing concern with social exclusion as a social phenomenon is not restricted to the effect of social insurance, but social insurance can have an impact on tendencies towards exclusion. Two strategies seem to be being adopted to deal with this. On the one hand, there is the relaxing of contribution conditions and the making of entitlement depend upon social category. On the other hand, there is an emphasis being placed upon non-contributors being provided with an non-insurance based income with entitlement being on the basis of the recipient fulfilling certain obligations (such as RMI in France). The latter course involves a clearer separation between insurance and non-insurance based schemes and between the treatment of recipients of each form of support, while the former includes within social insurance those who would otherwise be excluded from benefit receipt.

However, while there are indications that social insurance is adapting to an extent (ie, through the creation of 'fictitious' contribution periods or more extensive contribution crediting for carers), it can be argued that this adaptation has been insufficient in the light of a growing number of people who are not, or are only partially, covered by social insurance programmes and thus increasingly resort to means tested programmes.   On the other hand, it can be argued that a social insurance programme which, in reference to the German terminology, comprises too large a scope of 'insurance alien' elements, ie, benefit entitlements to those who are credited with 'fictitious' contribution rights without having actually made monetary contributions, is in danger of losing legitimacy in the eyes of the actual contributors.   In other words, the dilemma, or tension, remains between defining contributions and thus benefit rights sufficiently widely, to an extent which would make social insurance more inclusive by bringing in those who are not in full-time, secure employment, and at the same time defining them narrow enough so as not to endanger the political stability and support for social insurance by 'net' contributors.

Stretching the propensity to subsidise a social insurance system too far might undermine the 'moral infrastructure' (Hinrichs, 1996) upon which social insurance ultimately rests and thus lead to resentment of middle income groups, as shown in the case of the Czech Republic in this volume.   Yet, if the involvement of middle and higher income earners is a crucial element which makes social rights based on social insurance principles more resilient to political retrenchment than social rights based on universal principles (Ganßmann, 1993b), the question is not merely how to devise a system of social protection that can adapt to new types of risk, family formation and labour market change, and thus maximise solidarity, but also how to devise a system that maximises social legitimacy.   In the light of the contributions in this book, it seems that such a system is more likely to be found within rather than beyond the boundaries of social insurance.

Bibliography

Abrahamson, P. and Hansen, F. K. (1996) *Poverty in the European Union*, Copenhagen: Centre for Alternative Social Analysis.

Adamik, M. (1990) 'Parenting policy at the end of the eighties in Hungary', Paper given at conference on parenting policy, University of Columbia, New York, May.

Adam Smith Institute (1989) *Needs reform: the overhaul of social security*, London: Adam Smith Institute.

Adamy, W. and Bäcker, G. (1993) 'Bedarfsorientierte Mindestsicherung für Arbeitslose', *Arbeit und Sozialpolitik*, vol 3, no 4, pp 41-8.

Ágh, A. (1989) 'The triangle model of society and beyond', in V. Gáthy (ed), *State and civil society*, Budapest: Institute of Sociology, Hungarian Academy of Sciences.

Alber, J. (1987) *Vom Armenhaus zum Wohlfahrtsstaat*, Frankfurt: Campus Verlag.

Alber, J. (1988) 'The West German welfare state in transition', in R. Morris (ed), *Testing the limits of social welfare*, Hanover: Brandeis University Press.

Alber, J. (1989) *Der Sozialstaat in der Bundesrepublik 1950-1983*, Frankfurt: Campus Verlag.

Alber, J. (1992) *Das Gesundheitswesen der Bundesrepublik Deutschland. Entwicklung, Struktur und Funktionsweise*, Frankfurt: Campus Verlag.

Albert, M. (1991) *Capitalisme contre capitalisme*, Paris: Seuil.

Alcock, P. (1992) 'Social insurance in crisis?' *Benefits*, vol 5, pp 6-9.

Alcock, P. (1996) 'The advantages and disadvantages of the contribution base in targeting benefits', *International Social Security Review*, vol 49, no 1, pp 31-50.

Amarel, J. Ferreira do (1996) 'Segurança social refém do crescimento do PIB', *O Público*, 17 May 1996.

Amitsis G. (1992) 'Social security in Greece', *Basic Income Group Bulletin*, no 1, pp 12-145.

Andersen, D. and Høgelund, J. (1995) 'Arbejdsgiveres betaling af dagpengegodtgørelse for 1 og 2 ledighedsdag' [Employers' payment of unemployment compensation during the 1st and 2nd day of unemployment], *Arbejdsnotat*, no 3, Copenhagen: Danish National Institute of Social Research.

Andersen, R. (1971) *Grundprincipper i socialpolitikken* [Basic principles in social policy], Albertslund: Det Danske Forlag.

André, I. M. (1996) 'At the centre on the periphery? Women in the Portuguese labour market', in M. D. García-Ramon and J. Monk (eds), *Women in the European Union*, London: Routledge.

Árvay, J, and Vértes, A. (1993) 'Research work on the assessment of the real performance of the private sector in Hungary', mimeo, Budapest.

Atkinson, A.B. (1991) 'A national minimum? A history of ambiguity in the determination of benefit scales in Britain' in T. Wilson and D. Wilson (eds), *The state and social welfare*, Harlow: Longman.

Atkinson, A.B. (1995) *Incomes and the welfare state*, Cambridge: Cambridge University Press.

Atkinson, A.B. and Micklewright, J. (1989) 'Turning the screw: benefits for the unemployed 1979-88', in A. Dilnot and I. Walker (eds), *The economics of social security*, Oxford: Oxford University Press.

Bäcker, G. (1995) 'Der Sozialstaat – ein Auslaufmodell? Die Krise der Sozialpolitik als politische Krise', *WSI Mitteilungen*, vol 48, no 6, pp 345-57.

Bäcker, G. and am Orde, B. (1993) 'Sozialpolitik 1992', in M. Kittner (ed), *Gewerkschaftsjahrbuch 1993*, Cologne: Bund Verlag.

Baldwin, P. (1990) *The politics of social solidarity: class bases of the European welfare state 1875-1975*, Cambridge: Cambridge University Press.

Baldwin, S. and Falkingham, J. (eds) (1994), *Social security and social change*, Hemel Hempstead: Harvester Wheatsheaf.

Banco de Portugal (1994) *Report of the directors and economic and financial survey for the year 1993*, Lisbon: Banco de Portugal.

Barr, N. and Coulter, F. (1990) 'Social security: solution or problem?' in J. Hills (ed), *The state of welfare*, Oxford: Oxford University Press.

Barreto, A. (ed) (1996) *A situação social em Portugal 1960-1995*, Lisbon: Instituto de Ciências Sociais, Universidade de Lisboa.

Beck, U. (1992) *Risk society*, London: Sage.

Bennett, F. (1993) *Social insurance: reform or abolition?* London: IPPR.

Berghman, J. (1991) 'Basic concepts of social security', in D. Pieters (ed) *Social security in Europe: miscellanea of the Erasmus programme of studies relating to social security in the European communities*, Brussels: Bruylant.

Berghman, J. (1996) 'The resurgence of poverty and the struggle against exclusion: a new challenge for social security?' Paper presented at the ISSA European Conference 'Adapting to new economic and social realities: what challenges, opportunities and new tasks for social security?', Aarhus, Denmark, 19-21 November.

Birmingham, D. (1993) *A concise history of Portugal*, Cambridge: Cambridge University Press.

Blackwell, J. (1992) 'Changing work patterns and their implications for social protection' Paper given at 'Social Security: 50 Years after Beveridge', International Conference, University of York, 27-30 September.

Blackwell, J. (1994) 'Changing work patterns and their implications for social protection', in S. Baldwin and J. Falkingham (eds), *Social security and social change*, Hemel Hempstead: Harvester Wheatsheaf.

BMAS (Bundesministerium für Arbeit und Sozialordnung) (1993) *Teilzeitarbeit. Ein Leitfaden für Arbeitnehmer und Arbeitgeber*, Bonn: BMAS.

BMAS (Bundesministerium für Arbeit und Sozialordnung) (1994) *Sozialbericht 1993*, Bonn: BMAS.

BMAS (Bundesministerium für Arbeit und Sozialordnung) (1996) *Programm für mehr Wachstum und Beschäftigung. Maßnahmen im sozialpolitischen Bereich*, April, Bonn: BMAS.

Boleat, M. (1995) 'Private insurance and social risks since World War II', in R. Silburn (ed), *Social insurance: the way forward*, Nottingham: Benefits Research Unit, vol 1, no 3, pp .

Bonoli, G. and Palier, B. (1996), 'Reclaiming welfare', *South European Society and Politics*, vol 1, no 3, pp 240-51.

Bouget, D. (1996) 'The French social welfare system and the Juppé plan', *Working Paper 3*, Copenhagen: Centre for Welfare State Research.

Bradshaw, J. and Millar, J. (1991) *Lone parent families in the UK*, Department of Social Security, Research Report no 7, London: HMSO.

Bradshaw J., Ditch J., Holmes, H. and Whiteford, P. (1993a), *Support for children: a comparison of arrangements in fifteen countries*, London: HMSO.

Bradshaw, J., Ditch, J., Holmes, H. and Whiteford, P. (1993b) 'A comparative study of child support in fifteen countries', *Journal of European Social Policy*, vol 3, no 4, pp 255-71.

Cabinet Office (1995) *Deregulation task force*, Report, London: HMSO.

Campos, A. Correia de (1990) *Estado-providência: perspectivas e financiamento. O caso da Saúde*, Lisbon: Escola Nacional de Saúde Pública.

Carlson, E. (1979) 'Concentration of rising Hungarian mortality among manual workers', *Sociology and Social Research*, vol 73, no 3, pp 194-203.

Carreira, H.M. (1996a) *As políticas sociais em Portugal*, Lisbon: Gradiva.

Carreira, H.M. (1996b) 'Segurança social: a acentuação da crise', *O Público*, 19 February.

Castel, R. (1995) *Les métamorphoses de la question sociale*, Paris: Fayard.

Castle-Kanerova, M. (1996a) 'Social security in the Czech Republic: the market, paternalism or social democracy?' in M. May, E. Brundson and G. Craig (eds), *Social Policy Review*, no 8, pp 286-302.

Castle-Kanerova, M. (1996b) *Evaluating equal opportunities in the Czech Republic*, PHARE, Brussels: EC Publications.

Castles, F.G. (1995) 'Welfare state development in southern Europe', *West European Politics*, vol 18, no 2, pp 291-313.

Castles, F.G. and Mitchell, D. (1992) 'Identifying welfare state regimes: the links between politics, instruments and outcomes', *Governance*, vol 5, no 1, pp 1-26.

Cattacin, S. (1996) 'Die Transformation des Schweitzer Sozialstaates', *Swiss Political Science Review*, vol 2, no 1, pp 89-102.

CFQF (Commission Fédérale Pour les Questions Féminines) (1988) 'Propositions de la Commission fédérale pour les questions féminines en vue de la 10e révision de l'AVS', *Questions au Féminin*, vol 1, p 88, Berne: CFQF.

Clark, G., Hockley, T. and Smedley, I. (1995) 'The insurance of medical risks', in Association of British Insurers (eds) *Risk insurance and welfare*, London: Association of British Insurers.

Clasen, J. (1992) 'Unemployment insurance in two countries: a comparative analysis of Great Britain and West Germany in the 1980s', *Journal of European Social Policy*, vol 2, no 4, pp 279-300.

Clasen, J. (1994a) *Paying the jobless. A comparison of unemployment benefit policies in Great Britain and Germany*, Aldershot: Avebury.

Clasen, J. (1994b) 'Social security: the core of the employment-centred social state', in J. Clasen and R. Freeman (eds) *Social policy in Germany*, Hemel Hempstead: Harvester.

Clasen, J. and Freeman, R. (eds) (1994) *Social policy in Germany*, Hemel Hempstead: Harvester.

Clasen, J. and Gould, A. (1995) 'Stability and change in welfare states: Germany and Sweden in the 1990s', *Policy and Politics*, vol 23, no 3, pp 189-201.

Clogg, R. (1992), *A concise history of Greece*, Cambridge: Cambridge University Press.

Cm 615 (1989) *The government's expenditure plans 1989/90 to 1991-92*, Chapter 15, Department of Social Security, London: HMSO.

Cm 2687 (1994) *Jobseeker's Allowance*, London: HMSO.

Cm 2813 (1995) *Social Security departmental report, the government's expenditure plans 1995/96 to 1997/98*, London: HMSO.

Cm 3242 (1996) *A new partnership for care in old age*, London: HMSO.

Cmnd 9517 (1985) *Reform of social security*, London: HMSO.

Cmnd 9691 (1985) *Reform of social security: programme for action*, London: HMSO.

Commission on Social Justice (1994) *Social justice: strategies for national renewal*, London: Vintage.

Constituição da República Portuguesa (1991) *As 3 versões após 25 de abril 1989/1982/1976*, Oporto: Porto Editora.

Convery, P. (1994) 'Unemployment benefits: values decline', *Unemployment Unit Working Brief*, vol 53, pp 14-15.

Corkill, D. (1993) *The Portuguese economy since 1974*, Edinburgh: Edinburgh University Press.

Corkill, D. (1996) 'Portugal votes for change and stability: the election of 1995', *West European Politics*, vol 19, no 2, pp 403-9.

Czech Social Security and Health Insurance Legislation (1995), compiled by Trade Links, Prague.

Deacon, A. (1992) 'Whose obligations? Work and welfare in the 1990s', *Benefits*, vol 5, pp 14-17.

Deacon, B. and Hulse, M. (1997) 'The making of post-communist social policy: the role of international agencies', *Journal of Social Policy*, vol 26, no 1, pp 43-62.

Dehlinger, E. and Brennecke, R. (1992) 'Die Akzeptanz der sozialen Sicherung in der Bevölkerung der Bundesrepublik Deutschland', *Zeitschrift für Gesundheitswesen*, vol 54, pp 229-43.

Dertilis G. (1976), *Social change and military intervention in politics: Greece: 1881-1928*, PhD thesis, University of Sheffield.

Diário da República (1995) *Número 266/95 Suplemento*, 17 November.

Dich, J.S. (1964) *Socialpolitikkens teori: læren om de offentlige tilskud* [Theory of social policy: the public subsidies] (with an English summary), Copenhagen: Dansk Videnskabs Forlag.

Dich, J.S. (1973) *Den herskende klasse* [The ruling class], Copenhagen: Borgen.

Dilnot, A. (1995) 'The assessment: the future of the welfare state', *Oxford Review of Economic Policy*, vol 11, no 3, pp 1-10.

Dilnot, A., Disney, R., Johnson, P. and Whitehouse, E. (1994) *Pensions policy in the UK: an economic analysis*, London: Institute for Fiscal Studies.

Direcção-Geral dos Regimes de Segurança Social (1995) *Redução da taxa social única*, Lisbon, January.

Döring, D. (1995a) 'Anmerkungen zum Gerechtigkeitsbegriff der Sozialpolitik mit besonderer Berücksichtigung liberaler Vorstellungen zur Sozialversicherungspolitik', in D. Döring, F. Nullmeier, R. Pioch and G. Vobruba (eds) *Gerechtigkeit im Wohlfahrtsstaat*, Marburg: Schüren Presseverlag.

Döring, D. (1995b) 'Soziale Sicherung in der Defensive: Einige kritische Betrachtungen zur gegenwärtigen Sozialpolitik', in D. Döring and R. Hauser (eds) *Soziale Sicherheit in Gefahr*, Frankfurt: Suhrkamp.

Dretakis, M. (1994), 'The reduction in income resulted in a reduction in the birth rate' (Athens), *Eleftherotypia* (Greek daily), 21 September.

DSS (1995) *Social security statistics*, London: HMSO.

Dupeyroux J.J. (1993, 12th edn) *Droit de la sécurité sociale*, Paris: Dalloz.

Eardley, T., Bradshaw J., Ditch J., Gough I. and Whiteford, P. (1996) *Social assistance in OECD countries: country reports*, London: HMSO

Economist Intelligence Unit (1995) *Country reports (1st, 2nd, 3rd and 4th quarters)*, London: EIU.

Edebalk, P.G. (1994) 'Möllermodellen', *Socialvetenskaplig tidskrift*, vol 1.

Edebalk, P.G. (1996) *Välfärdsstaten träder fram: Svensk socialförsäkring 1884-1955*, Lund: Arkiv förlag.

Esping-Andersen, G. (1990) *The three worlds of welfare capitalism*, Cambridge: Polity Press.

Esping-Andersen, G. (ed) (1996a) *Welfare states in transition*, London: Sage.

Esping-Andersen, G. (1996b) 'Frozen Fordism: the impasses of labour shedding and familialism in continental European social policy', Paper presented at the MIRE conference on 'Comparing social welfare systems in southern Europe', Florence, February.

Eurobarometer (1993), *Europeans and the family: results of an opinion survey*, Report no 39, prepared by N. Malpas and P. Lambert, Brussels: Commission of the European Communities.

European Commission (1993) *Social protection in Europe*, Luxembourg: Office for Official Publications of the European Communities.

European Commission (1994) *Employment in Europe*, Luxembourg: Office for Official Publications of the European Communities.

European Commission (1995) *Social protection in Europe*, Luxembourg: Office for Official Publications of the European Communities.

European Commission (1996) *Employment in Europe*, Luxembourg: Office for Official Publications of the European Communities.

Eurostat (1991) *A social portrait of Europe*, Luxembourg: Office for Official Publications of the European Communities.

Eurostat (1994), *Social protection expenditure and receipts 1980-1992*, Luxembourg: Office for Official Publications of the European Communities.

Eurostat (1995) *Social protection in the European Union*, Focus no 15, Luxembourg: Office for Official Publications of the European Communities.

Euzeby, A. (1994) 'Chères charges sociales', *Le Monde*, 1 February, p 7.

Ewald, F. (1986) *L'état providence*, Paris: Grasset.

Fassmann, M. (1994) 'Mzdy, dane a pojistne', *Pohledy*, no 6, pp 6-10.

Fassmann, M. (1996) 'My a Evropska Unie, IV Socialni Ochrana', *Pohledy*, no 5, pp 1-7.

Fawcett, H. and Papadopoulos, T. (1996) 'Social exclusion, social citizenship and de-commodification: an evaluation of the adequacy of support for the unemployed in the European Union', Discussion Paper no 42, Nuffield College, Oxford: Centre for European Studies.

Ferge, Z. (1979) *A society in the making*, Harmondsworth: Penguin.

Ferge, Z. (1986) 'The changing Hungarian social policy', in E. Øyen (ed) *Comparing welfare states and their futures*, Aldershot: Gower.

Ferge, Z. (1988) 'The trends and functions of social policy in Hungary', in J-P. Jallade (ed) *The crisis of redistribution in European welfare states*, Stoke-on-Trent: Trentham Books.

Ferge, Z. (1995) 'Challenges and constraints in social policy', in C. Gombár, E. Hankiss, L. Lengyel and G. Várnai (eds) *Question marks: the Hungarian government 1994-1995*, Budapest: Centre for Political Research.

Ferge, Z. (1996) 'The change of the welfare paradigm: the individualisation of the social', Plenary Paper given at the British Social Policy Association conference, Sheffield: Sheffield Hallam University, July.

Ferrera M. (1994) *EC citizens and social protection*, Luxembourg: Commission of the European Communities.

Ferrera, M. (1996) 'The "southern model" of welfare in social Europe', *Journal of European Social Policy*, vol 6, no 1, pp 17-37.

Finansministeriet (1995) *Pensionsopsparingens udbredelse og dækning* [Pension savings' coverage and replacement], Copenhagen: Ministry of Finance.

Finansministeriet (1996a) *Ældres indkomster og formuer* [Income and wealth of the elderly], Copenhagen: Ministry of Finance.

Finansministeriet (1996b) *Budgetredegørelsen 96: velfærdssamfundets veje* [Budget statement: possible routes of the welfare society], Copenhagen: Ministry of Finance.

Fitoussi, J.P. and Rosanvallon, P. (1996) *Le nouvel âge des inégalités,* Paris: Seuil.

Flora, P. (ed) (1986) *Growth to limits: the western European welfare states since World War II,* Berlin: De Gruyter.

Flora, P. and Heidenheimer, A.J. (eds) (1981) *The development of welfare states in Europe and America,* New Brunswick, NJ: Transaction Books.

Flora, P., Alber, J. and Kohl, J. (1977) 'Zur Entwicklung der westeuropäischen Wohlfahrtsstaaten', *Politische Vierteljahresschrift,* 18, pp 707-72.

Forster, D. and Józan, P. (1990) 'Health in Eastern Europe', *The Lancet,* no 335, pp 458-60.

Fotopoulos, T. (1985) *Dependent development: the Greek case* [in Greek], Athens: Exantas.

Fortopoulos, T. (1992) 'Economic restructuring and the debt problem: the Greek case', *International Review of Applied Economics,* vol 6, no 1, pp 38-64.

Fotopoulos, T. (1993) *The neoliberal consensus and the crisis of growth economy* [in Greek], Athens: Gordios.

Friedrich, W., Asmussen, J. and Burkhardt, N. (1996) *Zprava o statni politice socialni ochrany: Ceska Republika,* Cologne: ISG/WSF Consortium.

Gábor I. (1979) 'The second (secondary) economy', *Acta Oeconomica,* vol 22, nos 3-4, pp 291-311.

Gábor, I. and Galasi, P. (1985) 'Second economy, state and the labour market', in P. Galasai and G. Sziráczki (eds) *Labour market and second economy in Hungary,* Frankfurt/New York: Campus Verlag.

Galasi, I. (1985) 'The major domains of the second economy', in P. Galasai and G. Sziráczki (eds) *Labour market and second economy in Hungary,* Frankfurt/New York: Campus Verlag.

Galasai, P. and Sziráczki, G. (eds) (1985) *Labour market and second economy in Hungary*, Frankfurt/New York: Campus Verlag.

Gallagher, T. (1983) *Portugal: a twentieth-century interpretation*, Manchester: Manchester University Press.

Ganßmann, H. (1993a) 'After unification: problems facing the German welfare state', *Journal of European Social Policy*, vol 3, no 2, pp 79-90.

Ganßmann, H. (1993b) 'Sind soziale Rechte universalisierbar?', *Zeitschrift für Soziologie*, vol 22, no 5, pp 385-94.

George, V. and Taylor-Gooby, P. (eds) (1996) *European welfare policy: squaring the welfare circle*, London: Macmillan.

Gilbert, B. (1966) *The evolution of national insurance in Great Britain: the origins of the welfare state*, London: Michael Joseph.

Gilliand, P. (1988) *Politique sociale en Suisse*, Lausanne: Réalités Sociales.

Glennerster, H. (1992) *Paying for welfare: the 1990s*, Hemel Hempstead: Harvester Wheatsheaf.

Goodman, A. and Webb, S. (1994) *For richer, for poorer: the changing distribution of income in the United Kingdom 1961-91*, London: Institute for Fiscal Studies.

Götting, U., Haug, K. and Hinrichs, K. (1994) 'The long road to long-term care insurance in Germany', *Journal of Public Policy*, vol 14, no 3, pp 285-309.

Gregg, P. and Wandsworth, J. (1994) *More work in fewer households?*, Discussion paper 72, London: National Institute of Economic and Social Research.

Greve, B. (1996) 'Indications of social policy convergence in Europe', *Social Policy and Administration*, vol 30, no 4, pp 348-67.

Guillemard, A.-M. (1986) *Le déclin du social*, Paris: Presse Universitaire de France.

Guimarães, M.L.O. (1991) *'Rendimento social mínimo: o desafio social máximo!'*, Paper presented to a conference of the Partido Socialista, Porto, March.

Hall, P. (1986) *Governing the economy: the politics of state intervention in Britain and France,* Cambridge: Polity Press.

Hann, C. (1990) 'Second economy and civil society', *Journal of Communist Studies,* vol 6, pp 21-44.

Hansard (1994) House of Commons 24 November, c281w.

Hansen, H. (1997) *Elements of social security in seven countries* (6th edn), Copenhagen: Centre for Welfare State Research (forthcoming).

Hantrais, L. (1995) *Social policy in the European Union,* London: Macmillan.

Hauser, R. (1995a) 'Problems of the German welfare state after unification', *Oxford Review of Economic Policy,* vol 11, no 3, pp 44-58.

Hauser, R. (1995b) 'Das empirische Bild der Armut in der Bundesrepublik Deutschland: ein Überblick', *Aus Politik und Zeitgeschichte,* vol 31-2, pp 24-34.

Hauser, R. (1995c) 'Reformperspektiven des Systems der sozialen Sicherung bei veränderten Rahmenbedingungen', in D. Döring and R. Hauser (eds), *Soziale Sicherheit in Gefahr,* Frankfurt: Suhrkamp.

HC132 (1995) *Minutes of evidence to Social Security Select Committee,* London, 25 January.

Heimann, E. (1929) *Soziale Theorie des Kapitalismus: Theorie der Sozialpolitik,* Tübingen: J.C.B. Mohr (reprinted in Frankfurt: Suhrkamp Verlag, 1980).

Hennock, E.P. (1987) *British social reforms and German precedents: the case of social insurance 1880-1914,* Oxford: Clarendon Press.

Hills, J. (1993) *The future of welfare,* York: Joseph Rowntree Foundation.

Hills, J. (1995a) 'Funding the welfare state', *Oxford Review of Economic Policy,* vol 11, no 3, pp 27-43.

Hills, J. (1995b) *Joseph Rowntree Foundation inquiry into income and wealth,* vol 2, York: Joseph Rowntree Foundation.

Hinrichs, K. (1991) 'Irregular employment patterns and the loose net of social security: some findings within the West German development', in M. Adler, C. Bell, J. Clasen and A. Sinfield (eds) *The sociology of social security,* Edinburgh: Edinburgh University Press.

Hinrichs, K. (1994) 'Retrenchment or reconstruction of social policy in Germany? The case of health care policy', Paper presented at 'The state and economic crisis in 20th-century Germany', University of Nottingham, 14-16 April.

Hinrichs, K. (1996) 'Social insurances and the culture of solidarity: the moral infrastructure of interpersonal redistributions – with special reference to the German health care system', (mimeo) Bremen: Centre for Social Policy Research, University of Bremen.

Hirsl, M. (1994) 'Vyvoj zamestnanosti, realnych prijmu a nazoru na zivotni uroven v Ceske Republice', *Pohledy,* no 4, pp 4-9.

Hirsl, M., Rusnok, J. and Fassmann, M. (1995) 'Zprava o socialni politice a vyvoji socialnich podminek v Ceske Republice, 1989-1994', *Pohledy,* nos 1-2, pp 1-16.

Hockerts, H.G. (1980) *Sozialpolitische Entscheidungen im Nachkriegsdeutschland. Alliierte und deutsche Sozialversicherungspolitik 1945-1959,* Stuttgart: Nomos.

Hockerts, H.G. (1981) 'German post-war social policies against the background of the Beveridge Plan: some observations preparatory to a comparative analysis', in W.J. Mommsen and W. Mock (eds) *The emergence of the welfare state in Britain and Germany,* London: German Historical Institute, Croom Helm.

IMF (International Monetary Fund) (1992) *Report for the insurance system in Greece,* Athens: IMF

Immergut, E. (1992) *Health politics: interests and institutions in western Europe,* Cambridge: Cambridge University Press.

Immergut, E. (1996) 'The normative roots of the new institutionalism: historical-institutionalism and comparative policy studies', in A. Benz and W. Seibel (eds) *Beiträge zur Theorieentwicklung in der Politik – und Verwaltungswissenschaft,* Baden-Baden: Nomos.

Ingerslev, O. and Pedersen, L. (1996) *Marginalisering 1990-1994* [Marginalisation 1990-1994], vol 96, p 19, Copenhagen: Danish National Institute of Social Research.

ISA (Informationen zur Sozial – und Arbeitsmarktpolitik) (1995) 'Arbeitslosigkeit und Sozialhilfe: Ausgrenzung stoppen', Deutscher Gewerkschaftsbund, Bundesvorstand, June.

Jacobs, H. (1995) *Evaluierung von Maßnahmen der 'Hilfe Zur Arbeit' in Bremen*, Bremen: Centre for Social Policy Research.

Janyska, A. (1996) 'Zavadeni systemu socialni podpory v okrese olomouc', *Socialni Politika*, vol 22, no 4, pp 8-10.

Jessop, B. (1993) 'Towards a Schumpetreian workfare state? Preliminary remarks on post-Fordist political economy', *Studies in Political Economy*, vol 40, no 1, pp 7-39.

Jessop, B. (1994) 'The transition to post-Fordism and the Schumpeterian workfare state', in B. Burrows and B. Loader (eds) *Towards a post-Fordist welfare state?* London: Routledge.

Join-Lambert, M.T. (1994) *Politiques sociales,* Paris: Dalloz, PFNSP.

Juppé, A. (1996) 'Discours du 15 novembre 1995 devant le parlement', *Droit Social,* vol 3, March, pp 221-6.

Karabelias, F. (1989) *State and society in the period after the restoration of democracy (1974-1988)* [in Greek], Athens: Exantas.

Katrougalos, G.S. (1996) 'The south European welfare model: the Greek welfare state, in search of an identity', *Journal of European Social Policy*, vol 6, no 1, pp 39-60.

Katzenstein, P. (1984) *Corporatism and change: Austria, Switzerland, and the politics of industry*, Ithaca, NY: Cornell University Press.

Katzenstein, P. (1985) *Small states in world markets*, Ithaca, NY: Cornell University Press.

Keller, B. and Seifert, H. (1993) 'Regulierung atypischer Beschäftigungsverhältnisse', *WSI Mitteilungen,* vol 9, pp 538-45.

Kerschen, N. (1995) 'The influence of the Beveridge Report on the French social security plan of 1945', in MIRE *Comparing social welfare systems in Europe,* vol I, Oxford Conference, Paris: Mission Interministerielle Recherche et Experimentation.

Klevmarken, A. (1995) 'Sjukförsäkringens incitamentseffekter', in SOU (eds) *Ohälsoförsäkring och samhällsekonomi: olika aspekter på modeller, finansiering och incitament*, Stockholm: SOU.

Knudsen, R. (1987) *Sociale kontantydelser 1976-1987* [Cash benefits 1976-1987], Copenhagen: Danish National Institute of Social Research.

Konopasek, Z. (1995) 'Bezva finta, ktera by se nemusela vyplatit', *Lidove Noviny*, 5 April, p 8.

Korpi, W. (1995) 'Un état-providence fragmenté et contesté: le développment de la citoyenneté sociale en France', *Revue Française de Science Politique: la protection sociale en perspective*, vol 45, no 4, pp 632-67.

Kremalis, K. and Yfantopoulos, J. (1992) 'Changes in the social security policy in Greece during the eighties', in B. Greve (ed) *Social policy in Europe*, Copenhagen: Danish National Institute of Social Research.

Kriesi, H. (1995) *Le système politique suisse*, Paris: Economica.

Kvist, J. and Petersen, J.H. (1997) *Statutory and supplementary pensions: implications for welfare state typologies*, (forthcoming).

Kvist, J. and Ploug, N. (1996) 'Social security in northern Europe: an institutional analysis of cash benefits for the unemployed', CWR Working Paper 1/96, Copenhagen: Centre for Welfare State Research.

Kvist, J. and Sinfield, A. (1996) 'Comparing tax routes to welfare in Denmark and the United Kingdom', Copenhagen: Danish National Institute of Social Research.

Kvist, J. and Torfing, J. (1996) 'Changing welfare state models', CWR Working Paper 5, Copenhagen: Centre for Welfare State Research.

Labour Party (1996) *The road to the manifesto*, London: Labour Party.

Lampert, H. and Bossert, A. (1992) *Sozialstaat Deutschland*, Munich: Verlag Vahlen.

Land, H. (1994) 'The demise of the male breadwinner – in practice but not in theory', in S. Baldwin and J. Falkingham (eds) *Social security and social change,* Hemel Hempstead: Harvester Wheatsheaf.

Lantto, K. (1994) 'Vad bör göras åt sjukpenningen?', *Ekonomisk Debatt,* vol 22, p 135.

Leibfried, S. (1993) 'Towards a European welfare state?', in C. Jones (ed) *New perspectives on the welfare state in Europe,* London: Routledge.

Leibfried, S. and Pierson, P. (1995) 'Semisovereign welfare states: social policy in a multitiered Europe' in S. Leibfried and P. Pierson (eds) *European social policy: between fragmentation and integration,* Washington DC: Brookings Institution.

Leibfried, S., Leisering, L., Buhr, P., Ludwig, M., Mädje, E., Olk, T., Voges, W. and Zwick, M. (1995) *Zeit der Armut. Lebensläufe im Sozialstaat,* Frankfurt: Suhrkamp.

Leisering, L. (1992) 'Selbststeuerung im Sozialstaat: zur Verortung der Rentenreform 1992 in der Sozialpolitik der 80er Jahre', *Zeitschrift für Sozialreform,* vol 38, no 1, pp 3-38.

Leisering, L. (1996) 'Grenzen des Sozialversicherungsstaats? Sozialer Wandel als Herausforderung staatlicher Einkommenssicherung', in F.X. Kaufmann (ed) *Sozialpolitik im französisch-deutschen Vergleich,* Wiesbaden: Verlag Chmielorz.

Lewis, J. (1992) 'Gender and the development of welfare regimes', *Journal of European Social Policy,* vol 2, no 3, pp 159-73.

Lijphart, A. (1984) *Democracies. Patterns of majoritarian and consensus government in twenty-one countries,* New Haven and London: Yale University Press.

Lister, R. (1994) '"She has other duties": women, citizenship and social security', in S. Baldwin and J. Falkingham (eds) *Social security and social change: new challenges to the Beveridge model,* Hemel Hempstead: Harvester.

Lopes, J. da Silva (1996) 'A economia Portuguesa desde 1960', in A. Barreto (ed) *A situação social em Portugal 1960-1995,* Lisbon: Instituto de Ciências Sociais, Universidade de Lisboa.

Lykketoft, M. (1994) *Sans og samling: en socialdemokratisk krønike,* Copenhagen: Samleren.

Maia, F. (1985) *Segurança social em Portugal: evolução e tendências*, Lisbon: Instituto de Estudos para o Desenvolvimento.

Maia, F. (1993) *População idosa e segurança social: anos 90*, Lisbon: Universidade Internacional.

Maltby, T. (1994) *Women and pensions in Britain and Hungary: a cross national and comparative case study of social dependency*, Aldershot: Avebury.

Manow-Borgwardt, P. (1994) 'Die Sozialversicherung in der DDR und der BRD, 1945-1990: Über die Fortschrittlichkeit rückschrittlicher Institutionen', *Politische Vierteljahresschrift*, vol 1, pp 40-61.

Maratou-Alipranti, L. (1995) 'Family obligations in Greece', in J. Millar and A. Warman (eds) *Defining family obligations in Europe*, Social Policy Papers, no 23, Bath: University of Bath.

Marinakou, M. (1996) '"Latin rim" or semiperipheral welfare states? The case of Greece', Paper presented at the conference on 'Social research and social policy in southern Europe', Greek National Centre of Social Research, Athens, 13-14 September 1996.

Mendes, F.R. (1995) 'Por onde vai a segurança social portuguesa?', *Análise Social*, vol 30, nos 131-2, pp 405-29.

Merrien, F-X. (1990) 'Etats et politiques sociales: contribution à une théorie néo-institutionnaliste', *Sociologie du Travail*, no 3, pp 267-94.

Meslé, F. (1991) 'Mortality in East European countries', *Population*, vol 46, pp 599-650.

Miegel, M. and Wahl, S. (1985) *Gesetzliche Grundsicherung: private Vorsorge – der Weg aus der Rentenkrise*, Stuttgart: Verlag Bonn aktuell.

Ministry of Finance (1982) *The social insurance system, no 5: public finance in Hungary*, Budapest: Ministry of Finance, Budapest.

Ministry of Labour and Social Affairs (1996), series of statistical data and informal discussions, Prague.

MIRE (1995) *Comparing social welfare systems in Europe*, vol I, Oxford Conference, Paris: Mission Interministerielle Recherche et Experimentation.

MISSOC (1996) *Social protection in the member states of the community*, Brussels: Commission of the European Communities.

Moran, M. (1994) 'Health care policy', in J. Clasen and R. Freeman (eds) *Social policy in Germany*, Hemel Hempstead: Harvester.

Mouzelis, N. (1990) *Post Marxist alternatives* [in Greek], Athens: Themelio.

Mozzicafreddo, J. (1992) 'O estado-providência em Portugal: estrategias contraditorias', *Sociologia – Problemas e Práticas*, no 12, October.

Neidhart, L. (1970) *Plebiszit und pluralitäre Demokratie: Eine Analyse der Funktionen des Schweitzerischen Gesetz- referendums*, Berne: Francke.

Neves, Ilídio das (1993) *A segurança social Portuguesa: problemas, realidades e perspectivas*, Lisbon: Colecção Estudos.

Nielsen, H.K. (1994) *Frihed i fællesskab: moderne socialisme* [Freedom in community: modern socialism], Copenhagen: Samleren.

NISI (National Institute for Social Insurance) (1935) *Social insurance in Hungary*, Budapest: National Institute for Social Insurance.

'No Turning Back' Group of Conservative MPs (1993) *Who benefits? Reinventing social security*, London: Conservative Political Centre.

Nullmeier, F. and Rüb, F.W. (1994) 'Erschöpfung des Sozialversicherungsprinzips? Gesetzliche Rentenversicherung und sozialstaatlicher Republikanismus', in B. Riedmüller and T. Olk (eds) *Grenzen des Sozialversicherungsstaates*, (Leviathan, special issue, no 14), Opladen: Westdeutscher Verlag.

Nyrup Rasmussen, P. (1996) *Statsministerens übningstale 1996* [Opening speech of the Prime Minister].

O Público (1995a) 'Eleições Legislativas', *O Público*, 2 October.

O Público (1995b) 'O rendimento mínimo', *O Público*, 10 November.

O Público (1996a) 'Dívidas à segurança social', *O Público*, 8 March.

O Público (1996b) 'Um terço das empresas devem à segurança social', *O Público*, 15 March.

O Público (1996c) 'Pensões mínimas aumentadas', *O Público*, 9 May.

O Público (1996d) 'Rendimento mínimo avança', *O Público*, 10 May.

O Público (1996e) 'Mínimo, à experiênca', *O Público*, 2 July.

OECD (1990) *Economic surveys – Greece*, Paris: OECD.

OECD (1994a) *The reform of health care systems: a review of seventeen OECD countries*, Paris: OECD.

OECD (1994b) *New orientations in social policy*, Paris: OECD.

OECD (1994c) *Employment outlook*, Paris: OECD.

OECD (1995) *Social and labour market policies in Hungary*, Centre for Co-operation with the Economies in Transition, Paris: OECD.

OECD (1996) *Tax expenditures: recent experiences*, Paris: OECD.

Offe, C. (1990) 'Akzeptanz und Legitimität strategischer Optionen in der Sozialpolitik', in C. Sachße and H.T. Engelhardt (cds) *Sicherheit und Freiheit: zur Ethik des Wohlfahrtsstaates*, Frankfurt: Suhrkamp.

Offe, C. (1991) 'Smooth consolidation in the West German welfare state: structural changes, fiscal policies, and populist politics', in F.F. Piven (ed) *Labour parties in postindustrial societies*, Cambridge: Polity Press.

Offe, C. (1994) 'A non-productivist design for social policies', in J. Ferris and R. Page (eds) *Social policy in transition: Anglo-German perspectives in the new European Community*, Aldershot: Avebury.

Oudin, J. (1992) *Rapport d'information fait au nom de la commission des finances, du contrôle budgétaire et des comptes économiques de la nation sur les aspects financiers de la protection sociale,* Information report of the Sénat, no 31, 28 October 1992.

Palier, B. and Bonoli, G. (1995) 'Entre Bismarck et Beveridge, "crises" de la sécurité sociale et politique(s)', *Revue Française de Science Politique,* vol 45, no 4, pp 668-99.

Papadopoulos, T. (1996) '"Family", state and social policy for children in Greece', in J. Brannen and M. O' Brien (eds) *Children in families: research and policy,* London: Falmer Press.

Papadopoulos, T. (1997) *Welfare support for the unemployed: a comparative analysis of social policy responses to unemployment in twelve European Union member states,* DPhil thesis, University of York.

Papadopoulos, Y. (1996) 'Les mécanismes du vote référendaire en Suisse: l'impact de l'offre politique', *Revue Française de Sociologie,* vol 37, pp 5-35.

Parker, H. (1989) *Instead of the dole,* London: Routledge.

Pechmann, J. (1988) *World tax reform,* Washington DC: Brookings Institution.

Pedersen, L. (1996) *Orlov, ledighed og beskæftigelse* [Leave, unemployment and employment], no 10, Copenhagen: SFI.

Pedersen, P. (1995), 'Sygedagpenge, fortidspension og arbejdsskadeforsikring: synspunkter i den danske diskussion', in SOU (eds) *Ohälsoförsäkring och samhällsekonomi: olika aspekter på modeller, finansiering och incitament,* Stockholm: SOU.

Pellet, R. (1995) 'Etatisation, fiscalisation et budgétisation de la sécurité sociale', *Droit Social,* vol 3, pp 296-305.

Pereirinha, J. (1992) *Observatory on national policies to combat social exclusion,* Lille: Commission of the European Communities.

Petersen, J.H. (1972) *Socialpolitisk teori* [Social policy theory], vol I, Odense: Odense University Press.

Petersen, J.H. (1974) *Socialpolitisk teori* [Social policy theory], vol II, Odense: Odense University Press.

Petersen, J.H. (1985) *Den danske alderdomsforsørgelses udvikling I: oprindelsen* [The development of old age retirement provision, part I: the origins], Odense: Odense University Press.

Petersen, J.H. (1995), 'Leuven lectures: three essays on trends towards a transformation of the Danish welfare state', CHS Working Paper 1995, no 1, Odense: Odense University.

Petmesidou, M. (1991) 'Statism, social policy and the middle classes in Greece', *Journal of European Social Policy*, vol 1, no 1, pp 31-48.

Petmesidou, M. (1996) 'Social protection in southern Europe: trends and prospects', *Journal of Area Studies*, no 9, pp 95-125.

Piachaud, D. (1996) 'Means testing and the Conservatives', *Benefits*, vol 15, pp 5-8.

Pick, M. (1996), 'Kratkodoby vyhled ekonomiky CR', *Pohledy*, no 6, pp 11-17.

Pierson, P. (1994) *Dismantling the welfare state: Reagan, Thatcher and the politics of retrenchment*, Cambridge: Cambridge University Press.

Pieters, D. (ed) (1990) *Introduction to the social security law of the member states of the European Community*, Brussels: Bruylant.

Pieters, D. (1994) *Introduction into the basic principles of social security*, Deventer: Kluwer Law and Taxation Publishers.

Pioch, R. (1996) 'Basic income: social policy after full employment', in A. Erskine (ed) *Changing Europe: some aspects of identity, conflict and social justice*, Aldershot: Avebury.

Ploug, N. and Kvist, J. (1994) *Overførselsindkomster i Europa: systemerne i grundtræk* [Cash benefits in Europe: the basics of the systems], *Social Security in Europe*, vol 2, Copenhagen: Danish National Institute of Social Research.

Ploug, N. and Kvist, J. (1996) *Social security in Europe: development or dismantlement?* Deventer: Kluwer Law and Taxation Publishers.

PRD (Parti Radical Démocratique) (1988) 'Avenir de l'AVS: rapport final d'un groupe de travail du Parti radical-démocratique suisse', *Revue Politique*, vol 67, no 2, pp 34-45.

Priester, K. (1993) 'Lean welfare: mit Pflegeversicherung und Karenztagen zum Umbau des Sozialstaats', *Blätter für Deutsche und Internationale Politik*, vol 9, pp 1086-98.

PSS/USS (Parti Socialiste Suisse/ Union Syndicale Suisse) (1987) *Droits égaux dans l'AVS: propositions du Parti socialiste suisse et de l'Union syndicale suisse pour la révision de l'AVS*, Berne: PSS/USS.

Redmond, G. (1992) *Unemployment and de-commodification*, Masters dissertation, University of Bath.

Rehfeld, U. and Luckert, H. (1989) 'Die versicherungsfremden Leistungen in der Rentenversicherung: Eine Schätzung von Häufigkeiten und Volumen', *Deutsche Rentenversicherung*, vols 1-2, pp 42-71.

Renard, D. (1995) 'The relation between assistance and insurance in the constitution of the French welfare state' in MIRE.

Répássy, H. (1991) 'Changing gender roles in Hungarian agriculture', *Journal of Rural Studies*, vol 7, pp 23-29.

Riksförsäkringsverket (1995) *Socialförsäkringsstatistik: fakta 1995*, Stockholm: Riksförsäkrings Verlet.

Ritter, G. (1983) *Sozialversicherung in Deutschland und England: Entstehung und Grundzüge im Vergleich*, Munich: C.H. Beck.

Robolis, S. (1993) 'A view from the South: reforms in Greece', *Journal of European Social Policy*, vol 3, no 1, pp 56-59.

Robolis, S. (1997) 'Comments on the amendment concerning the social security funds reserves' (Athens), *Eleftherotypia* (Greek daily), 15 February.

Rosa, E. (1996) 'Segurança social: nem tudo são défices', *O Público*, 29 May.

Rosa, M.J.V. (1996) 'O envelhecimento e as dinâmicas demográficas da população Portuguesa a partir de 1960: dos dados ao dilema', in A. Barreto (ed) *A situação social em Portugal 1960-1995*, Lisbon: Instituto de Ciências Sociais, Universidade de Lisboa.

Rosanvallon, P. (1995) *La nouvelle question sociale: repenser L'État Providence*, Paris: Seuil.

Rosewitz, B. and Webber, D. (1990) *Reformversuche und Reformblockaden im deutschen Gesundheitswesen*, Frankfurt: Campus Verlag.

Santos, Boaventura de Sousa, (1990) *O estado e a sociedade em Portugal (1974-1988)*, Oporto: Edições Afrontamento.

Santos, Boaventura de Sousa, (1991) *State, wage relations and social welfare in the semiperiphery: the case of Portugal*, Coimbra: Centro de Estudos Sociais.

Sapelli, G. (1995) *Southern Europe since 1945*, New York: Longman.

Schmähl, W. (1993) 'The "1992 reform" of public pensions in Germany: main elements and some effects', *Journal of European Social Policy* , vol 3, no 1, pp 39-51.

Schmidt, M.G. (1988) *Sozialpolitik: Historische Entwicklung und internationaler Vergleich*, Opladen: Leske and Budrich.

Secretaria de Estado da Segurança Social (1985) *Lei da segurança social, Lei no 28/84 de 14 de Agosto*, Lisboa.

Secretaria de Estado da Segurança Social (1993) *Trabalhadores independentes: nova legislação*, Lisboa.

Secretaria de Estado da Segurança Social (1996) *Prestações familiares, portaria no 35/96 de 10 de Fevereiro*, Lisboa.

Sécurité Sociale, periodical published monthly by the Swiss Federal Office for Social Insurance (OFAS/BSV).

Sik, E. and Svetlik, I. (1988) 'Similarities and differences', in A. Evers and H. Wintersberger (eds) *Shifts in the welfare mix*, Vienna: ECSWTR.

Silburn, R. (1995) 'Social Insurance: key themes and issues from the first phase', in R. Silburn (ed) *Social insurance: the way forward*, Nottingham: Benefits Research Unit.

Sinfield, A. (1996) 'Blaming the benefit: the costs of the distinction between active and passive programmes', Paper presented at the ETUC/ETUI Annual Conference on Social Protection in Europe, Brussels, 7-8 November.

Skatteministeriet (1994) *Skattepolitisk redegørelse, juni 1994* [Statement of the Treasury], Copenhagen: Skatteministeriet.

Skocpol, T. and Amenta, E. (1986) 'States and social policies', *Annual Review of Sociology*, vol 12, pp 131-57.

Socialdemokratiet (1995) *Velfærd med vilje* [Willing welfare], Copenhagen: The Social Democratic Party.

Socialkommissionen (1992) *Uden arbejde: overførselsindkomster til midtergruppen* [Without work: cash benefits for the middle aged], Copenhagen: Socialkommissionen.

Socialkommissionen (1993) *Reformer: Socialkommissionens samlede forslag* [Reforms: the proposals of the Social Commission], Copenhagen: Socialkommissionen.

Socialministeriet (1991) *Rapport om bruttoficiering af den sociale pension* [Report on making the social pension taxable], Committee on the Equalisation of Pensioners and Transformation of Social Assistance Under the Ministry of Social Affairs, Copenhagen: Ministry of Social Affairs.

Socialni Politika (1996) 'Nezamestnanost v zari', *Socialni Politika*, vol 22, no 11.

SOU (Statens Offentliga Utredningar) (1996), *En allmän och aktiv försäkring vid sjukdom och rehabilitering* 113, Stockholm: SOU.

Sozialpolitische Umschau (various issues), Presse- und Informationsamt der Bundesregierung, Bonn.

Spicker, P. (1993) 'Can European social policy be universalist?', in R. Page and J. Baldock (eds) *Social Policy Review no 5*, University of Kent, Canterbury: Social Policy Association.

Ståhlberg, A. (1989) 'Redistribution effects of social policy in a lifetime analytical framework', in B. Gustafsson and A. Klevmarken (eds) *The political economy of social security*, Amsterdam: North-Holland.

Ståhlberg, A. (1990) 'Lifetime income redistribution of the public sector: inter- and intragenerational effects', in I. Persson (ed) *Generating equality in the welfare state: the Swedish experience*, Oslo: Norwegian University Press.

Ståhlberg, A. (1991) 'Lessons from the Swedish pension system', in T. Wilson and D. Wilson (eds) *The state and social welfare: the objectives of policy*, London and New York: Longman.

Ståhlberg, A. (1995a), 'Pension reform in Sweden', *Scandinavian Journal of Social Welfare*, no 4, pp 267-73.

Ståhlberg, A. (1995b) 'Women's pensions in Sweden', *Scandinavian Journal of Social Welfare*, no 4, pp 19-27.

Stathopoulos, P. (1996) 'Greece: what future for the welfare state?', in V. George and P. Taylor-Gooby (eds) *European welfare policy*, London: Macmillan.

Statisztikai Ékönyv (1994, 1995) *Magyar statisztikai ékönyv* (Statistical yearbook of Hungary), Budapest: Central Statistical Office.

Steffen, J. (1994) 'Die wesentlichen Änderungen in den Bereichen Arbeitslosenversicherung, Rentenversicherung, Krankenversicherung und Sozialhilfe (HLU) in den vergangenen Jahren', mimeo, Arbeiterkammer Bremen.

Stone, A. (1992) 'Le néo-institutionalisme: défis conceptuels et méthodologiques', *Politix*, vol 20, 156-68.

Swain, N. (1992) *Hungary: the rise and fall of feasible socialism*, London: Verso.

Szalai, J. (1990) 'Social participation in the context of restructuring and liberalization: the Hungarian case', Paper given at IV World Congress for Soviet and East European Studies, Harrogate.

Szalai, J. (1991), 'Hungary: early exit from the state economy', in M. Kohli, M. Rein, A.-M. Guillemard and H. Van Gunsteren (eds) *Time for retirement*, Cambridge: Cambridge University Press.

Szelényi, I. (1989) 'Eastern Europe in an epoch of transition: towards a socialist mixed economy?', in V. Nee and D. Stark (eds) *Remaking the economic institutions of socialisms in China and Eastern Europe*, Stanford: Stanford University Press.

Széman, Z. (1989) *Pensioners on the labour market: a failure in welfare*, Budapest: Institute of Sociology, Hungarian Academy of Sciences.

Széman, Z. (1993) 'Age discrimination and the labour market in Hungary', Paper given at roundtable on 'Age discrimination in the labour market', XVth Congress of the International Association of Gerontology, Budapest, July.

SZOT (1975) *Social insurance in Hungary*, Budapest: SZOT.

Titmuss, R. (1958) *Essays on the welfare state*, London: Allen and Unwin.

Toft, C. (1995) 'Constitutional choice, fiscal federalism and the provision of unemployment compensation in Britain, Germany and Denmark', Paper presented at the 51st Congress of the International Institute of Public Finance, Lisbon.

Tomeš, I. (1968) 'Basic features of old age pension schemes in socialist countries of Eastern Europe', *International Social Security Review*, vol 21, pp 412-23.

Townsend, P. and Walker, A. (1995) *The future of pensions: revitalising National Insurance*, Fabian Society Discussion Paper no 22, London: Fabian Society.

Trabalho and Segurança Social (1996a) *Proposta de orçamento de estado para 1996*, vol 6, no 3, March.

Trabalho and Segurança Social (1996b) *Rendimento mínimo: regime de atribuição, lei no 19-A/96, de 29 de Junho*, vol 6, no 8, August.

Tsakloglou, P. (1988) *Aspects of inequality and poverty in Greece: 1974-1982*, PhD thesis, University of Warwick.

Tsoukalas, K. (1987) *State, society and work in postwar Greece* [in Greek], Athens: Themelio.

TSR (Télévision Suisse Romande) (1995), *AVS 10e, 62 ou 64?*, 10 June.

Unemployment Unit (1995) *Working Brief 65*, June.

Vesterø-Jensen, C. (1985) *Det tvedelte pensionssystem* [The dual pension system], Roskilde: Forlaget Samfundsøkonomi og Planlægning.

Vobruba, G. (1990) 'Lohnarbeitszentrierte Sozialpolitik in der Krise der Lohnarbeit', in G. Vobruba (ed) *Strukturwandel der Sozialpolitik*, Frankfurt: Suhrkamp.

Vodicka, J. (1996), 'Pred jednanim o navrhu zakona o socialni pomoci', *Socialni Politika*, vol 22, no 11, pp 2-6.

von Nordheim Nielsen, F. (1996), 'Danish occupational pensions in the 1980s: from social security to political economy', in M. Shalev (ed) *The privatization of social policy? Occupational welfare in America, Scandinavia and Japan*, London: Macmillan.

Wadensjö, E. (1991) 'Partial exit: Sweden', in M. Kohli, M. Rein, A.M. Guillemard and H. van Gunsteren (eds) *Time for retirement: comparative studies of early exit from the labor force*, Cambridge: Cambridge University Press.

Wagner, A. (1995) 'Langzeitarbeitslosigkeit: Vielfalt der Formen und differenzierte soziale Lage', *WSI Mitteilungen*, vol 48, no 12, pp 739-59.

Wagner, A. (1996) 'Early retirement in Germany: current situation and prospects', Paper presented to ILM Conference on 'Unemployment in theory and practice', Robert Gordon University, Aberdeen, June.

Walker, A. (ed) (1996) *The new contract between the generations: intergenerational relations and social policy*, London: University College Press.

Walker, A. and Maltby, T. (1997) *Ageing Europe*, Buckingham: Open University Press.

Walker, R. (1995) 'Responding to the risk of unemployment', in Association of British Insurers (eds) *Risk, insurance and welfare*, London: Association of British Insurers.

Walter, J. (1989) *Basic income: freedom from poverty, freedom to work*, London: Marion Boyars.

Webb, S. (1994) 'Social insurance and poverty alleviation', in S. Baldwin and J. Falkingham (eds) *Social security and social change*, Hemel Hempstead: Harvester Wheatsheaf.

Webb, S. (1995) 'Social security policy in a changing labour market', *Oxford Review of Economic Policy*, vol 11, no 3, pp 11-24.

Wilensky, H.L. (1975) *The welfare state and equality: structural and ideological roots of public expenditures*, Berkeley: University of California Press.

Wolf, J. (1991) 'Sozialstaat und Grundsicherung', *Leviathan*, vol 3, pp 386-410.

Zeniskova, M. (ed) (1995) *Novela socialniho pojisteni, bilance*, Prague: Ministry of Labour and Social Affairs.

Zizkova, J. (1994) 'Chudoba a moznosti jejiho reseni', *Socialni Politika*, vol 20, no 10, pp 15-17.

Zizkova, J. (1996) 'Nad socialni reformou v CR a jejim dalsim postupem', *Socialni Politika*, vol 22, no 6, pp 2-3.

Index

absenteeism, in Sweden 45-6, 52, 54
ACOSS (*Agence Centrale des Organismes de Sécurité Sociale*) 89
Agricultural Insurance Organisation (OGA), Greece 179, 185, 195
agricultural workers
  female, Hungary 12, 212-13, 214, 215, 243
  Portugal 167-8, 243
AHV/AVS (Swiss pensions) 113, 119-22
Aide Social 90
allocation de solidarité spécifique 95
allocation unique dégressive 94-5
Arbeitslosengeld (German unemployment benefit) 64
Arbeitslosenhilfe (German unemployment support scheme) 18, 64
arbejdsloshedsforsikring (Danish unemployment insurance) 19, 24-5
arbejdsmarkedspensioner (Danish labour market pension) 28-30
ASSEDICS (*Associations pour l'Emploi dans l'Industrie et le Commerce*) 89
Association of Insurance Funds, Germany 66
assurance maternité 92
ATP (Labour Market Supplementary Pension, Denmark) 21, 23, 24, 27-8, 36
ATP (Swedish public national supplementary pension) 43, 45, 47-51
Austria 109

Bakros, Lajos 220
Balladur, Edouard 98
basic income 4, 245
  proposals for UK 149
Basic Law of Social Security, Portugal (1984) 11, 152, 155, 166
Beamte (tenured public sector employees) 61
benefit ceilings 5, 6, 249
benefits
  calculation of 15, 18
  flat-rate 5, 11, 18, 242
  funding of 6-7, 15
  in kind 6, 240
    German health insurance 66
  relationship with contributions 18-19, 61, 63, 64, 69
  relationship with income 18
  transportable 247
  types of 6
  universal or selective 9, 17
Benefits Agency, UK 132
Beveridge, William 45, 69, 135-6, 137, 138, 144
Bismarckian tradition 10, 68, 84, 107, 111
Bonn demonstration (1996) 79
Bonoli, Giuliano ix, 10-11, 107-29

CAFS (*Caisses d'Allocations
    Familiales*) 88
caisses autonomes 87
caisses mutuelles 86, 87
cantons, Swiss 107-9, 111, 112,
    114
care insurance 3, 4, 67-8, 77,
    248
  private for long-term 11, 143
carers, pension credits for 63
cash transfers 6, 15
Castle-Kanerova, Mita ix, 13,
    223-39
'categorical' insurance *see*
    selectivity
Cavaco e Silva, Aníbal 165,
    173, 175
Central and Eastern Europe
    (CEE) 12, 205, 217
Centre Democrats, Denmark
    31, 34
Centre Party, Sweden 58
charges sociales ('social burden')
    96
Christian Democratic Union
    (CDU), Germany 69, 77
Christian Democrats,
    Switzerland 110, 121
Christian People's Party,
    Denmark 31, 34
citizens' income 4
citizenship condition 4, 47, 237
Civic Democratic Party, Czech
    Republic 223
Civic Forum, Czech Republic
    225
civil servants
  Denmark 22, 23, 36
  France 87, 101, 102
  Germany 61, 83
  Greece 191
  Portugal 153, 156, 158
Civil Servants' Pensions Act,
    Denmark (1919) 22

Clasen, Jochen ix, 1-13, 60-83,
    240-50
class, and social insurance 1
CNAF (*Caisse Nationale
    d'Allocations Familiales*) 88
CNAMTS (*Caisse Nationale
    d'Assurance Maladie des
    Travailleurs Salariés*) 88
CNAVTS (*Caisse Nationale
    d'Assurance Vieillesse des
    Travailleurs Salariés*) 88
Commission on Social Justice,
    UK 148-9
Common Fund of Engineers,
    Architects and Surveyors,
    Greece 181
communism, in Czech Republic
    224
Communist Party, Greece 194,
    196
companies' insurance schemes
    41
compensation for loss of
    income principle 41, 44, 45
compulsory membership 6, 242
conditionality of benefits 18-
    19, 19-20, 37, 38, 241, 249
consensual politics 108-10,
    126-7
conservatives 1, 7
  Denmark 31, 33
  UK 146, 149
contribution, *see also*
    compulsory membership;
    voluntary insurance
contribution crediting 48, 63,
    249
contributions
  earnings-related 135-6
  level of 5, 242
  relationship with benefits 18-
    19, 61, 63, 64, 69
  tripartite basis 6-7
Contributions Agency, UK 132

'corporatist-conservative model'
85, 100, 104
cotisations sociales 85, 98
coverage, degree of 3, 5, 17
CPAMS (*Caisses Primaires
d'Assurance Maladie*) 88
CRAMS (*Caisses Regionales
d'Assurance Maladie*) 88
cross-national differences 4, 6-
8, 242-5
CSG (*contribution sociale
généralisée*) 95, 98, 102,
103, 105
Czech General Health
Insurance 232
Czech Ministry of Labour and
Social Affairs 228, 229
Czech Office for Social Security
227-8
Czech Republic 13, 206, 223-
39, 247
employment insurance 225,
231-2
health insurance 232-3
informal economy 232
pension insurance 228-30
sickness insurance 230-1
social assistance 223, 226,
227, 234-5
social expenditure 226
social insurance 223, 226,
227-34, 240, 248, 250
future 235-9
social protection 5, 226-7
social security, since 1990
224-6
state social support 223, 226,
227, 233-4
Czechoslovakia 224; *see also*
Czech Republic

Danish Confederation of Trade
Unions *see* LO
Danish Constitution (1849) 22

Danish Federation of
Employers (DA) 29
debt, national
Hungary 207
Portugal 12, 171
demographic changes 3, 140,
142, 146, 246
Denmark 9, 14-39
Labour Market
Supplementary Pension *see*
ATP
multitiered welfare state 14-
39
pensions 9, 25-31 Table 1
social expenditure 172
social security
characteristics 5, 6, 9, 22-31
future 35-9
history 22-3, 36
institutional design 23-4
policy changes 31-5
retrenchment or
restructuring 14-39
tax/benefit reform (1994) 34-
5
unemployment insurance
scheme 19, 24-5
universal tax-financed
benefits 9, 14, 23, 36
voluntary unemployment
insurance 6, 240
dentistry 143
Department of Social Security,
UK 132
dependency ratio, adverse 70-1
dyrtidsregulieringen (Danish
indexation of pensions) 33

early retirement 246
Germany 74
Sweden 9, 40, 54-6
earnings ceiling 6
ecological movements 245
efterlon (Danish early
retirement pay) 24

eligibility criteria 2, 15, 17
embourgeoisement 219
employment
  changes in patterns 3
  comparative in EU 96
  criteria of participation in 6
entitlement
  criteria of left and right 4
  link with paid employment or
    education 7, 15
equivalence principle 18-19,
    61, 63, 64, 69
Erskine, Angus ix-x, 11, 130-
    50, 240-50
ethnocentrism 20
Europe
  social insurance in 240-50
  see also Central and Eastern
    Europe
European integration 3, 246-7
European Monetary Union 247
  Germany and 83
  Greece and 12, 202
European Union 90, 127
  and Czech Republic 224
  employment rates 96
  recommended public debt-
    GDP ratio 171
  relative poverty in 165
  retirement age 221
  social expenditure as % of
    GDP 158, 163
  state subsidies 181
exclusion, social 15, 98-100,
    249
expenditure, social 3, 8, 246

family see households
Farmers' Party, Switzerland 110
Federal Commission for
    Women's Issues,
    Switzerland 120
Federal Labour Office,
    Germany 62, 64

Federal Republic of Germany,
    former 61
federalism, Swiss 107-10
Federation of Swiss Trade
    Unions 120, 121
financing 15, 21
  by tax or contributions 5, 19
Finland, income testing 18
fiscal policy 9, 20, 150
folkepensionen (Danish national
    old age pension) 25
Folketinget (Danish parliament)
    23
Forrer law, Switzerland 111
Fowler Reviews of Social
    Security, UK 136
France, 4, 5, 10, 84-106, 119,
    240
  crises of welfare state 10, 85,
    95-105
  demonstrations (1995) 102,
    103, 104
  family benefits 94-5, 104
  healthcare 104
  industrial injury and
    occupational illness 93
  invalidity insurance 92-3
  maternity insurance 92
  old age pensions 93, 104
  sickness insurance 91-2
  social insurance
    access and coverage 91-5
    administration 88-9
    characteristics of 85-91,
      241
    compared with social
      assistance 90-1, 100-2
    management and financing
      89-91, 101
  students' and artists'
    insurance cover 21
French Constitution (1996) 105
functional equivalence 20

Fund of Financial Stabilisation for Social Security (FEFSS), Portugal 167

gender issues
Greece 190
and labour market, UK 141-2
in Swiss pensions 119-22, 125
generational contract 76, 80, 145
German Democratic Republic (GDR), former 61
German unification 60, 72-5
Germany 1-2, 4, 5, 9-10, 14, 21, 60-83
accident insurance 65
early retirement schemes 74
earnings-related insurance 10, 61-2, 68, 70
health insurance 65-7, 72-3, 74
long-term care insurance 10, 67-8, 77, 248
party politics and suggestions for change 75-9
pensions 62-3, 71, 73
social expenditure 60, 207
social insurance
characteristics 10, 22, 61-2, 68, 240
future 79-83
history 68-70
retrenchment or reconstruction 60-1, 72-5, 78-9
unemployment insurance 6, 18, 63-5
Ghent system 44-5, 57
Greece 12, 151, 164, 169, 177-204
crisis of statism 177, 200-3
EC membership (1981) 196, 198

family allowances 183, 189-90
healthcare 184, 187, 198
neo-liberal consensus 200-2
old age pensions 185-7
patronage legacy 12, 191-2, 199, 248
social expenditure 181-5 Figs 1-3
social insurance 178-85, 240
administration 178-80
financing 12, 180-1
fragmentation of 177, 178-80, 192-4, 241
future 202-3
history 190-202
statism legacy 194-7
unemployment benefits 184, 187-9
Greek Constitution (1975) 178, 196
Greek Orthodox Church 191
Green Party, Germany 82
Greens, UK 149
groupements mutualistes 87
guardian's allowance, UK 131-2

Hampson, Jack x, 11, 151-76
health expenditure, per capita, Switzerland compared to USA 112
healthcare
'co-payments' in German 71, 73, 81
costs 3, 246
Hedin, S.A. 43
Hinterbleibenenrente ('survivor's' pension) 63
Horthy, Miklós 212
households
lone-parent 3, 142
no-earner 3
patterns of 140, 141-2, 244-5
single-person 3

'work-rich' and 'work-poor'
141
Hungarian Socialist Workers
Party 208
Hungary 12-13, 205-22, 240,
247
female agricultural workers
12, 212-12, 215
pensioners in labour force
214-15, 216-17
pensions system 208, 212-17
per capita debt 206
secondary economy 208, 218-
19
social expenditure 207
social insurance
characteristics 210-11, 219-
20
future 220-2
history 206-8, 248
role of 209-10
'hypothecated tax' 131, 144,
147

IKA (Greek Institute for Social
Insurance) 178-9, 180, 181,
185, 187, 194
ILO (International Labour
Organisation), definition of
unemployment 160
IMF (International Monetary
Fund) 13, 200, 207, 219,
220, 221, 247
income, loss of
compensation principle 41-2,
44, 45
risk 243-4
relationship with benefit 18
income distribution 15
income maintenance 19, 91,
131-2
income support, UK 131-2, 135
income tax, UK 147, 149
indemnités journalières 91
index-linking of pensions

Czech Republic 228-9
Portugal 162, 175
Sweden 47, 49
individualisation 237, 240, 245
institutional context
Germany 77
Switzerland 108-9, 126-9
'insurance alien' benefits,
Germany 63, 78, 249, 250
international financial agencies,
conditions for credit 13,
200, 207, 221
Ireland, Northern 131
social expenditure 172

Japan 96
job creation
France 97
Switzerland 122, 123
Job Seekers Allowance (JSA),
UK 134, 137-9, 144, 148
Juppé, Alain 95, 97, 103-5

Kádár, János 219
KAS (Swedish cash assistance)
57
Klaus, Vaclav 225
Kohl, Helmut 70
Krankenkassen/caisses maladie
112
Kvist, Jon x, 9, 14-39

labour market
changes in 2-3
female participation 3, 141-2,
244-5
labour market policy, and
benefits policy, UK 136,
138-9, 140
Labour Party, UK 147-8
Länder
new (of former GDR) 61, 72,
82
old (of former FRG) 61, 81-2

'Latin Rim' countries 7, 151, 155
Lawyers' Fund, Greece 181
leave-of-absence from unemployment 38
Lebensstandardsicherung see status maintenance
legislation, timing of social insurance 3
Liberal Democrats, Switzerland 110, 120
liberals 1, 7
  Denmark 31, 37
life chances, promotion of 15
LO (Danish Confederation of Trade Unions) 23, 29

maladie professionelle 93
male breadwinner model *see* nuclear family assumption
Maltby, Tony x, 12-13, 205-22
market economies, wage labour in 243-4
marketisation process 217, 235, 239
Masaryk, T.G. 224
maternity insurance 92, 133, 161
means testing
  France 10, 104
  Hungary 13, 220
  and the right 4
  role of 2, 250
  UK 11, 135, 136, 150
Mendes, Ribeiro 170, 175
Mexico, social expenditure 207
migration patterns 246-7
minimum standards, principle of 15, 19, 45
Minimum Subsistence Amount Act (1991), Czech Republic 225
minimum vieillesse 93
minimum wage, France 97

Ministry for Health, Welfare and Social Security (MHWSS), Greece 179
Ministry of Solidarity and Social Security, Portugal 175-6
Moderate Party, Sweden 58
Möller, Gustav 44-5
moral hazard 51-2
'moral infrastructure' of social insurance 10, 79-80, 250
mothers, 'baby years' per child credited to in Germany 63
multitiered social security, Denmark 9, 20-2, 35-7
mutualité sociale agricole 87

National Health Service, UK 132, 143
National Insurance, UK 6, 145, 248
  administration 132
  funding of 131, 132-3, 139-40
  the scale of 133-4
National Pension Act, Denmark (1956) 22
Nazism 69
'neo-institutionalist school' 108
Netherlands, The 109
  disability schemes 20
New Democracy, Greece 200, 201
New Economic Mechanism, Hungary 206, 209, 214
Nordic countries 22, 109
Norway, unemployment insurance scheme 19
nuclear family assumption 2, 75, 140, 236, 244

occupational insurance, negotiated 9, 41-2, 47, 137
OECD 207, 220

OGA *see* Agricultural Insurance
  Organisation, Greece
Öreségi nyugdíjak (Hungarian
  old age pension) 208
Organisation for the
  Employment of the Labour
  Force (OAED), Greece 180,
  187, 189
OTF (*Országos
  Társadalombiztosítási
  Föigazgatóság*), Hungary
  210

Palier, Bruno x-xi, 10, 84-106
Panhellenic Socialist Movement
  (PASOK) 197-200, 201-2
Papadopoulos, Theodoros N.
  xi, 12, 177-204
parents, 'free' pension rights
  during children's infancy in
  Sweden 48
part-time employment 244
pay-as-you-go principles 3, 4,
  246
pay-as-you-go schemes
  Germany 61, 70, 80
  Greece 185, 246
  Portugal 166
  Sweden 41, 45-6, 49
  UK 4, 131
Pension Reform Act, Germany
  (1957) 69; 91989) 71
pensions de retraite 93
Pensionsforsikringsanstalten
  (*PFA*) (Danish Pension
  Insurance Institution) 22-3
Plan Juppé, Le 103-5
poor
  deserving and non-deserving
    20
  'working' 97
Poor Law 5
Popular Party, Portugal 174
Portugal 11-12, 151-76, 240

'centres of social security'
  153, 157
dictatorship 152, 154, 172
family benefits 163-4
guaranteed minimum income
  (1996) 152, 165-6, 174
healthcare 153, 158-9
invalidity pensions 163
legislation 11, 152, 155
maternity benefits 161
old age pensions 161-3, 174-
  5
sickness and health policies
  158-9
social expenditure 157-8,
  163, 171-2
'social pension' 155, 162-3
social protection
  characteristics (post-1974)
    155-8, 248
  comparative assessment
    164-6
  economic and political
    factors 170-4
  financial and demographic
    issues 166-70
  future 174-6
  history 153-5
social security for self-
  employed 155, 159, 161,
  169
unemployment support 155,
  159-60
Portuguese Constitution (1933)
  154; (1976) 155, 173
poverty
  Czech Republic 225, 235
  Hungary 206, 213, 214, 219,
    220, 222
  traps 97
  in UK 142-3
  see also relative poverty
*prestations d'accidents du
  travail* 93

*prestations d'assurance
invalidité* 92-3
prestations d'assurance maladie
91-2
prestations en espèces 91
prestations familiales 94-5
Previdencia Social (Portuguese
New State policies) 154-5
private pensions
Czech Republic 229
Denmark 9, 29, 30
UK 11, 137, 140, 153-4, 146-
7
private provision 4-5, 7, 9, 245,
246
compared with social
insurance 5-6

qualification criteria 5
quality of life 38

RDS (*Remboursement de la
Dette Sociale*) 103
realrenteafgiften (Danish
taxation of pension fund
income) 32
redistribution 15, 42, 64-5, 66,
68, 80, 249
referendums, Switzerland 11,
108-10, Table 2; 121-2,
125, 127-9
régime général 86, 87-9, 90, 91-
4, 96
régimes complémentaires 86
régimes non-non 87
régimes particuliers 87, 104
régimes spéciaux 87, 104
reintegration 15, 19-20
relative poverty, in EU 165
Rendimento Mínimo Garantido
(RMG) (Portuguese
guaranteed minimum
income) 152, 165-6, 174
residence condition 4, 47
retirement age 221, 246

Czech Republic 228
and gender equality in Swiss
pensions 121, 125
Hungary 213, 215, 217, 221
Swedish flexible 48
for women, Portugal 161-2
retrenchment thesis 11, 14, 38-
9, 110, 124-7
rights, links with obligations
38, 249
risks
covered 3, 8
marginal 19
new types of 243, 245
pooling of 241
RMI (*Revenu Minimum
d'Insertion*) (minimum
income scheme) 99-100,
249
Romania 206
Romany population, Czech
Republic 236
Rome, Treaty of 246

Salazar, Antonio de Oliveira
154, 172
savings plans 245
Scandinavia 9, 14; *see also*
Denmark; Finland;
Norway; Sweden
Schmidt, Helmut 70
sécurité sociale, la 84-106
segurança social (Portuguese
social security) 153
seguro social (Portuguese social
insurance) 153
selectivity 17, 37, 61
self-employed insurance
France 87
Hungary 214
optional sickness in Czech
Republic 231
Portugal 155, 159, 161, 169
UK lack of provision for 148

SERPS (state earnings related pensions scheme, UK) 6, 132, 133, 134, 136, 137, 146
service sector 244
Serviço Nacional de Saúde (Portuguese National Health Service) 153, 158
Singapore model 232
Slovakia 206
small countries 109
SMIC (minimum wage, France) 97
Smith, John 148
social assistance
　defined 5, 16
　dependency on 141-2
　and minimum level of subsistence 19
social class *see* class
social control 20
'social democracy' principle 1-2, 7, 89, 101, 155
Social Democratic Party
　Czech Republic 223, 225
　Portugal 165, 171, 173
Social Democratic Party (SPD), Germany 77, 82
Social Democrats
　Denmark 31, 33-5, 37, 38
　Sweden 58
　Switzerland 110, 112, 120, 121, 122
social inclusion, Portugal 165, 175-6
social insertion policies 99-100
social insurance
　attitudes to 1
　challenges and policy responses 246-50
　and class 1
　compared to private provision 5-6
　concept of 1-13
　crucial criterion 7

defining 5-6, 16, 131
　gaps in 3
　historical function and current challenges 242-5
　and income maintenance 19
　pressures on programmes 8
　traditional assumptions of 2-3
Social Insurance Fund, Hungary 210-11
Social Liberals, Denmark 34
social partners 5, 89, 101-2, 105, 109
social policy
　changes 8
　'conservative-revolutionary dual nature' 1
　and economic freedom 119
　from above or from below 2
　and tax policy 20
　typology of regimes 151
social protection schemes 5-6
　changing role of 15
　cross-national differences 6-7, 8
　hybrid forms 6, 18
　mix of 7, 9
social security
　administration 21
　defining 16, 20, 131-2
　financing 15, 21
　institutional design of 17-19, 38-9
　legislation 21
　multitiered 9, 20-2, 35-7
　objectives of 19-20
　public and private schemes 21-2
　regulation 21
　in theory 16-22
　universal tax-financed 16
Social Security Act, UK (1986) 136; (1989) 138
Socialist Party, Portugal 165, 174
socialists 1

Solidarité Nationale 90-1
Solidarity Fund, Hungary 210, 217
solidarity principle 227, 229, 237, 242, 249, 250
  in Germany 10, 63, 68, 78, 80
Spain 151, 164
Ståhlberg, Ann-Charlotte xi, 9, 40-59
state, role of 6, 152, 241, 246
state earnings related pension scheme, UK *see* SERPS
state intervention, France 100-2, 103-5, 128
state provision 6, 9
status maintenance 5, 15, 61, 69, 237, 242, 249
stigmatisation 15
Sträng, Gunnar 45
Sweden 5, 9, 40-59
  early retirement pension 9, 40, 54-6
  occupational injury insurance 40, 56-7
  old age pensions 9, 40, 47-51
  sickness insurance reforms 9, 40, 51-4
  social security
    characteristics 5, 41-3
    future 58-9
    history 43-4
    problems 45-7
  unemployment insurance 9, 40, 57-8
  voluntary unemployment insurance 6, 57, 240
Swedish Committee on Sickness and Occupational Injuries 52, 56
Swedish legislation 43-5
Swedish Occupational Health and Safety Act (1975) 55
Swiss Constitution (1976) 114
Switzerland 10-11, 107-29, 240
  health insurance 11, 111-13, 115-19, 124
  old age pensions 11, 113, 115, 119-22, 125, 127
  social assistance 111, 114, 124
  social insurance
    characteristics 111-14
    future 127-9
  social policy reforms (1990s) 115-24
  unemployment insurance 11, 114, 122-4
  welfare retrenchment in 11, 110, 124-7
SZOT (Hungarian Central Council of Trade Unions) 210

tax policy, and social policy 20
tax subsidies 6, 15
taxa social única (Portuguese contributions) 156
temporary employment 244
terminology 6, 20
ticket modérateur 92
trade unions, *see* unions
transfers, rationing through filters 17-18
transitional countries 7, 12-13, 205-6
Treasury, UK 133
tvaergaende ordninger (Danish collective agreement between employers and employees) 29

UCANSS (*Union des Caisses Nationales de Sécurité Sociale*) 89
UK 7, 11, 130-50
  incapacity benefits 134-5, 147
  long-term care provision 143, 148, 149
  maternity pay 133

pensions 132, 133, 134, 136,
137, 139-40, 141-2, 144-5,
148, 149
pressures for change 139-45
recent policy changes 135-9
sickness benefit 132, 147
social assistance 14, 131, 135,
136-7, 141-3, 144-5
social expenditure 133, 136,
172, 207
social insurance
characteristics 4, 5, 11, 18,
131-5, 241
future 146-50
relationship with social
assistance 144-5, 146
withering of 146-8, 240,
248
unemployment insurance 6,
18, 134, 136, 137-9, 147,
243
private 143
UNEDIC (*Union Nationale
pour l'Emploi dans
l'Industrie et le Commerce*)
89
unemployment 3, 244, 246
cross-national differences in
insurance 6
Czech Republic 231, 236
France 96
Germany 60, 70, 72-5
Greece 12, 189, 202
Hungary 12, 207
ILO definition 160
Portugal 12, 172-3
Sweden 46
Switzerland 10, 110, 115,
123 Table 3
UK 136, 137-9, 140, 148
*Union Régionale des Caisses
d'Assurances Maladie* 105
unions 1
France 100-2, 105, 106n
Hungary 210

Swedish 44-5, 57
UK 145
universalism 5-6, 16, 17, 22,
36, 37, 155
URSSAF (*Unions Locales de
Recouvrement des
Cotisations*) 89
USA
employment rates 96
reliance on social assistance
14

Venizelos 192, 194
versicherungsfremde Leistungen
(insurance alien benefits)
63, 78, 249, 250
virksomhedsbaserede ordninger
(Danish company based
pension) 29
voluntary unemployment
insurance 6, 24, 41, 57, 240

welfare capitalism 151
welfare states 2, 14
degree of 'de-
commodification' in 4
and European integration 3
Fordist Keynesuian 3
indicators of development 4
institutional design 17-19, 38-
9
post-Fordist Schumpeterian 3
recommodification in 98, 100
theories of development 3-4
typologies 4, 7
widows' pension
Germany 63
Hungary 216
Portugal 163
Sweden 40
women
labour force participation 3,
141-2, 244-5
in Portugal 161-2

in part-time employment,
  Germany 81
pension rights 244-5
and unemployment benefit,
  UK 148

working class, and social
  insurance 1
World Bank 13, 207, 219, 220

Yugoslavia, former 205-6